WITHDRAWN

POZNAŃ STUDIES
IN THE PHILOSOPHY OF THE SCIENCES AND THE HUMANITIES

VOLUME 88

EDITORS

Jerzy Brzeziński
Andrzej Klawiter
Piotr Kwieciński (assistant editor)
Krzysztof Łastowski
Leszek Nowak (editor-in-chief)

Izabella Nowakowa
Katarzyna Paprzycka (managing editor)
Marcin Paprzycki
Piotr Przybysz (assistant editor)
Michael J. Shaffer

ADVISORY COMMITTEE

Joseph Agassi (Tel-Aviv)
Étienne Balibar (Paris)
Wolfgang Balzer (München)
Mario Bunge (Montreal)
Nancy Cartwright (London)
Robert S. Cohen (Boston)
Francesco Coniglione (Catania)
Andrzej Falkiewicz (Wrocław)
Dagfinn Føllesdal (Oslo)
Bert Hamminga (Tilburg)
Jaakko Hintikka (Boston)
Jacek J. Jadacki (Warszawa)
Jerzy Kmita (Poznań)

Leon Koj (Lublin)
Władysław Krajewski (Warszawa)
Theo A.F. Kuipers (Groningen)
Witold Marciszewski (Warszawa)
Ilkka Niiniluoto (Helsinki)
Günter Patzig (Göttingen)
Jerzy Perzanowski (Toruń)
Marian Przełęcki (Warszawa)
Jan Such (Poznań)
Max Urchs (Konstanz)
Jan Woleński (Kraków)
Ryszard Wójcicki (Warszawa)

Poznań Studies in the Philosophy of the Sciences and the Humanities
is partly sponsored by SWPS and Adam Mickiewicz University

Address: dr Katarzyna Paprzycka · Instytut Filozofii · SWPS · ul. Chodakowska 19/31
           03-815 Warszawa · Poland · fax: ++48 22 517-9625
           E-mail: PoznanStudies@swps.edu.pl · Website: http://PoznanStudies.swps.edu.pl

KNOWLEDGE CULTURES

COMPARATIVE WESTERN AND AFRICAN EPISTEMOLOGY

Edited by

Bert Hamminga

AMSTERDAM–NEW YORK, NY 2005

The paper on which this book is printed meets the requirements of "ISO 9706:1994, Information and documentation - Paper for documents - Requirements for permanence".

ISSN 0303-8157
ISBN: 90-420-1996-4
©Editions Rodopi B.V., Amsterdam - New York, NY 2005
Printed in The Netherlands

CONTENTS

Bert Hamminga, Introduction 7

Yoweri Kaguta Museveni, The Power of Knowledge 11

Kwame Anthony Appiah, African Studies and the Concept of Knowledge 23

Bert Hamminga, Epistemology from the African Point of View 57

Bert Hamminga, Language, Reality and Truth: The African Point of View 85

Leszek Nowak, On the Collective Subjects in Epistemology:
   The Marxist Case and a Problem for the African Viewpoint 117

Bert Hamminga, The Poznań View: How To Mean What You Say . . . 129

Contributors 141

Index and Glossary 143

INTRODUCTION

Why compare the western ideas of knowledge with the African? And why do so in *Poznań Studies in the Philosophy of the Sciences and the Humanities*? One of the key interests of western philosophy is to characterize the specifics of the Modern western concept of knowledge, the concept that arose out of the late Mediaeval and early Renaissance revolution of thought. Such a characterization involves a difficulty similar to that of making the fish understand its water: one needs other environments to explain the specifics of one's own in which one grew up, taking it for granted. One needs alternative concepts of knowledge for comparison. These are not readily at hand in western society.

A usual and highly effective method of creating a window with a view on the modern western concept of knowledge is the study of Greek and Mediaeval philosophy and science. By pondering the in many respects so very surprising epistemological taxonomies and rules of argument of Greek and Mediaeval culture, one gains access to such questions as: what would pre-modern philosophers have thought about modern westerners? Where and why do modern westerners disagree with pre-modern views on what is knowledge and how to acquire it? Surely the analogy with the fish may well hold, insofar as this is nothing but a small jump above the surface of the epistemological fluid in which modern western man swims, but any such attempt, however restricted in its power to give self-insight should clearly be worth any philosopher's trouble.

In finding different epistemological concepts that might help us mirror western culture, time is not the only dimension through which one can travel. Space can do the job, as long as substantially different cultures still exist. The culture of Sub-Saharan Africa is the substance from which we, in this book, have tried to put together an epistemological mirror. That was no easy task. Complete precision is even impossible. Like western culture, African culture is *under way*. It may, conventionally, be thought to have arisen from a "classical" tribal state, cherished by anthropologists, the subject of romanticism both by westerners and many a modern African, to become something that is now evolving rapidly, partly converging to the western world view – which itself is in its own revolution, not free of African influences, though usually not identified as such.

But we hope our volume is not only relevant to western, but even to African philosophy. It should be conceded, though, that Africans have a long-standing advantage over westerners in understanding the culture with which they came into contact. As far as westerners are concerned: in both the scientific and the artistic literature, accounts, stories and anecdotes abound which feature westerners penetrating Africa without the slightest awareness that their own cultural education could be enhanced by the richness of human cultures of the continent, maintaining this conviction remarkably stubbornly, whatever they were confronted with during their stay, even if this was to last the rest of their lives. Africans, however, since the first advent of westerners in Africa, have been motivated – the hard way – to penetrate the white man's mind. To Africans, learning properly to understand the brutal, powerful white man, quickly after his first entry in the continent, became a matter of life and death.

Yet this volume does not engage in the comparative normative evaluation of the methods of knowledge acquisition of the different cultures. This is because it easily leads to conclusions that are far from novel, such as that the western attitude has led to greater technical capabilities in many fields (like flying, killing people and polluting the environment). On the other hand it leads to similar arguments from the African side that might raise western skeptical rationalist emotions that are not helpful to the problem at hand, such as that, in Africa, knowledge traditionally comes from ancestors – dead, but existing and acting ancestors. Norms rest on evaluation principles, and there are no such interculturally accepted principles available. Simply put: priorities diverge widely among the cultures and we shall not discuss who has the best ones. There are better things to do than to raise the typical western competitive discussions on "what's the best" that in western philosophy of science overshadow so many of the more interesting and civilized scholarly questions.

"Scientific" literature on African thought abounds. A lot of it, written both by western scientists and Africans trained scientifically in the western sense, is so much occupied with the western rituals of knowledge acquisition that it immediately sinks, – often never to be seen again – into statistical analysis of data obtained from random samples and their control groups. At the beginning of every attempt to understand, however, is the problem of getting your concepts right. "Knowledge", "truth", "finding the truth", yes, virtually all abstract concepts are bound to leave an African and a westerner talking in such terms in utter confusion. Africans traditionally have a profoundly different use and interpretation, yes, a different idea about the nature of language! This volume involves making two efforts: enhancing the western understanding of the way in which Africans engineer their knowledge, and enhancing African understanding of how this differs from western style of knowledge engineering ("science" in the western sense of that word). These two efforts require some common skills that are hard to acquire, but that are completely different in other respects. The volume concentrates on the former effort, which we think is the one of which the results are still lagging: showing what westerners can learn about themselves by trying to *genuinely* understand the logic of the African way of thinking.

Some illustrations, updates on related research, sequel research and links can be found on *http://mindphiles.com/knowledgecultures*.

Bert Hamminga

Yoweri K. Museveni

THE POWER OF KNOWLEDGE

Abstract. In this article I reflect on the role of knowledge formation and knowledge acquisition in my personal life, starting from my childhood in traditional African context, then dealing with my period as a student and a freedom fighter, and finally during my leadership of Uganda, initially in need of drastic recovery and development, later in need of stable concentration on economic development rather than political rivalry and rent-seeking.

Being asked to write, as someone embedded in African culture, about my views and perception of knowledge, I think it is most efficient to present them largely in the form of an account of my personal experiences of being confronted with others having and acquiring knowledge, bestowing it on me, and of myself bestowing my acquired knowledge on others. This article contains the relevant parts of my *Sowing the Mustard Seed* (London: Macmillan 1997), to which readers interested in the broader context of recent Ugandan history are referred.

Early Years, Education

I was born among the Banyankole Bahima nomads of southwestern Uganda in about the year 1944. I use the word "about" because my parents were illiterate and so did not know the date. In such circumstances dates were associated with events. Parents would tell their children: "You were born when such and such an event took place". We who know how to read and write can now look back and use all sorts of sources to find out what was happening at the time. That is how I came to the conclusion that my numerical birth date must be 1944 or 1945, but more likely 1944.

My first conscious experiences with knowledge were of course in learning and being taught. Traditionally, the educational system of our oral culture featured a number of types of learning and teaching.

First, there was the on-the-job practical training: girls would be with their mothers, boys with their fathers, and you would learn how to do things and how not to do them. This concerned production-related skills: cooking, dealing with cows, milking, cleaning, making repairs, etc.

Second, concerning intellectual knowledge, there was philosophy and morality and so on, a collective intellectual and moral teaching: almost every night we would sit three hours, from about 8 PM to 11 PM, with our elders who would tell us stories. Those stories often featured animals as persons, some of them acting well, some badly; some would make mistakes, others would try to correct them. The way the story ended would show which persons were good examples and which were bad ones. This is called *okuterama*, and the storytelling was called *okugana*, fables with a meaning, showing what happened to a person who was experiencing a vice-like jealousy, greediness etc.

Then, third, there was private intellectual and moral teaching: during the day's work, lots of subjects would be discussed and stories told that did not directly relate to the practical job at hand. This differed from the okuterama at night in that girls would be with their mothers and boys with their fathers, instead of everybody being together.

Finally, boys could be sent to the regiments of the King (that is, the King of the Banyankole Bahima). Then, they would go to the palace to be trained as a soldier in such things as archery, bravery, wrestling and other fighting skills, standards of behavior in the army, in general martial arts and warfare, but also chess-like analytic games like omweso. This was nearest to the idea of schools as they were introduced by the time I was born. Those boys who went into the Seventh Regiment of the King, for instance, would be called "Abaseveni", from which I got my name "Museveni", though I personally was not in that regiment.

All these modes of learning were oral. There was, traditionally, no alphabet, hence no knowledge traded by written language. So the evening sessions (*oftarama*) were not only for the children to listen, but also for adults to refresh and keep up the collective knowledge of the tribe, for instance by scraping back together details remembered by different persons. No wonder the traditional idea was that knowledge comes from the past, from remembering. In my youth, there was a start to school education for few of the children, from which I could profit because my father saw its value and even moved his kraal nearer to my school to facilitate my travel.

So I was among what was then still a minority of the children that learned to read. Reading was of course a great advantage, because it opened other options to learn than listening to storytellers. Now I could even "listen" to what had been said by someone long dead! For me, learning to read was not a surprising or spectacular affair, because as children we saw people around us who were able to read, and this made us eager to learn it too. We were not the pioneers among our people in learning to read, but a curiosity at the time in my family was that my sister also went to school. My father argued against it but my mother got her way.

For my A-level examinations, I took English, History and Economics as my subjects. We were not taught much African history and the literature was mostly European – Tennyson, Yeats and, of course Shakespeare; we learned many of the famous speeches. Although this kind of education was irrelevant to our situation we still could learn from it since all societies are basically the same. Reading *The Merchant of Venice*, as we did in Senior Three, we could see the conflict in the old society, where the new merchant class was being viewed as ravenous and greedy. It was clear that Shakespeare was denigrating Shylock as an undesirable character for wanting his pound of flesh; but capitalism is exactly like that, and it should be made to work to the benefit of society. Even if we did not appreciate all these implications at the time, the stories were interesting and we could see later how they applied when we learned more about societies.

What interested me most in history was the formation of states in Europe – particularly in Italy and Germany during the 19th century. I understood more when I went to university and learned about the evolution of capitalism, and the whole idea of markets. The French Revolution also fascinated me, and bourgeois opposition to the taxes imposed by the feudal order because it interfered with trade – which was also the reason that the Prussian Junkers wanted a unified government. Therefore, although there was often little direct African relevance in our curriculum at that time, I did not feel our education suffered because of it. Subsequently, one can read other more relevant books, once one has learned the skills, the discipline, and especially the habit of reading – and that we did learn at Ntare School.

Later, at Dar es Salaam University we found a very good political and intellectual atmosphere with a lot of modernist revolutionary thinkers such as Walter Rodney, and other lecturers from Europe. We became exposed to new ideas and this gave us a very good chance to become familiar with pan-Africanist and anti-colonialist ideas, the most dramatic of which was the exposure to the role imperialism had played in distorting socio-economic development in Africa. This played a large part in focusing our own political outlook as far as internal and external issues were concerned. We had previously had a vague nationalist feeling but it took definite shape because it was now backed by a coherent ideological outlook.

We became aware that the greatest danger to the welfare of Africans was imperialism in its modern manifestation of unbalanced, non-reciprocal foreign capital penetration, resulting in one-sided expatriation of dividends. This had led to a continuous net outflow of resources from the backward regions of the world to advanced Western Europe, North America and Japan. We discovered that by the 15th century, the initial unbalanced development of science and technology in the world had resulted in European predators starting the process of enslaving the peoples of Africa, Asia and Latin America. They had relied on the monopoly of gunpowder and the process had gone through various stages: the slave trade, the looting of precious raw materials, and eventually, colonization and effective occupation of the whole continent which completely distorted the development of Africa.

For the degree course we started off with three subjects in the first year, then continued with two for the second and third years. I began with Law, together with Economics and Political Science. At Dar es Salaam they had a unique way of teaching Law as a subject, rather than as a profession. After the first year I dropped Law because I did not find the way they were teaching it very useful. We had to spend a lot of time on case law and, of course, it was heavily loaded towards European culture. I remember a particular case called Amkeyo vs. Regina. Amkeyo was a man in Kenya who had stolen a cow, slaughtered it, eaten it and buried its skin in his hut. Now, according to the British laws of evidence, and their concept of marriage, a wife cannot give evidence against her husband because, before the law, they are one person. So how can a man give evidence against himself?

Nobody knew where the cow skin was – there was some suspicion that Amkeyo had eaten the cow, but there was no proof. Later on Amkeyo quarreled with his wife and she reported him to the police who came and dug up the missing cow skin from his hut. I don't know who advised Amkeyo about this British law, but when he went to court, he argued that his wife was not a competent witness to give evidence against him since they were one person! However, the British judge said: "No. Natives do not really marry so they cannot benefit from this law. This law cannot be used by people like you. It is only for people who really marry – yours is only woman purchase!" So the judge allowed the wife to testify against her husband because, according to him, she was not really his wife. When I read that case, I thought we were wasting time learning a lot of rubbish. It was just like acting – like being on a stage! In any case, the law of two people "being one" was to me an absurd one – the fact that if I committed a crime, my wife could not report me! What they should have taught us was principles of modern law as Part A of such a course, and Part B could have been the application of those principles to our society. That would have been a better approach, but these lecturers were stuck on European case law.

As far as the other subjects were concerned, there was a lot of nonsense in Political Science as well. I disliked constructing models: "Let us assume this, let us assume that", and so on. My question was: "But why do you assume? Why don't you study reality? Why do you waste so much time constructing models when you have reality?" We used to have a number of conflicts with the lecturers who were mainly from Europe and America. There were a few African lecturers but they were heavily western-influenced.

Teaching and Arguing: Improving Bahima Nomad Life

But before I went to the University of Dar es Salaam, after having finished my school education, in my early twenties I joined my friend Mwesigwa Black in his effort to teach the Bahima Banyankole. Because of their nomadic way of life, most of their children still did not go to school and modern ideas about animal husbandry, hygiene and health did not percolate through to them. They did not believe in supplementing their pastoralist activities by cultivating food or cash crops. Their quality of life therefore deteriorated in all fields: nutrition, education, health, science and technology, literature and art, community cohesion, fertility and social progress in general.

The problems were not entirely of their own making. When the colonialists came, they had interfered with the socio-economic systems they found in place. The production, for instance, of the rich and nutritious finger millet, a staple food in Ankole, went into steep decline. The colonialists called on the "natives" to shift from food to cash crops such as coffee and cotton. They did nothing to build up the cattle industry, as it would have competed with that of the white farmers in Kenya. It was partly through this neglect that the cattle in Ankole were decimated by tsetse fly and tick-borne diseases such as East Coast fever. Because the Bahima in Ankole were dependent on cattle, they became impoverished and large numbers of them dispersed all over Uganda to the areas of Masaka, Mpigi, Mubende, Luwero, Busoga, Bukedi, Teso, Lango and Acholi. Some of them even crossed into Tanzania. Wherever they went, they faced exploitation and persecution. They worked for little or no pay or were branded as "foreigners" and told to go back to their homelands. They lived as serfs all over the country, in spite of being extremely diligent cattle herders.

The local collaborator chiefs in Ankole, although mostly Bahima, were busy protecting their own interests and did not mobilize these poor people to reorient their lives in order to survive new situations. The settlement of the people was even obstructed by local government authorities who wanted to prevent the peasants from gaining legal control over their pieces of land. The peasants in the area filled in forms (the legal requirement for land being leased to them), but the authorities would not allow them to complete the process. The hope of the United Peoples Congress reactionaries was that the peasants would be forced to migrate out of the areas so that the people in power could grab it for their own use or give it to their cronies.

To a limited extent, a small group of the cultivating Banyankole somehow benefited from the situation by growing the then prized cash crops, especially coffee, but not cotton. The Banyankole roasted the experimental cotton seed to show that cotton could not grow in Ankole, a trick the colonialists fell for. Nevertheless, the quality of life deteriorated in Ankole although there were superficial trappings of "development", such as the introduction of woven cloth to replace cow hides and bark cloth, the elimination of mass killer diseases such as smallpox, and some literacy and education for a small fraction of the population.

As a result there was some awareness of the existence of a new type of knowledge, coming from other sources than elders and ancestors. I would not want to use the word "science" exclusively for this new type of knowledge, because our people traditionally had science too, which originated from many types of crafts, like making iron. But an example of the new type was a European cure for a skin disease. For this, sulfur drugs came into use, which cured the disease. As a result of such kinds of useful knowledge having come from outside, when you were known to come from the culture of the educated (called the *abashomeire*), even if you were young, as I was at the time, it was held possible that you had some knowledge to bring and you would be listened to with curiosity and interest.

Mwesiga Black and I walked from kraal to kraal in the present Kazo and Nyabuzi counties of Mbarara district, urging peasants to refuse to vacate their land. We encouraged them to till and fence it, in spite of obstructions by the district administration run by the UPC (United Peoples Congress, the party of the then president Milton Obote, chiefly supported by protestants and northern tribes).

The problem with the cattle keepers of Ankole was not that they did not know how to look after cattle – it was that they lacked education. They lacked some knowledge that was indispensable for adapting to the changed circumstances. If their cows died they thought it was just bad luck, or that they had "bad bones". So our task was to educate them about modern cattle keeping methods. We would approach the most influential man in the neighborhood and explain to him what we were trying to do. We would spend the night in the area and the next day the influential man would gather the people in his area and we would talk to them about fencing their land and treating their cows with modern medicines.

When they said: "How can we afford to pay for the fencing of our pasture?", we would ask them: "How many cattle do you lose in a year from wandering away and getting lost because your land is not fenced?" It was our aim to make them understand that if they fenced their land they would not lose their cattle. They should begin to see that it would be worth their while to sell a few cows to pay for the fencing in the knowledge that they would benefit from more cows in the long run. We used the same argument when they said that they could not afford to buy modern medicines when their cows became sick. We pointed out the numbers they were losing each year from preventable diseases and showed them that this would no longer be the case if they bought modern drugs.

Winning the Bahima over was not only due to their giving us a chance to come with our ideas because they had become aware of the existence of new types of knowledge brought by Abashomi. Our message was not as simple as coming up with a practical, short-term, convincing power like sulfur drugs to cure some skin disease. What we supplied were arguments for new solutions to recent, new problems. But they should do the work of changing methods. Fortunately, in supplying our line of thought we could quote information available to the Bahima, though they were not interpreting it correctly: they knew that cows were doing well in government experimental stations, though they were fenced in and not treated according to the nomadic method. Those cows did not move around.

But, since such cows were using drugs that were considered unaffordable, the Bahima thought they should stick to their own science, at a lower technological base: move around with their cows in the nomadic way and find virgin areas in order to avoid overgrazing and vectors (ticks and other insects carrying bacteria), which tend to multiply if a cow herd remains in one place for long.

We also used a fighting metaphor to encourage replacement of nomadism by fencing and medicine use: do not run away from disease, stay, face it and fight against it.

Though we were given a chance to state our ideas, the strong Bahima traditions meant that their reception was a skeptical one. In so far as it involved reasoning about the results of actions that they had never seen tried, some 20% would follow them initially. Trust in a line of thought without having seen the predicted result was generally considered to be too precarious to base a change of method upon. So there would be little implementation before we had set the example by building our own non-government model farm from scratch, near them, so they could see the good state of the cows there. Then the people could see with their own eyes the truth of our reasoning.

As a result of our intensive mobilization campaign, peasants did settle down on the land and, to a large extent, abandoned their nomadic way of life. Their new sedentary cattle farming method caused the number of cows to increase and finally the die-hards supporting the traditional methods would be won over.

Because of the use of ancient cattle-breeding practices, not only were cattle dying from preventable diseases; children were not going to school either. If people did not fence their land, in order to prevent their cattle roaming into other people's homes and gardens, they had to keep their children at home to restrain the cows – to act as a human fence. Another reform resulting from our campaign was the elimination of the ancient and labor-intensive practice of the daily removal of cow dung from cattle enclosures – a task I was only too familiar with from my own childhood: it was the children's task to remove it, with their bare hands! These enclosures (for the night) had been necessary because in the past, cattle raiders and wild animals had to be discouraged. Fencing the entire pasture eliminated the children's tasks of watching over cattle and removing dung. Moreover, the dung now fertilized that whole area. This simple reform saved much time and labor – especially the children's. So the effect of our education in spreading knowledge was multiplicative: after implementing the time-saving improvements children could go to school and thus the Bahima would get even more education.

Later Teaching and Arguing: Helping to Understand the Monetization of the Economy

Later, as president, part of my efforts to eliminate rural poverty was to further the recognition among the people that the introduction of money in the economy had changed their household problem situation, and that the new problems called for new solutions. Before the introduction of money, the main purpose of production had been the procurement of food for self-supply. People were not used to evaluate their work. They did not link their needs with their means. That became necessary when needs changed and having money to spend became a prerequisite to fulfill certain needs. Money became needed for school fees. People were used to travel by using their legs. Now roads were opening markets but to go to the market, you had to pay the bus fare. Medicine had become necessary for people as well as cattle. Chemicals had become required to grow crops in a competitive way. Once people became confronted with money deficits, they did not catalogue their means. They did not factor it in. They could not cope with the problem by the traditional methods. They needed knowledge in order to create equilibrium between their incomes and their expenses, or, even better, a surplus.

With money now needed for things like school, health, transport and clothing, production should also become the solution to financial problems. I was regularly going into the rural areas to teach how to adapt the management of the household to the new conditions of living in a world with money. This necessitated production, partly for a market in order to have a money revenue that could be used for the new needs.

We have advised people to survey the market and if the price of a particular crop goes down, they should switch to another one. In other words, they should receive maximum money returns from their plots of land. The source of poverty in this respect has been small-scale farmers producing low-value crops on a small scale and being unable to balance their household budgets as a result. I think that the rural economy will eventually crystallize into two forms of production. People with small pieces of land will produce more and more high value crops, plus their own food crops, whereas medium and large scale farmers will produce low value crops, but on a large scale.

Another aspect of the rural poverty problem was the conceptual confusion that persisted as to who should play what role in the economy. If somebody does not have enough money to meet his needs, he blames the government: "I am poor and it is the fault of the government". In recent years I have been going round the country clarifying matters for the people by defining who is supposed to do what. I do this mostly by using local imagery in order to illustrate the concepts. I have been using the example of *olubimbi* or *ogrugyezi*, words in our local languages meaning the piece of land marked out of a farm for an individual to cultivate with his hoe. In the army, the equivalent would be the arc of fire one is supposed to cover. It is the role of the government to ensure peace and to build the infrastructure, such as constructing roads, because these problems are too large for private people to solve. Once the government has done that, then the individual must do his part, which is to use his land optimally to get enough income for his household.

Another image I use is *okulembeka*, which is tapping rainwater running off the roof to use in the home. The imagery here is that it is possible for God to make rain but if the individual does not take the trouble to tap the water to use in his own house, it is not up to God to do it for him. This sort of imagery has helped the people to realize that if there are moneymaking possibilities in the country, the individual must take the trouble to look for avenues to tap money into his household in order to balance his needs with his income. This is because people have simply been producing goods or crops without tabulating the household requirements and the money they need to offset those needs. The focal point is the household and if its income is boosted, poverty will be eliminated and development will be sustainable.

During my rural teaching sessions, therefore, which I normally carry out at the headquarters of every county I visit, I use an illustration of three columns ("Ebyetaaga", "Obugaaga", "Emyooga") on a blackboard. The first column, headed *Ebyetaaga* (needs), is for household needs, the second, headed *Obugaaga* (family assets), includes both physical assets and non-physical ones, such as education. The third, headed *Emyooga* (activities) is to work out how to use what is in column two to offset the requirements of column one (and the requirements of investment in column two). (For an illustration of the President Museveni's teaching, see http://mindphiles.com/knowledgecultures – B.H.)

This procedure of planning and budgeting was well known, but used chiefly for partial problems like planning, if you had a number of sons, for the bride prices or dowries (containing many items, among which cows were the key ones) you would have to pay to the families of the daughters your sons were going to marry. Maybe you would go the King, who might help you. So there was the idea of budget analysis, but now, to cope with the transition from a subsistence-barter economy to a money-exchange economy, the idea of budget analysis should be applied to encompass the entire household. Our teaching task here was not so much to introduce the idea of what in western economics is called "rational" planning and budgeting, but to make use of this known idea and extend it for the purpose of the transition from old solutions to old problems of a purely commodity economy to new solutions to the new problem of producing for the money surplus that the modern economy necessitates.

I have been teaching like this for a long time, but more intensively in the recent past, because we have now put some of the infrastructure in place. Originally, when there were no good roads anywhere in the country, you could not tell people to use roads to tap money where there were none. Although there are some areas that are still remote and cut off by a lack of infrastructure, there is no good reason why many areas in the country should not now do better economically.

Ancestors

While teaching, some people tend to refer to the wisdom of ancestors. In my opinion this shortcut shows a lack of confidence on the teacher's part and is to be avoided. The ancestors no doubt were wise and respectable people, but they had their own problems, which they solved in their own way. That is the past. Now, we have new problems and we should use our own sense of logic and available and obtainable knowledge to solve the problems of today! So teachers should avoid romanticizing, and should not go for such short cuts and quick results by trying to quote ancestral authority. Moreover, there is a danger to it, because this approach involves those fellows who claim to be intermediaries between the ancestors and us. They can interpose their own self-interest and start telling lies. I do not believe that education means pushing against the power of the ancestors. Our ancestors did their work then, we have our own challenges now.

Is Africa a Backward Continent?

The technological backwardness of traditional African cultures should not be exaggerated. Historically all major technical revolutions, like those from stone to bronze age and bronze to iron age, occurred in Sub-Saharan African in roughly the same time as elsewhere. The arrears are a relatively recent and I believe temporary phenomenon that should not be overstated.

There are some aspects in which African cultures still seem to be in the lead. Here I think of the vocabularies of Bantu languages. They have traditionally been developed in an oral context. From the literal point of view, they have not been fully explored by far, that is, existing written accounts of those vocabularies in dictionaries are far from complete. For many words denoted by word combinations in English (think of a word like "forehead"), Bantu languages have separate words (here *obuso*). Words without counterparts in western languages tend to be absent from "Bantu dictionaries" because they usually are forged by westerners merely searching for the Bantu counterparts of western words, thus missing Bantu words that have no, or only unsatisfactory counterparts in western language. Hence those dictionaries are very incomplete. In fact the vocabulary of Bantu languages is richer than for instance that of English. An integration of these Bantu vocabularies, say in the form of an enhancement of Swahili, would be an enrichment, not only to the literal form of African expression, but to global culture as well. Clearly, the range of vocabularies limits knowledge, or at least its expression. Now writing has become integrated in African culture, this program of bringing to bear the full power of African language on the written word clearly should be on the African agenda.

Conclusion

The power of the types of knowledge that I have discussed is their ability to enrich and improve the quality of life, hence ultimately the vitality of a population. Lack of such knowledge is the cause of poverty, disease and social conflict. I have come to understand, as I wrote already in my book *Sowing the Mustard Seed*, that lack of knowledge is a major factor in many of the mistakes that have occurred in Africa since the 1960s. One important example of lack of knowledge resulted in the ruinous idea that the nationalization of industries enhances production and employment. This in turn was fed by a second type of ignorance prompting the idea that a plant run by foreign investors is a "foreign plant". Nationalization, it was thought, would make it "our own plant". The mistake here is thinking that whether a plant is foreign or domestic is to be judged by its ownership. But what really matters is who is put to work for a wage in the factory and who will receive the tax revenues, who will profit from the demand raised by the factory for the raw materials it needs, and who will profit from the spending of the wage earned by the workers of that factory. Those will clearly all be domestic beneficiaries, no matter who owns the firm. If ownership of firms in your country is left to those who know best how to run them, they will boost your country no matter who these owners are. A third, equally ruinous idea that seems hard indeed to root out is that entrepreneurs, whether foreign or domestic, seeking reinvestable profit by hiring labor as cheaply as possible, and using it for production as efficiently as possible, are usurpers of the public and cause poverty!

But it is not only economic knowledge that is at stake. The same holds for all kinds of scientific knowledge: 90% of the diseases are avoidable by immunization, proper nutrition, and proper hygiene, measures requiring relatively little money and effort. The AIDS epidemic grew to its devastating size from lack of knowledge: it is not difficult or expensive for anyone to avoid becoming infected as soon as one obtains the relevant knowledge.

Yoweri K. Museveni
President of Uganda

Kwame Anthony Appiah

AFRICAN STUDIES AND THE CONCEPT OF KNOWLEDGE

Bima ya beto ke dya bambuta me bikisa
[What we eat – our ancestors have shown us]
Mbiem proverb

Abstract. This article summarizes my views on epistemological problems in African studies as I have expressed them previously in different contexts, mainly my book *In My Father's House* (1992), to which I refer the reader for further details. I start with an attempt to expose some natural errors in our thinking about the traditional-modern polarity, and thus help understand some striking and not generally appreciated similarities of the logical problem situation in modern western philosophy of science to the analysis of traditional African epistemic procedures. This similarity rests upon both types of analysis dealing with *procedures crucially hinging upon knowledge claims*.

The Nature of Belief

I propose to begin in a place whose strangeness for most Europeans and Americans and whose naturalness for many Africans are a measure of the distance between Nairobi and New York; namely, with what, with some unhappiness, I shall call African "religion". For one of the marks of African traditional life is the extent to which beliefs, activities, habits of mind, and behavior in general are shot through with what Europeans and Americans would call "religion". Indeed, it is because understanding traditional religion is so central to the conceptual issues that modernization raises that philosophical discussion of the status of traditional religion has been so central in recent African philosophy. And the urgency and the relevance of the issue to central questions of public policy is one of the reasons why there is greater excitement to be found in philosophical discussion of religion in Africa than in philosophy of religion in the West.

If I am reluctant to use the term *religion* without qualification, it is because religion in the contemporary West is, by and large, so different from what it is in traditional life that to report it in western categories is as much to invite misunderstanding as to offer insight. But the examples I want to discuss should help make this point for me. Let us begin, then, with an account of a traditional ceremony.

In: Hamminga, B. (ed.), *Knowledge Cultures. Comparative Western and African Epistemology* (*Poznań Studies in the Philosophy of the Sciences and the Humanities*, vol. 88), pp. 23-56. Amsterdam/New York, NY: Rodopi, 2005.

The place is somewhere in rural Asante. The time is the ethnographic present – which is to say, the past. As we arrive, a male figure dressed in a fiber skirt and with charms about his neck is dancing to the accompaniment of drumming and singing. Suddenly he leaps into a nearby stream and emerges clasping something to his breast. This he places in a brass pan and pounds with clay (which we later discover comes from the sacred river Tano) and the leaves or bark of various plants, some gold dust, and an aggrey bead.

During the pounding, the figure utters words, which we may translate as follows:

> God, Kwame, Upon-whom-men-lean-and-do-not-fall; Earth Goddess, Yaa; Leopard and all beasts and plants of the forest, today is sacred Friday: and you, Ta Kwesi, we are installing you, we are placing you, so that we may have life, that we may not die, that we may not become impotent. To the village head of this village, life; to the young men of the village, life; to those who bear children, life; to the children of the village, life.
>
> Spirits of the trees, we call upon you all, to let you come here now, and let all that is in our heads be placed in this shrine.
>
> When we call upon you in darkness, when we call upon you in the day, if we say to you "Do this for us", that will be what you will do.
>
> And these are the rules that we are placing here for you, god of ours: if a king comes from somewhere and comes to us or our children or our grandchildren, and says he is going to war, and he comes to tell you; and if he is going to fight and will not have a victory, it is necessary that you should tell us; and if he is going and he will have a victory, tell the truth also.

The peroration continues, and the spirit is asked repeatedly to tell the truth about the sources of the evil that make men ill. The priest ends by saying:

> We have taken sheep and a chicken, we have taken palm wine, which we are about to give you that you may reside in this village and preserve its life.
>
> Perhaps on some tomorrow the King of Asante may come and say "My child So-and-so is sick", or perhaps "Some elder is sick"; or he may send a messenger to ask you to go with him; and in such a case you may go, and we will not think you are fleeing from us.
>
> The mouths of all of us speak these things together.

Then the sacrifices of the animals are made, and their blood is allowed to flow into the brass pan. While this is going on, perhaps some other priest will go into trance and sing the song of some other minor local spirit.

This account is a rough paraphrase of one that Captain R. S. Rattray (1955, pp. 147-9) published in the 1920s and, with few modifications, you could find just such a ceremony at the installation of a spirit – an *obosom* – in a shrine today.

Perhaps there is nothing puzzling in the ritual I have described. I have tried deliberately to give an account of a series of actions that:

1. people outside the culture are unlikely to believe could possibly succeed;
2. all of us could surely at least imagine believing in.

Yet this ritual is part of a religious world that is typical of the many traditional cultures whose modes of thought have struck western ethnography and philosophy as puzzling.

We can begin to see why, if we ask ourselves not what it is that is believed by these actors but *how they could have come to believe it*. Most intellectuals outside Asante think they know, after all, that there are no such spirits. That, for all the requests in the priest's prayer, no unseen agent will come to inhabit the shrine; no one will answer the questions "What made this person ill?" or "Would we win if we went to war?" or "How should we cure the king's elder?" Yet here is a culture where, for at least several hundred years, people have been setting up just such shrines and asking them just such questions and asking the spirits they believe are in them to perform just such tasks. Surely by now they should know, if they are rational, that it won't work.

Now, it is the appeal to a notion of rationality in this last question that will lead us into characteristically philosophical territory: and it is, in part, because of what it tells us about rationality, about the proper scope and function of reason, that the study of these rituals relates to similar studies of scientific procedures. And if we press the question how these beliefs can be sustained in the face of a falsity that is obvious, at least to us, we shall return, in the end, to the question whether we have really understood what is going on, much in the same way as this question could be pressed concerning theories known from the history of western science that are abandoned, will be abandoned, or ought to be abandoned according to adherents of some kind of position. And since falsity claims and truth claims are within the same discourse, this matter is relevant for philosophy of science generally.

It is as well, however, to begin with some distinctions. I have already made what is the first crucial distinction: between understanding the content of the beliefs involved in the actions in a religious performance, on the one hand, and understanding how those beliefs became established in the culture, o n the other. But we shall need more distinctions than this. For we need, I think, to bear in mind at least these three separate types of understanding: first, understanding the ritual and the beliefs that underlie it; second, understanding the historical sources of both ritual and belief; and, third, understanding what sustains them.

One of the advantages of making such distinctions – exactly the sort of distinction that is often held up as typical of the trivial logic chopping that makes academic philosophy so unpleasing to those who do not practice it – is that it allows us to set some questions to one side. So we can say, to begin with, that to understand these ritual acts what is necessary is what is necessary in the understanding of any acts: namely to understand what *beliefs and intentions* underlie them, so that we know *what the actors think they are doing*, what they are trying to do. Indeed if we cannot do this we cannot even say what the ritual is. To say that what is going on here is that these people are inviting a spirit to take up its place in a shrine is already to say something about their beliefs and their intentions. It is to say, for example, that they believe that there is a spirit, *Ta Kwesi*, and believe too that asking the spirit to do something is a way of getting that spirit to do it; it is to say that they want the spirit to inhabit the shrine.

Perhaps this is obvious, though it runs counter to the principles of currents like behaviorism. So perhaps I do not need to say that it is not just the performance of certain bodily movements by the priest and the other villagers that makes up this ritual. But it is important to remember that you and I could carry out these very movements in order to demonstrate the form of the ritual, and that if *we* did it in *that* spirit, we should not be inviting anyone – least of all *Ta Kwesi* – to do anything. It is thus precisely because we think these particular Asante acts are *intended* in a certain way that we know what is going on is a religious act. What makes it religious is what the people are trying to do.

Any theoretical account of this ritual must begin by trying to understand, therefore, what the beliefs and intentions are that form it. But that is not, of course, all there is to understanding the ritual. For there are certainly features of it – the use of gold dust and the aggrey bead in making up the contents of the brass pan, for example – that may still remain in need of explanation. We may well discover that though the priest means to put the gold dust into the pot, he does so only because this is, as he might say, part of "how the ancestors called a spirit" – that is, he might have no special reason of his own for using the gold dust.

What does it mean to say that this still needs explaining? The priest does lots of things in the performance of the ritual for no special reason of his own. He raises a stick up and down as he dances, and he does so deliberately: it is part of his intention in dancing to raise the stick up and down. Yet we may find nothing to explain in this.

I think the first step in answering the question "Why does the gold dust need explaining?" is to distinguish between two kinds of things that the priest does in the performance of the ritual. On the one hand, there are such things as the addition of the gold dust, which the priest believes are an essential part of what he is doing. To leave out the gold dust would be to fail to do something that is essential if the performance is to succeed in bringing the spirit to its new shrine. These essential components of the ritual are to be contrasted with what we can call the "accidental" components. Maybe the priest wipes the sweat off his nose as the dancing rises in crescendo, and, when asked, he tells us that this is, of course, something that the ritual could have done without. If the raising of the stick and the wiping of the sweat are incidental to the performance, then that is why we do not need to explain them to understand the ritual. So that part of why the gold dust needs explaining is that it is essential to the ritual action.

Now in saying that the gold dust is essential, we have already given part of its explanation. It is there because without it the act is believed to be less efficacious, perhaps not efficacious at all. But a question remains. Why does adding it make a difference? After all, all of us probably have ancestors, great-grandmothers, for example, who had remedies for the common cold, of which we take little or no notice. Why should the priest think that this piece of ancestral lore is worth holding onto, especially if he has no idea why the ancestors thought it an essential part of calling a spirit?

Here, I think, many cultural anthropologists will be disposed to say that the gold dust attracts our attention because it plainly symbolizes something. We can make up our own stories. Let us suppose, for the sake of argument, that what it symbolizes is the giving of riches to the spirit, a sort of spiritual sweetener for the contract between village and spirit that is in the making. The plausibility of this suggestion should not distract us from what is problematic in it. For if this *is* why the gold dust is there, why doesn't the priest know it? The obvious answer is that he doesn't know it because he is only carrying out the prescribed form. The people who designed the ritual, the people the priest calls the ancestors, knew why the gold dust was there. They put it there because they thought that part of a proper invitation to a powerful spirit was to give it some of your riches. For to do this is to do what you would do when asking any powerful person for a favor. It is true that spirits have no use for money – the spiritual economy is greased by something other than gold – but in handing over this gold dust you are treating the spirit as you would treat a human being you respect. For these ancestors, then, the handing over of the gold dust is an act whose efficacy depends upon the spirit's recognition that it is an expression of respect.

I do not know if anything like this is true; it would be a hard thing to find out. "The ancestors" are not around to ask. But notice that this explanation of the presence of gold dust as symbolic takes us out of the arena of understanding the ritual acts themselves into examining their origins. This resort to origins is not, however, what makes it true that the gold dust functions symbolically. Our priest might himself have been aware that the gold dust functions symbolically in this way. And I shall try in a moment to say a little more about what this means. But it is important to see that treating an element of a ritual as symbolic requires that there be someone who treats it symbolically, and that this someone be either the actor him- or herself, or the originator of the form of ritual action. Finding that the priest does not see the act as symbolic, we needed to look for someone else who did. There are more and less sophisticated versions of this sort of symbolist treatment. Durkheim, for example, appears to have thought (Skorupski 1976) that religious practices can symbolize social reality because, though the agent is not consciously aware of what they symbolize, he or she may be unconsciously aware of it. Lévi-Strauss, I think, believes something similar. I happen to think that this is a mistake, but whether or not Durkheim was right, he recognized, at least, that a symbol is always somebody's symbol: it is something that means something to someone.

But what is it exactly to use the gold dust as a symbol of respect? We are so familiar with this sort of symbolic act that we do not often reflect upon it. Here again, it is useful to make a distinction. Some symbols, of which words are the paradigm, are purely conventional. It is because there exists a complex interaction of beliefs and intentions between speakers of the same language that it is possible for us to use our words to express our thoughts to each other. This complex background makes it possible for us to refer to objects, and thus to use words to stand for those objects symbolically. But words are not the only purely conventional symbols, and speaking is not the only purely conventional symbolic act. In saluting a superior officer, a soldier expresses his recognition of the officer's superiority. And it is only because such a convention exists that the act of saluting has the meaning it has.

Now, the gold dust is not a purely conventional symbol. It is possible to use the gold dust in this context as a symbol of respect, because in other contexts the giving of gold dust is a sign of respect. After all, the reason that giving gold dust to a powerful figure in Asante is a sign of respect is not that there is a convention to this effect. People give gold dust to powerful people because gold dust is money and money is something that powerful people, like others, have a use for. To give someone money when you need him or her to do something for you is to seek to influence their acts, and thus to acknowledge that they have it in their power to do something for you. They know that you think they have that power because you both know that you would not be giving them the money otherwise. If the giving of gold dust along with a request occurs regularly in contexts where people require something of someone with powers they do not themselves have; and if, as in Asante, to ask someone in a position of power to do something for you is to show respect; then offering gold dust in conjunction with a request becomes a sign of respect

– in the simple sense that it is something whose presence gives evidence that the giver respects the receiver.

It is thus not *arbitrary* that the ancestors in my story chose gold dust as a symbol of respect, even though they realized that in placing the gold dust in the pan they were not in fact giving the spirit something that it could use.

Many symbolic ritual acts have this character. They are not arbitrary signs, like words or salutes; they are acts that draw their meaning from the non-ritual significance of relevantly similar performances. What makes them symbolic is the recognition by the agents that these acts in ritual contexts do not work in the standard way. The spirit comes not because we have given it some money but because we have done something that shows respect, and giving the gold dust shows respect because outside these ritual contexts the giving of gold dust is standardly accompanied by respect.

I have spent some time discussing the role of this symbol in this ritual because to many it has seemed that it is the distinguishing character of these religious acts that they are symbolic. Clifford Geertz (1973, p. 90) has famously remarked that religion is "a system of symbols". Now it is, of course, an impressive fact about many religious practices and beliefs that they have symbolic elements: the Eucharist is loaded with symbolism, and so is the Passover meal. But I want to argue that the symbolism arises out of the fundamental nature of religious beliefs, and that these fundamental beliefs are not themselves symbolic.

All my life, I have seen and heard ceremonies like the one with which I began. This public, ritual appeal to unseen spirits on a ceremonial occasion is part of a form of life in which such appeals are regularly made in private. When a man opens a bottle of gin, he will pour a little on the earth, asking his ancestors to drink a little and to protect the family and its doings. This act is without ceremony, without the excitement of the public installation of an *obosom* in a new shrine, yet it inhabits the same world. Indeed, it is tempting to say that, just as the public installation of a spirit is like the public installation of a chief, the private libation is like the private pouring of a drink for a relative. The element of ceremonial is not what is essential; what is essential is the ontology of invisible beings. So that in the wider context of Asante life it seems absurd to claim that what was happening, when my father casually poured a few drops from the top of a newly opened bottle of Scotch onto the carpet, involved anything other than a literal belief in the ancestors. The pouring of the drink may have been symbolic: there is no general assumption in Asante that the dead like whisky. But for the gesture of offering them a portion of a valued drink to make sense, the ancestors who are thus symbolically acknowledged must exist. It is true, as Kwasi Wiredu (1980, p. 42) has expressed the matter, that the proposition "that our departed ancestors continue to hover around in some rarified form ready now and then to take a sip of the ceremonial schnapps is . . . [one] that I have never heard rationally defended". But that it is never rationally defended is not, perhaps, so surprising: it is, after all, not usually rationally *attacked*. (Nor, as I say, do we need to suppose that a literal sip is at stake.) The proposition that there are planets hovering around the sun, larger than the earth, however small they may appear as we ponder the night sky, is not in the usual course of things rationally defended in Europe or America. It is not rationally defended not because anyone thinks there could be no rational defense but because it is taken, now, to be obviously true. And, in traditional Asante culture the existence of disembodied departed spirits is equally uncontroversial. I shall return to this issue later.

If I am right, and it is (as Tylor claimed) a commitment to disembodied agency that crucially defines the religious beliefs that underlie rituals like the one I have described, then there is, of course, an important question that needs to be answered – namely, why in many such rituals symbolism plays so important a part. And the answer is implicit in the account I gave earlier of the relationship between the installation of a chief and the installation of a spirit.

For, as any Asante could tell you, symbolism is a major feature of both of these ceremonies. And though there is a religious component in the installation of a chief, as there is in any public ceremony in Asante, that does not make the installation an essentially religious act. Symbolism is in fact a feature of all major ceremonial occasions in any culture, and the presence of symbolism in religious ceremonial derives from its nature as ceremonial and not from its nature as religious. In private and less ceremonial religious acts in a traditional culture (such as, for example, an appeal at a household shrine to the ancestors), there is still, of course, an element of symbolism. But it is important to recall here that in Asante culture relations with *living* elders where a request is being made in private are also ceremonious. All important contacts between individuals in traditional cultures are ceremonious. When Rattray (1955) reported a séance at the Tano shrine in the early part of this century, he described how, when the priest with the shrine "containing" the spirit on his head entered the trance in which he would speak for the spirit, the assembled priests and elders said, "Nana, ma akye" [Sir, good morning], as they would have done if a chief (or an elder) had entered. The formality of the response is somehow less striking to me than its naturalness, the sense it gives that the Tano spirit is simply a being among beings – addressed with ceremony for its status or its power and not because the scene is set apart from the everyday.

And once we have seen that the ritual setting is ceremonious, we need only the further premise that all ceremony has elements of symbolism to complete a syllogism: ritual entails symbolism. I do not myself have theories as to why human beings so closely bind together ceremony and symbolism. It is something many of us begin to do in our play as children, and it is surely as much a part of our natural history as, say, language. But that the prevalence of symbolism in religious ritual in Asante derives from the conception of relations between people and spirits as relations between persons seems to me, in the light of these facts, hard to deny. Case by case, the same claim can be made for religion in most non-literate cultures – in Africa and elsewhere.

If the emphasis in western theory on the distinctively symbolic character of traditional religious thought and practice is misleading, it is worth taking a moment to consider why it should have been so pervasive. And the answer lies, I think, in the character of religion in the industrial cultures in which this theorizing about religion takes place.

Christianity is a religion that defines itself by doctrine; heresy, paganism, and atheism have been, as a result, at various times central *topoi* of Christian reflection. In this respect Christianity is not, of course, unique; Islam, too, is defined by its doctrine and, like Christianity, its Book. Islamic evangelists have sometimes held that the simple acceptance of two items of doctrine – that God is one, and that Muhammad is his prophet – was sufficient to constitute conversion, though Christian missionaries have usually insisted on at least token assent to some more complex credo. But these differences seem relatively unimportant when we come to contrast Christianity and Islam, on the one hand, with many of the other systems of ritual, practice, and belief that we call religions. Never has the contrast been more sharply drawn than in a remark of Chinua Achebe's (1982): "I can't imagine Igbos traveling four thousand miles to tell anybody their worship was wrong!"

The extraordinary importance attached to doctrine in the Christian churches is not a modern phenomenon; growing up between Roman and Hellenistic paganism, on the one side, and Judaism on the other, and divided bitterly and regularly from the very beginning on topics that may seem to us wonderfully abstruse: the history of the church is, to a great extent, the history of doctrines. But, though doctrine is indeed central to Christianity in this way, it is important to remember what this means. "Doctrine" does not mean, precisely, beliefs (for it is easy to show, as Keith Thomas does in his marvelous *Religion and the Decline of Magic* (1973), that the character of the actual propositions believed by Christians has changed radically in the last two millennia); rather it means the *verbal formulae* that express belief. And this has proved something of an embarrassment for many Christians in the world since the scientific revolution.

It is a familiar theme in the history of theology that Christianity has followed in some measure Oscar Wilde's (1982, p. 418) epigram: "Religions die when they are proved true. Science is the record of dead religions". One powerful reaction among Christian intellectuals has been to retreat in the face of science into the demythologization of the doctrines whose central place in the definition of his religious tradition they cannot escape. And – as I think the work of Keith Thomas (1973), among others, shows – it is correct to say that the effect of demythologization has been to treat doctrines that were once taken literally as metaphorical or, to return to my theme, symbolic. This has led us, if I may caricature recent theological history, to the position where the statement that "God is love" can be claimed by serious men – Paul Tillich, for example – to mean something like "Love is tremendously important" and to treating the traditional doctrine of the triumph of the kingdom of God as a "symbolic" way of expressing a confidence that "love will win in the end". And similar demythologizing tendencies can be detected in liberal (or otherwise counter-normative) Jewish theology (certainly they are found in Martin Buber). It is not my business to say whether this is a healthy development, though it will no doubt be clear which way my sympathies lie. But even if, as I doubt, this is consistent with the main traditions of Christianity or Judaism, to treat the religious beliefs of traditional cultures as likewise symbolic is radically to misrepresent their character.

The intellectual reformulation of Christianity coexists with a change in the character of Christian lay life, at least insofar as it concerns intellectuals. For educated Christians in Europe prior to the scientific revolution and the growth of industrial capitalism, the belief in spiritual beings – saints, angels, principalities, and powers – had in many respects just the character I claim for traditional Asante religion. Through acts at shrines that westerners would call magical in Asante, the faithful sought cures for their ills, answers to their questions, guidance in their acts. As technological solutions to illness and a scientific understanding of it have developed, many people (and, especially, many intellectuals) have turned away from this aspect of religion, though, as we should expect, it remains an important part of Christianity in the non-industrial world and in those – significant – parts of the industrial world where the scientific worldview remains ungrasped.

But in the industrial world, the religious life of intellectuals has turned more and more toward the contemplative, conceived of as spiritual intercourse with God. If God's answer is sought to any questions of a technical character, it is those questions that have remained recalcitrant to scientific management (questions about one's relations with others) and questions that could not even in principle be addressed by science (questions of value). This is itself a very interesting development, but it has driven a great wedge between the religion of the industrial world and the religion of traditional cultures.

There is a further change in the nature of contemplative religion in the West. It connects with the observation I made earlier that symbolism characterizes the ceremonious, and that social relations of importance require ceremony in traditional cultures. As our relations with each other have become less ceremonious, so have our private religious acts. Prayer has become for many like an intimate conversation. But so it is for Asante tradition. It is just that the understanding of intimacy is different.

What Fuels Beliefs

I have largely been addressing the first group of questions I posed about religious ritual: those about the nature of the ritual and the beliefs that underlie it. I have said little about the origins of these beliefs; in predominantly non-literate cultures, such questions often cannot be answered because the evidence is lacking. For Christianity or Judaism it is possible to discuss such questions because we have records of the councils of Nicaea and Chalcedon, or because we have the extensive traditions of literate Jewish reflection. But if we are to face the question of the rationality of traditional belief we must turn, finally, to my third set of questions: those about *what keeps these beliefs, which outsiders judge so obviously false, alive.*

It is in asking these questions that some have been led by another route to treating religion symbolically. The British anthropologist John Beattie, for example, has developed a "symbolist" view of Africa's traditional religions, whose "central tenet" as Robin Horton (a philosopher-anthropologist who is a British subject and a long-time Nigerian resident) puts it, "is that traditional religious thought is basically different from and incommensurable with western scientific thought"; so that the symbolists avoid "comparisons with science and turn instead to comparisons with symbolism and art" (Horton 1972, pp. 21-33, 30).

The basic symbolist thought is neatly (if ironically) captured in this formulation of the Cameroonian philosopher M. Hegba:

> As a first approach towards magic and sorcery we could assume to have a symbolic language before us. . . . Someone flying in the air, turning himself into an animal, making himself invisible at will . . . that could be nothing but a code language to be deciphered. That would be reassuring (Hegba 1979, p. 219)[1].

---

[1] "Une première approche des phénomènes de la magie et de la sorcellerie serait de supposer que nous nous trouvons là en face d'un langage symbolique. . . . Un homme qui vole dans les airs, qui se transforme en animal, ou qui se rend invisible à volonté . . . pourraient n'être alors qu'un langage code dont nous devrions simplement découvrir la clef. Nous serions alors rassurés".

Simply put, the *symbolists are able to treat traditional believers as reassuringly rational only because they deny that traditional people mean what they say*. Now Robin Horton has objected – correctly – that this tale leaves completely unexplained the fact that traditional people regularly appeal to the invisible agencies of their religions in their explanations of events in what we would call the natural world (Horton 1972, pp. 21-33, 30). Horton could usefully have drawn attention here to a fact that Hegba (1979, p. 219) observes, when he moves from characterizing symbolism to criticizing it, namely that "le langage symbolique et ésotérique est fort en honneur en notre société". It is peculiarly unsatisfactory to treat a system of propositions as symbolic when those whose propositions they are appear to treat them literally *and display, in other contexts, a clear grasp of the notion of symbolic representation*.

I have mentioned Durkheim once already, and it is in his work that we can find the clearest statement of the connection between the urge to treat religion as symbolic and the question why such patently false beliefs survive. For Durkheim cannot allow that religious beliefs are false, because he thinks that false beliefs could not survive. Since if they are false they would not have survived, it follows that they must be true: and since they are not literally true, they must be symbolically true (Skorupski 1976, ch. 2). This argument is based on a misunderstanding of the relationship between the rationality of beliefs, their utility and their truth; it is important to say why.

Rationality, Utility and Truth of Beliefs

Rationality is best conceived of as an ideal, both in the sense that it is something worth aiming for and in the sense that it is something we are incapable of realizing. It is an ideal that bears an important internal relation to that other great cognitive ideal, Truth. And, I suggest, we might say that rationality in belief consists in being disposed so to react to evidence and reflection that you change your beliefs in ways that make it more likely that they are true. If this is right, then we can see at once why inconsistency in belief is a sign of irrationality: for having a pair of inconsistent beliefs *guarantees* that you have at least one false belief, as inconsistent beliefs are precisely beliefs that cannot all be true. But we can also see that consistency, as an ideal, is not enough. For someone could have a perfectly consistent set of beliefs about the world, almost every one of which was not only false but obviously false. It is *consistent* to hold, with Descartes in one of his skeptical moments, that all my experiences are caused by a wicked demon, and, to dress the fantasy in modern garb, there is no inconsistency in supporting the paranoid fantasy that the world is "really" a cube containing only my brain in a bath, a lot of wires, and a wicked scientist. But, though consistent, this belief is not rational: we are all, I hope, agreed that reacting to sensory evidence in *this* way does not increase the likelihood that your beliefs will be true.

Now the question of the utility, the survival value, of a set of beliefs is quite separate from that of both their truth and their reasonableness, thus conceived. Anyone who has read Evans-Pritchard's elegant discussion of Zande witchcraft beliefs will remember how easy it is to make sense of the idea that a whole set of false beliefs could nevertheless be part of what holds a community together. But the point does not need laboring: since Freud we can all understand why, for example, it might be more useful to believe that you love someone than to recognize that you do not.

With such an account of reasonableness, we can see why the apparently obvious falsehood of the beliefs of the Asante priest might be regarded as evidence of his unreasonableness. For how could he have acquired and maintained such beliefs if he was following the prescription always to try to change his beliefs in ways that made it more likely that they were true? The answer is simple. The priest acquired his beliefs in the way we all acquire the bulk of our beliefs: by being told things as he grew up. As Evans-Pritchard (1973, p. 202) says of the Zande people, they are "born into a culture with ready-made patterns of belief which have the weight of tradition behind them". And of course, so are we. On the whole, little has happened in his life to suggest they are not true. So too, in our lives.

Now it may seem strange to suggest that accepting beliefs from one's culture and holding onto them in the absence of countervailing evidence can be reasonable, if it can lead to having beliefs that are, from the point of view of western intellectuals, so wildly false. And this is especially so if you view reasonableness as a matter of trying to develop habits of belief acquisition that make it likely that you will react to evidence and reflection in ways that have a tendency to produce truth. But to think otherwise is to mistake the relatively deplorable nature of our epistemic position in the universe. It is just fundamentally correct that there is no requirement other than consistency that we can place on our beliefs in advance, in order to increase their likelihood of being true; and that a person who starts with a consistent set of beliefs can arrive, by way of reasonable principles of evidence, at the most fantastic untruths. The wisdom of epistemological modesty is, surely, one of the lessons of the history of natural science; indeed, if there is one great lesson of the failure of positivism as a methodology of the sciences, it is surely, as Richard Miller (1987, passim) has argued, that there are no a priori rules that will guarantee us true theories. The success of what we call "empirical method" seems, in retrospect, to have been, like evolution, the result of capitalizing on a series of lucky chances. If the priest's theory is wrong, we should see this as largely a matter of bad luck, rather than of his having failed culpably to observe the proper rules of an a priori method.

We may also fail to see how reasonable the priest's views should seem, because, in assessing the religious beliefs of other cultures, we start, as is natural enough, from our own. But it is precisely the absence of this, our alien, alternative point of view in traditional culture, which makes it reasonable to adopt the "traditional" worldview. The evidence that spirits exist is *obvious*: priests go into trance, people get better after the application of spiritual remedies, people die regularly from the action of inimical spirits. The reinterpretation of this evidence, in terms of medical-scientific theories or of psychology, requires that there be such alternative theories and that people have some reason to believe in them; but again and again, and especially in the area of mental and social life, the traditional view is likely to be confirmed. We have theories explaining some of this, the theory of suggestion and suggestibility, for example, and if we were to persuade traditional thinkers of these theories, they might become skeptical of the theories held in their own culture. But we cannot *begin* by asking them to assume their beliefs are false, for they can always make numerous moves in *reasonable* defense of their beliefs. It is this fact that entitles us to oppose the thesis that traditional beliefs are simply unreasonable.

The classical account of this process of defense in the ethnography of African traditional thought is Evans-Pritchard's *Witchcraft, Oracles and Magic among the Azande*. Toward the end of the book, he says (Evans-Pritchard 1973, pp. 199-201): "It may be asked why Azande do not perceive the futility of their magic. It would be easy to write at great length in answer to this question, but I will content myself with suggesting as shortly as possible a number of reasons". He then lists twenty-two such reasons. He mentions, for example, that since "magic is very largely employed against mystical powers . . . its action transcends experience" and thus "cannot easily be contradicted by experience", reinforcing a point made a few pages earlier: "We shall not understand Zande magic . . . unless we realize that its main purpose is to combat other mystical powers rather than to produce changes favorable to man in the objective world". He says that the practices of witchcraft, oracles, and magic presuppose a coherent system of mutually supporting beliefs:

> Death is proof of witchcraft. It is avenged by magic. The accuracy of the poison oracle is determined by the king's oracle, which is above suspicion. . . . The results which magic is supposed to produce actually happen after the rites are performed. . . . Magic is only made to produce events which are likely to happen in any case . . . [and] is seldom asked to produce a result by itself but is associated with empirical action that does in fact

produce it – e.g. a prince gives food to attract followers and does not rely on magic alone (Evans-Pritchard 1973, pp. 201-3).

And, though he acknowledges that Azande notice failures of their witchcraft, he shows too how they have many ways to explain this failure: there may have been an error in executing the spell, there may be an unknown and countervailing magic, and so on.

It is the fact that it is possible to make exactly these sorts of moves in defense of traditional religious beliefs that has led some to draw the conclusion that traditional religious belief should be interpreted as having the same purposes as those of modern natural science, which are summarized in the slogan "explanation, prediction, and control". For when scientific procedures fail, scientists do not normally react – as I once heard a distinguished physicist react to an hour in a lab studying the phenomena produced by Uri Geller, an illusionist who claimed that spoons seen to bend seemingly spontaneously in his vicinity did so by his mental force – by saying that we must "begin physics all over again". Rather, they offer explanations as to how the failure could have occurred consistently with the theory. Biochemists regularly ignore negative results, assuming that test tubes are dirty, or that samples are contaminated, or that in preparing the sample they have failed to take some precaution that is necessary to prevent the action of those enzymes that are always released when a cell is damaged. A skeptical Zande could well make the same sorts of observation about these procedures as Evans-Pritchard makes about Azande magic: "The perception of error in one mystical notion in a particular situation merely proves the correctness of another and equally mystical notion".

Philosophers of science have names for this: they say that theory is "underdetermined" by observation, and that observation is "theory-laden". And they mean by underdetermination the fact that French philosopher-physicist Pierre Duhem noticed in the early part of this century: that the application of theory to particular cases relies on a whole host of other beliefs, not all of which can be checked at once. By the theory-ladenness of observation, relatedly, they mean that our theories both contribute to forming our experience and give meaning to the language we use for reporting it. Sir Karl Popper's claim (Popper [1962] 1974) that science should proceed by attempts at falsification, as we all know after reading Thomas Kuhn ([1962] 1970), is incorrect. If we gave up every time an experiment failed, scientific theory would get nowhere. The underdetermination of our theories by our experience means that we are left even by the most unsuccessful experiment with room for maneuver. The trick is not to give up too soon or go on too long. In science, as everywhere else, there are babies and there is bathwater.

I have suggested we might assimilate the theories that underlie traditional religion and magic to those that are engendered in the natural sciences because both are explanatory systems of belief that share the problem of underdetermination. But there are other routes to this assimilation, and if we are to explore the plausibility of this idea, it will help if we assemble a few more pieces of the evidence.

Let me describe another ceremony, in which I participated some years ago in Kumasi. It was, as it happens, my sister's wedding, and the legal ceremony occurred in a Methodist church, in the context of a service in the language of the old English prayer book. "Dearly Beloved", it began "we are gathered here together in the sight of God". In the front row sat the king of Asante, his wife, the queen mother, and the king's son, Nana Akyempemhene, as grand a collection of the Asante traditional aristocracy as you could wish for. Afterwards we went back to the private residence of the king, and there we had a party, with the queen mother's drummers playing, and hundreds of members of the royal household.

But, not long after we began, the Catholic archbishop of Kumasi (remember, this is after a *Methodist* ceremony) said prayers, and this was followed (and remember this was a *Catholic* archbishop) by the pouring of libations to my family ancestors, carried out by one of the king's senior linguists. The words addressed to those ancestors were couched in the same idiom as the words of the priest that Rattray (1955; see Appiah in this volume, p. 24) heard. And the king of Asante is an Anglican and a member of the English bar; his son, a lawyer then in the Ghanaian Diplomatic Service, has a Ph.D. from Tufts; and the bride and groom met at Sussex University in England (and each had another degree as well) and were, respectively, a medical sociologist and a Nigerian merchant banker. These, then, are modern Africans, not merely in the sense that they are alive now, but they have that essential credential of the modern man or woman – a university's letters after their name. I shall argue, in a moment, that these letters are of more than metaphorical importance.

What are we to make of all of this? Or rather, what are Europeans and Americans to make of it, since it is all so familiar to me – to most contemporary Africans – that I find it hard to recover the sense of contradiction between the elements of this no-doubt remarkable "syncretism".

These ceremonies are what I want to call "nontraditional" – they are not traditional because they coexist both with some degree of belief in the Christianity that came with the colonials, on the one hand, and with some familiarity with the vision of the natural sciences, on the other. But they are not "modern" either – because the meanings attached to these acts are not those of the purely symbolic Eucharist of extreme liberal theology. The question, of course, is how all these elements can coexist, what it is that makes this conceptual mêlée not a source of intellectual tension and unease but a resource for a tremendous range of cultural activity.

The key to this question is, I think, to be found in following up the idea that we were led to earlier, the idea that *traditional religious theory is in certain respects more like modern science than modern religion – in particular that it shares the purposes of modern natural science, which we may summarize in the slogan "explanation, prediction and control"*. It is his systematic development of the analogy between natural science and traditional religion that has made the work of Robin Horton (1967, 1970, 1972, 1973, 1987) so important in the philosophy of African traditional religions, and it will be useful to begin with him.

Horton's basic point is just the one I made earlier: the fundamental character of these religious systems is that the practices arise from the belief, literal and *not symbolic*, in the powers of invisible agents. Horton argues persuasively, and I believe correctly, that spirits and such function in explanation, prediction, and control much as do other theoretical entities: they differ from those of natural science in being persons and not material forces and powers, but the logic of their function in explanation and prediction is the same.

Horton's view, then, is that religious beliefs of traditional peoples constitute explanatory theories and that traditional religious actions are reasonable attempts to pursue goals in the light of these beliefs – attempts, in other words, at prediction and control of the world. In these respects, Horton argues, traditional religious belief and action are like theory in the natural sciences and the actions based on it. As Hegba, in the francophone African tradition, says:

> Wishing neither to deny its limits nor to hinder the march to progress, science and liberation, it should be conceded that the African explanations of magic and sorcery are rational. Our popular beliefs are of stunning certainty, sometimes wrong, but would it not be a methodological mistake to assume their irrationality at the starting point of the study of a society? (Hegba 1979, p. 267).[2]

---

[2] "Sans méconnaître ses limites ni freiner la marche vers le progrès, la science et la libération, il faut admettre que l'explication africaine des phénomènes de la magie et de la sorcellerie est rationnelle. Nos croyances populaires sont déconcertantes certes, parfois fausses, mais ne serais ce pas une faute méthodologique grave que de postuler l'irrationnel au point de départ de l'étude d'une société?".

The Individual *versus* the Personal

Horton's thesis is not that traditional religion is a kind of science but that theories in the two domains are similar in these crucial respects. The major *difference* in the contents of the theories, he argues, is that traditional religious theory is couched in terms of *personal forces*, while natural scientific theory is couched in terms of *impersonal forces*.

Yet there is in the analogy between natural science and traditional religion much to mislead, too. A first way in which the assimilation risks being deceptive comes out if we remind ourselves that most of us are quite vague about the theoretical underpinnings of the medical theories that guide our doctors and the physical theories that are used to make and mend our radios. In this we are, of course, like the average nineteenth-century Asante, who was, presumably, quite vague about the bases on which herbalists and priests practiced their arts. In application, in use by non-specialists in everyday life, our theories about how the world works are often relied on in general outline in a practical way, without much articulation and without any deep investment in the details. In much contemporary African religious practice (and this includes the ceremony I have described) there is (within each community of practice, each sect or cult or community) a great deal more consensus on the proper forms of ritual and liturgical action than there is as to *what justifies it*; in this, religious practice in Africa differs little enough from religious practice in the contemporary industrialized world. Though the extent of literal belief in invisible agency may be somewhat greater in Africa than in the United States (and is probably much greater than in, say, Britain or Norway), there is both there and here a sense in which religious life can continue and be participated in with little curiosity about the literal beliefs of fellow participants, and little theoretical commitment on our own parts. In insisting on the role of *theory*, here, one is bound, as a result, to seem to be focusing on something that is far from central for those whose religious practices we are discussing, and thus distorting their experience in order to draw the analogy with natural science. But provided we bear in mind that no claim is being made beyond the claim that these religious practices operate on the assumption of a certain theory – that there are spiritual agencies of various kinds – and that this theory allows for explanation and prediction in the sort of way that scientific theories do, I do not think we need be led into misjudging the relative importance of theory and practice in traditional religion in this way.

Still, this worry comes close to a second difficulty with the assimilation of traditional religion and natural science – one Kwasi Wiredu (1980, ch. 3) has pointed out – namely, that it is, prima facie, very odd to equate traditional religious belief in West Africa with modern western scientific theory, when the obvious analogue is traditional western religious belief. I think it will be obvious from what I have already said that it seems to me that there need be no contest here: for the explanatory function of religious beliefs in traditional Europe seems to me to be identical in its logic with that of scientific theory also.

What *is* misleading is not the assimilation of the logics of explanation of theories from religion and science but the assimilation of traditional religion and natural science as institutions. This is, first of all, misleading because of the sorts of changes that I sketched in western religious life. For the modern westerner, as I have shown, to call something "religious" is to connote a great deal that is lacking in traditional religion and not to connote much that is present. But there is a much more fundamental reason why the equation of religion and science is misleading. And it is to do with the *totally different social organization of enquiry in traditional and modern cultures*. I shall return to this issue below.

Horton himself is, of course, aware that traditional religious beliefs are certainly unlike those of natural science in at least two important respects First of all, as I have already insisted, he points out that the theoretical entities invoked are agents and not material forces. And he offers us an account of why this might be. He suggests that this difference arises out of the fundamental nature of explanation as the reduction of the unfamiliar to the familiar. In traditional cultures nature, the wild, is untamed, alien, and a source of puzzlement and fear. Social relations and persons are, on the contrary, familiar and well understood. Explaining the behavior of nature in terms of agency is thus reducing the unfamiliar forces of the wild to the familiar explanatory categories of personal relations.

In the industrial world, on the other hand, industrialization and urbanization have made social relations puzzling and problematic. We move between social environments – the rural and the urban, the workplace and the home – in which different conventions operate; in the new, urban, factory, market environment we deal with people whom we know only through our common productive projects. As a result the social – at least the social as it is experienced in traditional societies – is relatively unfamiliar. On the other hand, our relations with objects in the city are relations that remain relatively stable across all these differing social relations. Indeed, if factory workers move between factories, the skills they take with them are precisely those that depend on a familiarity not with other people but with the workings of material things. As far as their skills pertain to dealing with people, it does not pertain to dealing with particular persons: the individuals you work with are substitutable. It is no longer natural to try to understand nature through personal social relations; rather, we understand it through machines and formal human interaction, through abstract depersonalized procedures whose workings are comfortably familiar (Horton 1967, p. 64).

In complex, rapidly changing industrial societies, the human scene is in flux. Order, regularity, predictability, simplicity, all these seem lamentably absent. It is in the world of inanimate things that such qualities are most readily seen. And this, I suggest, is why the mind in quest of explanatory analogies turns most readily to the inanimate. In the traditional societies of Africa we find the situation reversed. The human scene is the *locus par excellence* of order, predictability, regularity. In the world of the inanimate, these qualities are far less evident. Here, the mind in quest of explanatory analogies turns naturally to people and their relations.

Horton relies here on a picture of the function of scientific theory as essentially concerned to develop models of the unified, simple, ordered, regular underlying features of reality in order to account for the diversity, complexity, disorder, and apparent lawlessness of ordinary experience (Horton 1967, p. 51). His story works so well that it is hard not to feel that there is something right about it; it would indeed explain the preference for agency over matter, the first of the major differences Horton acknowledges between traditional religion and science.

Efficient Causality and Functional Explanation

And yet this cannot be quite right. All culture – in modest mood, I might say, all the cultures I have knowledge of – have the conceptual resources for at least two fundamental sorts of explanation. On the one hand, all have some sort of notion of what Aristotle called "efficient" causation: the causality of push and pull through which we understand the everyday interactions of material objects and forces. On the other, each has a notion of explanation that applies paradigmatically to human action, the notion that the American philosopher Daniel Dennett (1987) has characterized as involving the "intentional stance". This sort of explanation relates actions to beliefs, desires, intentions, fears, and so on – the so-called propositional attitudes – and is fundamental (in ways I suggested earlier) to folk psychology. We might say, analogously, that efficient causality is central to what cognitive psychologists now call "naive" or "folk physics".

These kinds of explanation are, of course, interconnected: when I explain the death of the elephant by talking of your need for food, your hunt, your firing the gun, there are elements of folk physics and of folk psychology involved in each stage of this narrative. To say that mechanical explanation is unfamiliar to pre-industrial peoples is, of course, to say something true.

Mechanical explanation is explanation in terms of machines, which are, of course, exactly what pre-industrial cultures do not have. But mechanical explanation is by no means the only kind of non-intentional explanation: there is more to folk physics than a view of machines. And the fact is that the stability of the causal relations of objects in the pre-industrial world is surely quite substantial: not only do people make tools and utensils, using the concepts of efficient causation, but their regular physical interactions with the world – in digging, hunting, walking, dancing – are as stable and as well understood as their familial relations. More than this, pre-industrial Homo is already Homo faber, and the making of pots and of jewelry, for example, involve intimate knowledge of physical things and an expectation of regularity in their behavior. Pots and rings and necklaces break, of course, and they often do so unpredictably. But in this they are not obviously less reliable than people, who, after all, are also notoriously difficult to predict.

What we need to bring back into view here is a kind of explanation that is missing from Horton's story: namely, functional explanation, which we find centrally (but by no means uniquely) in what we might call "folk biology". Functional explanation is the sort of explanation that we give when we say that the flower is there to attract the bee that pollinates it; that the liver is there to purify the blood; that the rain falls to water the crops.

This sort of explanation is missing from Horton's story for a very good reason namely, that the positivist philosophy of science on which Horton relies sought either to eradicate functional explanation or to reduce it to other sorts of explanation, in large part because it reeked of teleology – of the sort of Aristotelian "final" causation that positivism took to have been shown to be hopeless by the failure of vitalism in nineteenth-century biology. And, surely, what is most striking about the "unscientific" explanations that most pre-colonial African cultures offer is not just that they appeal to agency but that they are addressed to the question "Why?" understood as asking *what the event in question was for*, Evans-Pritchard in his account of Zande belief insists that the Azande do not think that "unfortunate events" ever happen by chance (Evans-Pritchard 1973, ch. 2): their frequent appeal to witchcraft – in the absence of other acceptable explanations of misfortune – demonstrates their unwillingness to accept the existence of contingency. But to reject the possibility of the contingent is exactly to insist that everything that happens serves some purpose: a view familiar in Christian tradition in such formulas as "And we know that all things work together for good to them that love God" (Rom. 8:28), or in the deep need people feel – in Europe and America as in Africa – for answers to the question "Why do bad things happen to good people?" Zande witchcraft beliefs depend on an assumption that the universe is in a certain sort of evaluative balance; in short, on the sort of assumption that leads monotheistic theologians to develop theodicies.

What Zande people will not accept, as Evans-Pritchard's account makes clear, is not that "unfortunate events" have no explanation – the granary falls because the termites have eaten through the stilts that support it – but that they are meaningless; that there is no deeper reason why the person sitting in the shade of the granary was injured. And in that sense they share an attitude that we find in Christian theodicy from Irenaeus to Augustine to Karl Barth: the attitude that the cosmos works to a plan. Pre-colonial African cultures, pre- and nonscientific thinkers everywhere are inclined to suppose that events in the world have meaning; they worry not about the possibility of the unexplained (what has no efficient cause nor agent explanation) but of the meaningless (what has no function, no point). And this marks those who accept the scientific worldview – a minority, of course, even in the industrialized world – from almost all other humans throughout history. For it is a distinctive feature of that scientific world view that it accepts that not everything that happens has a human meaning. To explain this difference between scientific and nonscientific visions we need, I think, to begin with the fact that the world, as the sciences conceive it, extends so hugely far beyond the human horizon, in time as in space. As Alexandre Koyré indicated in the title of his well-known study of the birth of modern celestial physics, the Newtonian revolution took the intellectual path From the Closed World to the Infinite Universe, and the Victorian dispute between science and religion had at its centre a debate about the age of the earth, with geology insisting that the biblical time scale of thousands of years since the creation radically underestimated the age of our planet. Copernicus turned European scientists away from a geocentric to a heliocentric view of the universe and began a process, which Darwin continued, that inevitably displaced humankind from the centre of the natural sciences. A recognition that the universe does not seem to have been made simply for us is the basis of the radically non-anthropocentric character of scientific theories of the world. This non-anthropocentrism is part of the change in view that develops with the growth of capitalism, of science, and of the modern state, the change to which, for example, Weber's account of modernization was addressed, and it contributes profoundly to the sense of the universe as disenchanted that Weberians have taken to be so central a feature of modernity (a claim that makes more sense as a claim about the life of professional intellectuals than as one about the culture as a whole).

"Open" and "Closed" Societies

But Horton in his original work made, as I said, a second important claim for difference: he summarized it by calling the cognitive world of traditional cultures "closed" and that of modern cultures "open". "What I take to be the key difference is a very simple one" he writes. "It is that in traditional cultures there is no developed awareness of alternatives to the established body of theoretical tenets; whereas in scientifically oriented cultures, such an awareness is highly developed" (Wilson 1970, p. 153). And it is here, when we turn from questions about the content and logic of traditional and scientific explanation to the social contexts in which those theories are constructed and mobilized, that Horton's account begins to seem less adequate.

We should begin, however, by agreeing that there clearly are important differences between the social contexts of theory formation and development in pre-colonial Africa, on the one hand, and post-Renaissance Europe, on the other. Modern science began in Europe just when her peoples were beginning to be exposed to the hitherto unknown cultures of the Orient, Africa, and the Americas. The first vernacular scientific works – Galileo's dialogues, for example – were written in Italy at a time when the Italian trading cities had for some time been at the centre of commerce between the Mediterranean, the Near and Far East, the New World, and Africa. In such a climate, it is natural to ask whether the certainties of your ancestors are correct, faced with cultures such as the China Marco Polo reported, whose technical ingenuity was combined with totally alien theories of nature.

This challenge to traditional western beliefs occurs not only in terms of the theory of nature but also recapitulates Greek discussions of the ways in which matters of value seem to vary from place to place; discussions that lead very naturally to moral as well as scientific skepticism of exactly the kind that we find in the early modern empiricists. And it seems no coincidence that those earlier Greek discussions were prompted by an awareness of the existence of alternative African and Asian worldviews, an awareness to be found in the first historians, such as Herodotus. (Herodotus's account of the Persian Wars begins with an extended discussion of the variety of religious and social customs found within the Persian empire.) It is, in other words, the availability of alternative theories of morals and nature that gives rise to the systematic investigation of nature, to the growth of speculation, and to the development of that crucial element that distinguishes the open society – namely, organized challenges to prevailing theory.

Remember the answer the priest gave to the question about the gold dust: "We do it because the ancestors did it". In the open society this will no longer do as a reason. The early modern natural scientists, the natural philosophers of the Renaissance, frequently stressed the unreasonableness of appeals to authority. And if modern scholarship suggests that they *over*stressed the extent to which their predecessors were bound by a hidebound traditionalism, it is still true that there *is* a difference – if only in degree – in the extent to which modernity celebrates distance from our predecessors, while the traditional world celebrates cognitive continuity.

Now, Horton's account of the sense in which the traditional world view is closed has – rightly – been challenged. The complexities of war and trade, dominance and clientage, migration and diplomacy, in much of pre-colonial Africa, are simply not consistent with the image of peoples unaware that there is a world elsewhere. As Catherine Coquery-Vidrovitch, a leading French historian of Africa, has pointed out:

> In fact, these reputedly stable societies rarely enjoyed the lovely equilibrium presumed to have been disrupted by the impact of colonialism. West Africa, for example, had been seething with activity ever since the eighteenth-century waves of Fulani conquest and well before the creation of units of resistance to European influence. . . . The Congolese basin was the site of still more profound upheavals linked to commercial penetration. In such cases the revolution in production rocked the very foundations of the political structure. As for South Africa, the rise of the Zulus and their expansion had repercussions up into central Africa. How far back do we have to go to find the stability alleged to be "characteristic" of the pre-colonial period: before the Portuguese conquest, before the Islamic invasion, before the Bantu expansion? Each of these great turning points marked the reversal of long-term trends, within which a whole series of shorter cycles might in turn be identified, as, for example, the succession of Sudanic empires, or even such shorter cycles as the periods of recession (1724-1740, 1767-1782, 1795-1811, and so on) and the upswing of the slave-trade economy of Dahomey. In short, the static concept of "traditional" society cannot withstand the historian's analysis (Coquery-Vidrovitch 1976, p. 91).

In particular – as Horton himself has insisted in "A Hundred Years of Change in Kalabari Religion" – African historians can trace changes in religious and other beliefs in many places long before the advent of Christian missionaries and colonial educators. The Yoruba were aware of Islam before they were aware of England, of Dahomey before they had heard of Britain. But Yoruba religion has many of the features that Horton proposed to explain by reference to a lack of awareness of just such alternatives.

It is also possible to find first-rate speculative thinkers in traditional societies whose individual openness is not to be denied. I think here of Ogotemmeli, whose cosmology Griaule (1948) has captured in *Dieu d'eau*, and Barry Hallen (1977) has provided evidence from Nigerian sources of the existence, within African traditional modes of thought, of styles of reasoning that are open neither to Wiredu's (1980, pp. 20-1, 37, 143) stern strictures nor to Horton's milder ones. To begin with, Hallen (1977, p. 82) says, when

Yoruba people answer the question "Why do you believe *x*?" by saying that "this is what the forefathers said", in the way that Wiredu objects to and Horton also takes to be typical, they are not trying to offer a *reasoned justification* for believing *x*. Rather they are taking the question as one about the *origin* of a belief or custom. They are giving the same sort of response westerners would be likely to if asked how they *came to* believe in shaving the hair off their faces. However if one goes further and asks a Yoruba to explain what a belief *means* a more sophisticated response is often forthcoming.

And, Hallen goes on to argue, in Yoruba culture this more sophisticated response often meets standards for being critical and reflective. Hallen takes as a model Karl Popper's ([1962] 1974) characterization of critical reflection on tradition, a gesture all the more significant given the Popperian provenance of the open-closed dichotomy. This requires:

1. Identifying the tradition *as* a tradition;
2. Displaying an awareness of its consequences; *and*
3. Being aware of at least one alternative and, on some critical basis, choosing to affirm or to reject it.

By this test the Yoruba *babalawo* – the diviner and healer – whom Hallen cites *is* critically appreciative of the tradition he believes in.

Hallen is right, then, to challenge the structure of Horton's original dichotomy of the open and the closed. On the one hand, as I said earlier, there is in post-Kuhnian history and sociology of science a good deal of evidence that these Popperian desiderata are hardly met in physics, the heartland of western theory. On the other, Horton's original stress on the "closed" nature of traditional modes of thought does look less adequate in the face of Africa's complex history of cultural exchanges and of Hallen's *babalawo*, or in the presence of the extraordinary metaphysical synthesis of the Dogon elder, Ogotemmeli (Griaule 1948). In a recent book – written with the Nigerian philosopher J. O. Sodipo – Hallen insists on the presence among Yoruba doctors of theories of witchcraft rather different from those of their fellow countrymen (Hallen and Sodipo 1986). Here, then, among the doctors, speculation inconsistent with ordinary folk belief occurs, and there is no reason to doubt that this aspect of contemporary Yoruba culture is, in this respect, like many pre-colonial cultures.

But in rejecting altogether Horton's characterization of the traditional world as "closed", we risk losing sight of something important. Such thinkers as Ogotemmeli are individuals – individuals like Thales and the other early pre-Socratics in the western tradition – and there is little evidence that their views have a wide currency or impact (indeed, it seems clear that the *babalawos* of

Hallen and Sodipo's acquaintance are not especially concerned to share or to spread their speculations). If "traditional" thought is more aware of alternatives and contains more moments of individual speculation than Horton's original picture suggested, it is also true that it differs from the thought of both theorists and ordinary folk in the industrialized world in its responses to those alternatives and its incorporation of these speculations.

Acquisition of Knowledge as a Social Ideal

Horton has recently come – in response, in part, to Hallen's (1977) critique – to speak not of the closedness of traditional belief systems but, borrowing a term from Wole Soyinka (1976), of their being "accommodative". He discusses work by students of Evans-Pritchard's that not only addresses the kind of static body of belief that is captured in Evans-Pritchard's (1973) picture of the Azande thought world but also stresses the dynamic and – as Horton admits – "open" way in which they "devise explanations for novel elements in experience", and "their capacity to borrow, re-work and integrate alien ideas in the course of elaborating such explanations". "Indeed", he continues, "it is this 'openness' that has given the traditional cosmologies such tremendous durability in the face of immense changes that the 20th century has brought to the African scene". Horton then contrasts this accommodative style with the "adversary" style of scientific theory, which is characterized by the way in which the main stimulus to change of belief is not "novel experience but rival theory" (Horton, unpublished).

And it seems to me that this change from the Popperian terminology of "open" and "closed" allows Horton to capture something important about the difference between traditional religion and science; something to do not with individual cognitive strategies but with social ones. If we want to understand the significance of social organization in differentiating traditional religion and natural science, we can do no better than to begin with those of Evans-Pritchard's answers to the question why the Azande do not see the falsity of their magic beliefs that mention social facts about the organization of those beliefs.

Evans-Pritchard wrote:

> Skepticism, far from being smothered, is recognized, even inculcated. But it is only about certain medicines and certain magicians. By contrast it tends to support other medicines and other magicians. . . . Each man and each kinship group acts without cognizance of the actions of others. People do not pool their ritual experiences. . . . They are not experimentally inclined. . . . Not being experimentally inclined, they do not test the efficacy of their medicines (Evans-Pritchard 1973, pp. 202-4).

And, he added

> Zande beliefs are generally vaguely formulated. A belief, to be easily contradicted by experience . . . must be clearly shared and intellectually developed.

Whatever the practices of imperfect scientists are actually like, none of these things is supposed to be true of natural science. In our official picture of the sciences, skepticism is encouraged even about foundational questions – indeed, that is where the best students are supposed to be directed. Scientific researchers conceive of themselves as a community that cuts across political boundaries as divisive as the (late and unlamented) cold war Iron Curtain, and results, "experiences", are shared. The scientific community is experimentally inclined, and, of course, scientific theory is formulated as precisely as possible in order that those experiments can be carried out in a controlled fashion.

That, of course, is only the official view. Three decades of work in the history and sociology of science since Thomas Kuhn's iconoclastic *The Structure of Scientific Revolutions* (Kuhn [1962] 1970) have left us with a picture of science as much more messy and muddled – in short, as a more human business. Yet while this work has had the effect of revising (one is inclined to say "tarnishing") our image of the institutions of scientific research, it has not revised the fundamental recognition that the production of scientific knowledge is organized around competing theoretical positions, and that the demand for publication to establish the success of laboratories and individual scientists exposes each competing theory to review by ambitious counter-theorists from other laboratories, with other positions. What we have learned, however (though it should have been obvious all along), is that there are serious limits placed on the range of positions that will be entertained. In 1981, for example, when Rupert Sheldrake's *A New Science of Life* was published, a correspondent in Nature suggested it might usefully be burned; this was inconsistent with official ideology because Sheldrake, a former research fellow of the Royal Society, who had studied the philosophy of science, had constructed a proposal, which, though provocative, was deliberately couched in terms that made it subject to potential experimental test. Still, it outraged many biologists (and physicists), and if there had not been a challenge from the *New Scientist* magazine to design experiments, his proposal, like most of those regarded as in one way or the other the work of a "crank", would probably simply have been ignored by his professional peers. (There is some conclusion to be drawn from the fact that the copy of Sheldrake's book listed in the catalogue at Duke University appears to be in the divinity school library!) The development of science is not a free-for-all with all the participants cheering each other on with the cry: "And may the best theory win". But science is, crucially, adversarial, and the norms of publication and reproducibility of results, even though only imperfectly adhered to, are explicitly intended to lay theories and experimental claims open to attack by one's peers, and thus make competition from the adventurous "young Turk" possible.

More important than the hugely oversimplified contrast between an experimental, skeptical, science and an un-experimental, "dogmatic" traditional mode of thought is the difference in images of knowledge that are represented in the differences in the social organization of inquiry in modern as opposed to "traditional" societies. Scientists, like the rest of us, hold onto theories longer than they may be entitled to, suppress, unconsciously or half consciously, evidence they do not know how to handle, lie a little; in pre-colonial societies there were, we can be sure, individual doubters who kept their own council, resisters against the local dogma. But what is interesting about modern modes of theorizing is that they are organized around an image of constant change: we expect new theories, we reward and encourage the search for them, we believe that today's best theories will be revised beyond recognition if the enterprise of science survive. My ancestors in Asante never organized a specialized activity that was based around this thought. They knew that some people know more than others, and that there are things to be found out. But they do not seem to have thought it necessary to invest social effort in working out new theories of how the world works, not for some practical end (this they did constantly) but, as we say, for its own sake.

The differences between traditional religious theory and the theories of the sciences reside in the social organization of inquiry, as a systematic business, and it is differences in social organization that account, I think, both for the difference we feel in the character of natural scientific and traditional religious theory – they are the products of different kinds of social process – and for the spectacular expansion of the domain of successful prediction and control, an expansion that characterizes natural science but is notably absent in traditional society. Experimentation, the publication and reproduction of results, the systematic development of alternative theories in precise terms, all these ideals, however imperfectly they are realized in scientific practice, are intelligible only in an organized social enterprise of knowledge.

Literacy Prompts Discussions on Matters of Consistency

What can have prompted this radically different approach to knowledge? Why have the practitioners of traditional religion, even the priests who are the professionals, never developed the organized "adversarial" methods of the sciences? There are, no doubt, many historical sources. A few familiar suggestions strike one immediately.

Social mobility leads to political individualism, of a kind that is rare in the traditional polity; political individualism allows cognitive authority to shift, also, from priest and king to commoner; and social mobility is a feature of industrial societies.

Or, in traditional societies, accommodating conflicting theoretical views is part of the general process of accommodation necessary for those who are bound to each other as neighbors for life. I remember once discussing differences between Ghana and America in cultural style with a fellow Ghanaian and an American. The American student asked what had struck us both as the most important cultural difference between Ghana and the United States when we first arrived. "You are so aggressive", said my Ghanaian friend. "In Ghana, we would not think that very good manners". Of course, what he had noticed was not aggression but simply a different conversational style. In Ghana, but not in America, it is impolite to disagree, to argue, to confute. And this accommodating approach to conversation is part of the same range of attitudes that leads to theoretical accommodations.

We could think of more differences in social, economic, and ecological background, which together may help to account for this difference in approach to theory. But it seems to me that there is one other fundamental difference between traditional West African culture and the culture of the industrial world, and that it plays a fundamental role in explaining why the adversarial style never established itself in West Africa. And it is that these cultures were largely non-literate.

Now literacy, as Jack Goody has pointed out in his influential book *The Domestication of the Savage Mind* (1977), has important consequences; among them is the fact that it permits a kind of consistency that oral culture cannot and does not demand. Write down a sentence and it is there, in principle, forever; that means that if you write down another sentence inconsistent with it, you can be caught out. It is this fact that is at the root of the possibility of the adversarial style. How often have we seen Perry Mason – on television in Ghana or the United States or England (for television, at least, there is only one world) – ask the stenographer to read back from the record? In the traditional culture the answer can only be: "What record?" In the absence of written records, it is not possible to compare the ancestor's theories in their actual words with ours; nor, given the limitations of quantity imposed by oral transmission, do we have a detailed knowledge of what those theories were. We know more about the thought of Isaac Newton on one or two subjects than we know about the entire population of his Asante contemporaries.

The accommodative style is possible because orality makes it hard to discover discrepancies. And so it is possible to have an image of knowledge as unchanging lore, handed down from the ancestors. It is no wonder, with this image of knowledge, that there is no systematic research: nobody need ever notice that the way that traditional theory is used requires inconsistent interpretations. It is literacy that makes possible the precise formulation of questions that we have just noticed as one of the characteristics of scientific theory, and it is precise formulation that points up inconsistency. This explanation, which we owe to Horton, is surely very plausible. Given the orality of traditional culture, it is possible to see how the accommodative approach can be maintained. With widespread literacy, the image of knowledge as a body of truths always already given cannot survive. But the recognition of the failures of consistency of the traditional worldview does not automatically lead to science; there are, as I have already observed, many other contributing factors. Without widespread literacy it is hard to see how science could have got started: it is not a sufficient condition for science, but it seems certainly necessary. What else, apart from a lot of luck, accounts for the beginnings of modern science? So many things: the Reformation, itself dependent not merely on literacy but also on printing and the wider dissemination of the Bible and other religious writings, with its transfer of cognitive authority from the Church to the individual; the experience with mechanism, with machinery, in agriculture and warfare; the development of universities. My claim is not that literacy explains modern science (China is a standing refutation of that claim); it is that it was crucial to its possibility. And the very low level of its literacy shaped the intellectual possibilities of pre-colonial Africa.

Literacy Prompts Generalization

For literacy has other significant consequences. Those of us who read and write learn very quickly how different in style written communication is from oral; we learn it so early and so well that we need to be reminded of some of the differences – reminded, in fact, of the differences that are really important. Here is one, whose consequences for the intellectual life of literate peoples are, I think, considerable.

Suppose you found a scrap of paper, which contained the following words: "On Sundays here, we often do what Joe is doing over there. But it is not normal to do it on this day. I asked the priest whether it was permissible to do it today and he just did this". A reasonable assumption would be that you were reading a transcription of words someone had spoken. And why? Because all these words – *here*, *there*, *this*, *today*, and even *Joe* and *the priest* – are what logicians call *indexicals*. You need the context in which the sentence is uttered. to know what they are referring to.

Every English speaker knows that *I* refers to the speaker, *you* to his or her audience; that *here* and *now* refer to the place and time of the utterance. And when we hear someone speak we are standardly in a position to identify speaker and audience, place and time. But when we write we have to fill in much of what context provides when we speak. We have to do this not only so that we avoid the uncertainty of indexicals but because we cannot assume that our readers will share our knowledge of our situation, and because, if they do not, they cannot ask us. But thinking about this – and trying to rephrase speech into writing to meet these demands – is bound to move you toward the abstract and the universal, and away from the concrete and the particular.

To see why literacy moves you toward universality in your language, consider the difference between the judgments of a traditional oracle and those of experts in a written tradition. A traditional thinker can get away with saying that if three oracles have answered that Kwame has engaged in adultery, then he has. But in a written tradition, all sorts of problems can arise. After all, everybody knows of cases where the oracles have been wrong three times because they were interfered with by witchcraft. To escape this problem, the literate theorist has to formulate principles not just for the particular case but more generally. Rather than saying, "Three oracles have spoken: it is so" or, as the Akan proverb has it, "Obosom anim, yeko no mprensa" [One consults a spirit three times] – he or she will have to say something like the following: Three oracles constitute good prima facie evidence that something is so; but they may have been interfered with by witchcraft. This is to be revealed by such and such means. If they have been interfered with by witchcraft, it is necessary first to purify the oracle.

And so on, listing those qualifying clauses that we recognize as the mark of written scholarship.

And to see why literacy moves you toward abstraction in your language, listen to traditional proverbs, orally transmitted. Take the Akan proverb "Aba a eto nyinaa na efifiri a, arika obi rennya dua ase kwan", which means (literally) "If all seeds that fall were to grow, then no one could follow the path under the trees". Its message is (usually) that if everyone were prosperous, no one would work. But it talks of seeds, trees, paths through the forest. The message is abstract, but the wording is concrete. The concreteness makes the proverb memorable – and in oral tradition all that is carried on is carried on in memory; there are, as I said, no records. But it also means that to understand the message – as I am sure only Twi-speaking people did before I explained it – you have to share with the speaker a knowledge of his or her background assumptions to a quite specific extent. The proverb works because, in traditional societies, you talk largely with people you know; all the assumptions that are needed to unpack a proverb are shared. And it is because they are shared that the language of oral exchange can be indexical, metaphorical, context-dependent.

Write, then, and the demands imposed by the distant, unknown reader require more universality, more abstraction. Because our reader may not share the cultural assumptions necessary to understand them, in contexts where communication of information is central our written language becomes less figurative. And so another nail is driven into the coffin of the inconsistencies of our informal thought.

For if we speak figuratively, then what we say can be taken and reinterpreted in a new context; the same proverb, precisely because its message is not fixed, can be used again and again. And if we can use it again and again with different messages, we may fail to notice that the messages are inconsistent with each other. After all, the proverb is being used now in this situation, and why should we think of those other occasions of its use here and now?

The impulse to abstract and universalise and move away from figurative language, and the recognition of the failures of consistency of the traditional world view, do not automatically lead to science; there are, as I have already observed, many other contributing factors. But, like literacy itself, these traits of literate cultures, while not sufficient to make for science, are ones it is hard to imagine science doing without.

In characterizing the possibilities of literacy, there is, as we have seen in many of the attempts to oppose tradition and modernity, a risk of overstating the case; our modernity, indeed, consists in part in our wishing to see ourselves as different from our ancestors. The communities of specialized knowledge that produce new physics and new ecology and new chemistry are small worlds of their own, with complex codes and practices into which ephebes are inducted not merely by the transmission of writings. Literate culture is still the culture of people who speak, and the mark of the autodidact, the person who has only book learning, is to be unfamiliar with the context of conversation needed to make a sound professional judgment. Physics textbooks do not tell you how to operate in the sociology and politics of the lab, and nowhere will you find it written exactly what it is about the major theorists in a field that makes their work important. More than this, the kind of checking for consistency that writing (and, now, the computer) makes possible is no guarantee that that possibility will be actualized or that, once inconsistencies are identified (as they seem to have been at the heart of the quantum theory), it will be clear what to do about them.

On the other side, there are many devices for supporting the transmission of a complex and nuanced body of practice and belief without writing. In Asante, for example, the figurative brass weights used for weighing gold dust are associated with proverbs that they represent, in ways that mean that the daily conduct of trade offered reminders of ideas of society and nature; and the same sorts of cultural coding are found in the patterns imprinted on the Adinkra cloth, or carved into our stools.

Still, intellectual style in cultures without widely distributed literacy was for that reason radically different from the style of contemporary literate cultures. And, complex as the real story is, the sorts of differences I have been discussing are real and have been important.

Literacy, then, makes possible the "modern" image of knowledge as something that is constantly being remade; what drives the culture to take up this possibility is, I believe, the economic logic of modernity.

Kwame Anthony Appiah
Harvard University
Barker Center

REFERENCES

Achebe, C. (1982). Interview with Anthony Appiah, D.A.N.Jones and John Ryle [and unpublished notes of that interview]. *Times Literary Supplement* 26 February 1982. New York: TLS.

Appiah, K. A. (1992). *In My Father's House: Africa in the Philosophy of Culture*. Oxford: Oxford University Press.

Coquery-Vidrovitch, C. (1976). The Political Economy of the African Peasantry and Modes of Production. In: Peter C.W. Gutkind and I. Wallerstein (eds.), *The Political Economy of Contemporary Africa*. Beverly Hills, Calif.: Sage Publications.

Dennett, D. (1987). *The Intentional Stance*. Cambridge, Mass.: Bradford Books.

Evans-Pritchard, E. E. (1973). *Witchcraft, Oracles and Magic Among the Azande*. Oxford: Clarendon Press.

Evans-Pritchard, E. E. (1974). *Nuer Religion*. New York: Oxford University Press.

Geertz, C. (1973). *The Interpretation of Cultures*. New York: Basic Books.

Goody, J. (1977). *The Domestication of the Savage Mind*. Cambridge: Cambridge University Press.

Griaule, M. (1948) *Dieu d'eau. Entretiens avec Ogotemmêli*. Paris: Editions du Chêne

Griaule, M. (1965). *Conversations with Ogotemmêli, An Introduction to Dogon Religious Ideas*. London: Oxford University Press.

Hallen, B. (1977). Robin Horton on Critical Philosophy and Traditional Thought. *Second Order* **6** (1).

Hallen, B. (1981). *An African Epistemology: The Knowledge-Belief Distinction.* Ife: University of Ife.

Hallen, B. and J. O. Sodipo, (1986). *Knowledge, Belief and Witchcraft: Analytic Experiments in African Philosophy.* London: Ethnographica.

Hegba. M. P. (1979). *Sorcellerie; chimère dangereuse?* Abidjan: INADES.

Horton, R. (1967). African Traditional Religion and Western Science. *Africa* **37** (1,2), 50-71 and 155-187.

Horton, R. (1970). A Hundred Years of Change in Kalabari Religion. In: J. Middleton (ed.), *Black Africa, Its Peoples and their Cultures Today.* London: Collier-MacMillan.

Horton, R. (1972). Spiritual Beings and Elementary Particles – A Reply to Mr. Pratt. *Second Order* **1** (1).

Horton, R. (1973). *Modes of Thought: Essays on Thinking in Western and Non-Western Societies.* London: Faber and Faber.

Horton, R. (1987). African Traditional Thought and Western Science. *Journal of the International African Institute* **37** (2).

Horton, R. (unpubl.). Traditional Thought and the Emerging African Philosophy Department: A Reply to Dr. Hallen. Unpublished Manuscript.

Kuhn, T. S. ([1962] 1970). *The Structure of Scientific Revolutions.* Chicago: Chicago University Press.

Lakatos, I. (1971) . History of Science and Its Rational Reconstructions. In: Buck and Cohen (eds.), *Boston Studies in the Philosophy of Science* **8**. Dordrecht: Reidel, pp. 91-136.

Miller, R. (1987). *Fact and Method.* Princeton: Princeton University Press.

Popper, K. R. ([1936] 1972). *The Logic of Scientific Discovery.* London: MacMillan.

Popper, K. R. ([1962] 1974). Towards a Rational Theory of Tradition. In: K. R. Popper, *Conjectures and Refutations.* New York: Basic Books.

Rattray, R. S. (1955). *Ashanti.* London: Oxford University Press.

Skorupski, J. (1976). *Symbol and Theory.* Cambridge: Cambridge University Press.

Soyinka, W. (1976). *Myth, Literature and the African World.* Cambridge: Cambridge University Press.

Thomas. K. (1973). *Religion and the Decline of Magic: Studies in Popular Beliefs in Sixteenth and Seventeenth Century England.* London: Weidenfeld & Nicolson.

Wilde, O. (1982). Phrases and Philosophies for the Use of the Young. In: Montgomery Hyde H. (ed.), *The Annotated Oscar Wilde.* New York: Clarkeston N. Potter Inc.

Wilson, B. (ed.) (1970). *Rationality.* Oxford: Basil Blackwell

Wiredu, K. (1980). *Philosophy and an African Culture.* Cambridge: Cambridge University Press.

Wiredu, K. (1993). African Philosophical Tradition. *The Philosophical Forum* **34**, 1-3.

Wiredu, K. (1996). *Cultural Universals and Particulars.* Bloomington and Indianapolis:Indiana University Press.

Bert Hamminga

EPISTEMOLOGY FROM THE AFRICAN POINT OF VIEW

Not knowing is bad.
Not wishing to know is worse.
Nigerian proverb

Abstract. In the traditional African view, knowledge is not acquired by labor but "given" by the ancestors. Second, it is immediately social: not "I" know, but "we" know. Thirdly, knowledge is not universal but *local tribal*: other tribes have different knowledge. Knowledge has it "biological variations" like all other things in nature. The ensuing logic is worked out in this article. Modern African society, changed as it is by the advent of western thought, should be understood in the awareness of the conflicting nature of the two ideas of knowledge.

This chapter contains the relevant part of my views on the African idea of epistemology as expressed in my recent book *Ik heb een fiets in Jinja* [I've got a bike in Jinja], Hamminga (2003), to be translated into English (updates: http://mindphiles.com/bike).

The African "Knowing Subject" Is Not an Individual Person

As an African, when I am born, some ancestor has been "born into" my mother. I will carry his name. I am not this ancestor himself. It is not "reincarnation". I *am* the vital power this ancestor is willing to invest in me. I am a link in the chain of vital power, the genealogical chain of procreation of my community. I pray often to my godfather when I need power. Give us power, I ask. The living people depend for their survival on the power of the ancestors. We *are* nothing but forces endowed with that power. We are a force finding food, shelter, and partners to procreate. And, the ultimate aim: to have vitally powerful children, as many as our own vital power allows. These are all instances of power growth. Vital power is what matters in life, we care for nothing else. We understand Darwin very well, and the Old Testament much better than modern western people do. The Old Testament describes our life and most of our consciousness far better than that of the 20th century westerner.

Our community is a tree (for an illustration of the tree model see Hamminga 2005, Web Appendix). (Dead) ancestors are roots giving energy to the adults.

In: Hamminga, B. (ed.), *Knowledge Cultures. Comparative Western and African Epistemology* (*Poznań Studies in the Philosophy of the Sciences and the Humanities*, vol. 88), pp. 57-84. Amsterdam/New York, NY: Rodopi, 2005.

Adults form the trunk. They in turn supply the branches, leaves and flowers, our children. The tree *knows*. "We" know. The tree is the knowing subject.

Westerners can be surprised to see us all getting excited (or sad) at the same moment. That is because we are one body, a tree. *We* sing, *we* dance, *we* weep, *we know*. We are "together", in such a far-reaching meaning of that word that westerners will have a hard time understanding and believing this togetherness. Ironically, the West sent Christians to teach us about togetherness. But we, here in Africa, are the experts. *Knowledge is one form of togetherness.*

Since togetherness is the highest value, we want share our views. All of them. Hence we always agree with everybody. Standing up and saying: "I have a radically different opinion" would not, as it often does in the West, draw attention to what I have to say. Instead, I am likely to be led before my clan leaders before I even had the chance to continue my speech. Among us, you simply never have radically different opinions. That is because, and that is why we are *together*. Togetherness is our ultimate criterion of any action, the pursuit of knowledge being just one of them.

The African's View on Western Philosophy and Science

If you ask Africans familiar with western philosophy and science what they would primarily say about it *in case they were to have to explain it to fellow Africans unfamiliar with the subject*, often the answer is: "It's critical". Now, what does that mean, if one African says that to another African in explaining the western idea of philosophy as well as science? The listening African is asked by the explaining African to take the following steps. First, consider yourself as an "independent", "isolated" individual. Second, build up your own *private* set of "reasons to believe". Third, on every occasion you have to decide whether to believe something or not, you should come – individually, on your own – to your own conclusions, using your own set of reasons to believe, if necessary expanding them for the purpose.

This might strike westerners as an underestimation of the social aspect of western thought and belief formation. Yet, from the African distance, it is not far beside the point. In any case, it stresses the scary leaps to loneliness Africans have to make if they wish to understand western belief formation, whether in philosophy or in science (and for westerners the reverse leaps, the subject of this paper, are even more difficult to make).

Westerners who are best at understanding the reverse leap – that is, the leap to "togetherness" – are those who have to co-operate closely and on a nearly instinctive level with others, like participants of team sports at a high level, or musicians, especially improvising musicians. I remember the comment by an

Ajax football player on a goal: "Yes, it went perfectly, we did not think, we just did it". Similar experiences can be heard in improvised music: musicians say that at their best moments they "dissolve into" their own music, they do not at that moment feel they consciously decide on some playing strategy, it just "happens" to them *together*. The way this attitude of participants turns a game or concert into a "collective" thing gives some clue on how everything – knowledge and its acquisition included – turns into a common thing once you adopt the traditional African attitude.

Among early modern western heros of thought and science, there is a strikingly frequent occurrence of independent minds that went their own individual, often lonely way, frequently laughed at, punished or even burned by their tribesmen. Africans ready to make such a choice for a dangerous solo tour through life are even scarcer than similar characters in the early modern western period, though they are now growing in numbers. Their courage should make everybody stand in awe. A part of a tree does not choose an individual existence. No part of a body – and that is all you are – can meaningfully survive cut off from the rest. And everything you do, including acquisition of knowledge and coming to beliefs, serves the purpose of enhancing the vital energy, the procreation of the tribe. Together. What you do if you isolate, individualize yourself is worse than dying: you will never be a root.

> Omwâná wa mwíno: tákúmála bugúmbá [The child of your sister (friend) can't take away your barrenness] (Cultural Research Centre 1999a, proverb 98; but in general there are many such proverbs about "bachelors").

New Proposals: The Role of Communication

The clan or tribe is the knowing subject. All knowledge is power. All power comes from the forces preceding us: our ancestors. These are three maxims that have a status comparable to the law of conservation of energy in western science: if some of your thoughts do not tally with it, that means you have made some error. So even if the tribe changes its mind, as for instance tribes, facing AIDS, nowadays do on sexual relations, this is an accommodation to new circumstances, according the traditional view agreed upon, yes *decreed* by the ancestors.

Scientists in the West might work for years on the basis of provisional beliefs not shared by their social or even scientific environment before deciding whether they were wrong or whether they should come out with their conclusions, even though they are inconsistent with general opinion. That is not what Africans mean by togetherness. If one member of the herd moves, it should either return or all should follow. And all this *now*. There is no bar on proposal by anyone. There is, if something is under discussion, remarkable freedom of speech for everybody and no kind of dictatorship.

It is not even sure beforehand who will get his or her way. That might depend on the subject. But at some stage matters become settled. There are no formal regulations for that to happen. Everybody feels ("Hears" as it is expressed in most Bantu languages, see Hamminga in this volume, p. 101) it. At that moment truth is *made*. Everybody conforms. Everybody. This is illustrated by a remark of Uganda president Yoweri Museveni, who in his autobiography, explains how he had to learn the use of the commanding type of leadership the hard way: only after serious human losses in the early stage of his liberation guerrilla did he start to cut short spontaneous procedures of common decision making among the fighters. "Originally, the group had been consultative – every decision was arrived at by consensus. But this practice was dangerous when it applied to military situations" (Museveni 1997, p. 80).

Now, this settling in the group looks, to westerners, most like the way westerners settle things individually: westerners usually buy the metaphor of doubt that one "voice" in you tells you to go somewhere, another to go elsewhere. That is a way to say you hesitate. It is an uncomfortable state of mind. If in an African group there are inconsistent proposals, the *group as a togetherness* is in quite a similar, uncomfortable state of mind. The state has to be resolved quickly. It decreases vitality, it inhibits action. Westerners do not have objections to the internal conflict of doubting as such, but, apart maybe from some philosophers, they do not want it to last for long. A westerner who keeps hearing conflicting voices goes into therapy. In the African group one feels the same, though not about oneself but about the community. They do not need therapy, they are well trained to reach community-wide consensus.

The term "voice" in the sense just used is a beautiful instrument to say what a "person" is in classical Africa: *a person is a voice in the tribe. Everybody* is a voice in the tribe. In most public events, sung and clapped refrains by everybody alternate with persons coming to the middle and performing song and dance, watched by everybody. And everybody will have his or her turn. Almost as soon as you can walk, you will participate, and you will keep doing so often even well after you have lost your ability to stand. It is the most important African way to represent, affirm and propagate established thought and science. This rhythmic and social (not the harmonic) tradition where everybody has his share came to the West with jazz, quickly degrading from science into personal lamentations (blues) and then pithily perverted in its recent western academic degeneration to "art" (jazz musicians learning to read their notes from paper) and perverted most of all in that vital insult to the drum, the fake western romanticism of "pop" music of the last half century, where a desired potential sexual partner is the victim of an uncivilized approach of brutish and savage singing.

The unconditional acceptance of each person *individually* by the group has the astonishing effect often observed by those westerners who did some teaching in Africa: ask a student to lecture on a subject in class and he or she will tell a coherent story, by heart, or with only a few words on a tiny scrap of paper. No shyness, no groping for sentences. They give themselves, because they did not learn to fear as students learnt in the West.

To the African it seems difficult to be an individual in the West because in western society they do not see a group in which they can be an individual. And that is why to the African, westerners seem to be a mass, a mob. Westerners look like each other: they wear similar clothes, although different ones with every new season (while the old ones were still perfect), they have the same opinions, the same interests, they watch the same TV programs. There is a fixed set of commodities a westerner needs to possess in order to take part in normal social intercourse. There is competition in having it a little bigger, a little shinier than your neighbor. To obtain these commodities, westerners neglect the care and extension of their families in favor of money earning activities. To Africans, the mass of westerners seems to consist of very similar "individuals", a homogenous sea to drown in.

Truth and Authority

The general rule always to agree with everybody holds most emphatically with respect to authorities. In the clan context, the elder's opinion is truth. All power, all truth comes up from the roots of the family tree, the dead ancestors, to the trunk, the elders, and passes up to parents and children, the branches, leaves and flowers.

This casts a light on the western strategy of convincing with *arguments*. From the African point of view, arguments are a sign of weakness, of lack of power and vitality. A good, forceful truth does not need arguments. Arguments are crutches that are needed only by weak, if not invalid opinions. Truth is not argued for but *felt* ("Heard" with capital H as we shall explain below, see Hamminga in this volume, p. 101) as a force coming from the speaking human. A strong man has strong truths. As far as truth is concerned, strength is not primarily felt through muscles but through age and wisdom. Wisdom does not exist of stockpiles of arguments. It consists of a wider and deeper understanding of the universe as possessed by those who have a deeper position in it. Wisdom is felt as a force.

Omúkulú táyoná: omúto n'âyoná [An elder never makes mistakes, it is the younger who makes mistakes] (Cultural Research Centre 1999a, proverb 759).

In the context of an artificial, perverse, foreign-imposed state bureaucracy this is elevated to a criterion by which an authority tests and shows his power: the authority likes to deliberately park his car in forbidden and inconvenient places, and displays weird opinions to test the obedience of his subordinates in agreeing with them. The general law that *the authority is right* is used, by the bureaucrat, to test whether or establish that he is an authority.

General Truths: What Is Meaningless to Doubt

Like western scientific knowledge, African knowledge has it layers. At the shallow level of practicalities there are the things about which we often disagree, like where best to hunt a specific animal or whether there will be rain (disagreement does not entail we believe to deal with *contingency*, see below p. 66). At the deepest level there are, as in western science, general laws acting like methodological rules: they are considered to be universal properties of the world, they act as filing and phrasing principles, and are used to prove *ex negatio* that someone is wrong (if he were right, the general law would be wrong, which nobody wishes to accept). It is not wrong to think about these general truths in terms of western concepts like "metaphysics", "paradigm", "hard core", "ground theory", "basic theory", but given the academic sophistication of the discussion surrounding these terms it is counterproductive at this stage to make a choice out of all these terms. In the African spirit, we simply coin all those different terms, like different sticks possibly capable of driving different cows in the same direction.

We turn now to those principles that a classical African deems unwise to doubt (if that question were ever to come up in someone's mind, which it often does not). First, the universe consists of *forces*. They exert *power* over each other. You have: non-living forces, living forces, formerly living forces (dematerialized forces, forces nevertheless!). Licking some kind of stone can stop you feeling sick when you are pregnant. A plant can cure your skin. Your dead father can give you power and advice. A bow can help you to hunt successfully. Everything has power, is active. More or less active. The African question to any unknown object is not "What is it?" but "What does it do?". In this context, it is interesting to remember that Newton opposed the Antique idea that everything is at rest unless it is moved by a force, by generalizing the notion of rest to a linear movement with constant speed, of which Antique "rest" (no movement) is a special case. This "generalized rest" would occur in the absence of forces exerted on the object. In the African tradition no notion of inertia whatsoever is meaningful, because everything is a force itself. It gets its power from outside, yes, but if it doesn't there is no force, so there "is" nothing.

In many African languages, the way to express that you got hit by a stone is: "A stone has beaten me". In Africa, you can buy fuel saving herbs to hang in your car.

The universe is a chain of forces "empowering" and "depowering" each other. God is the universal superforce, charging everything. God has important business, so he does not deal with humans directly. He leaves this to others: the young go to the elders, the elders to the ancestors, and to the diviner, who is in contact not only with the ancestors, but also with powerful spirits, people who died and whom we know only as a force.

There is not only a human chain of forces, there is also an animal chain, a plant chain, and a non-living chain. Transfer of power from everything to everything is possible.

Every force has something you may call a "meaning", an "intention", an "aim", a "function". In Lingala (Congo), it is called *ntína*, in Lusoga (Uganda) *ensónga*.

All these terms approach the idea in their own way. The universe, not only the biological part, but all of it, is functional. The stone is there to cure sickness when you are pregnant, and probably to do a lot of other things we do not know. *All knowledge acquisition is the discovery of the power of forces.* To discover what a thing "does". What the force is *for*. Burgman (1998) illustrates this with the Luo language, where one says literally that the grass "greens", the water "colds" and a woman "beautifuls". It is interesting to compare this to to Plato, *Phaidon* ([380BC] 1977), where Socrates is reported to say to Kebes, on his way to proving the immortality of the soul: "that nothing else has the power to make beautiful but the presence or the community with the beautiful or however you may wish to call such a being-together".

In their concept of God as omnipresent Supercharger of the universe, too big to be approached by individual humans, Africans are decisively *less* anthropocentric than western Christians and Muslims, even curiously enough more "modern" than them by *western* standards. Here we can learn from the type of western modernity advocated by Spinoza in his ethics ([1677] 1977). Spinoza, whose Jewish ancestors arrived in Amsterdam from Portugal which they had reached through Africa, maintains as basic principles of *Ethics* that "every thing thrives to keep existing" (and fails to do so only in a clash with something stronger), and that "God is all things in all aspects" (of which humans only know the spiritual and material aspect, a negligible subset of the aspects of things). Spinoza upholds a parallelism – a bijective attribution – between the material and spiritual appearance of things. By "spirit" Spinoza simply means, quite understandable to every African, the thing as it appears to us in the form of thought. But when the thing meets something stronger and dematerializes (stops "existing"), according to Spinoza, its spiritual attribute remains, perhaps in humans and certainly in God. From the epistemological viewpoint of *eternity* ("sub specie eternitate") everything exists by definition. The body of all thoughts is one aspect of God, the body of all material forces another. There will be infinitely more such aspects about which humans do not know. Finally, according to Spinoza, the aim of man's life is utility, that is survival. The primary means is the acquisition of intuitive (!) knowledge, that is acquiring "adequate" ideas. Adequate ideas make you stronger, inadequate ideas hurt you.

Spinoza's "utility" is less "consumer" or "commodity"-centered than the recent western economic concept of utility that suggests the influence of free-moving, atomic, individual desire as a factor determining our lives. Spinoza is thinking of what enhances the power to survive like abilities to maintain good shelter and food, possibly, but not necessarily procured by exchange of labor and goods on markets. In that sence he is closer to the traditional African than to the modern western point of view.

Most of that is perfectly clear to *every* African you meet, even though in the West, Spinoza's ideas have largely remained specialized voodoo for modernists. But Spinoza is generally considered to have been "ahead of his time" in the West. (Note the notoriously western linear concept of time and the idea of natural progress in this short expression!) Though dead more than four hundred years, Spinoza is still too "modern" (in the western sense!) to be a Christian's (or, for that matter, Jew's or Muslim's) favorite philosopher. From the African point of view there is some reason here to consider the possibility that westerners and Africans have common ancestors.

In their relation with God, Africans are decisively less anthropocentric than the original zealots of the three mayor mesopotamic religions: Catholicism, Protestantism and Islam. In the African view, the criterion of truth is personal advantage in the struggle for survival. Which of the three main mesopotamic religions enhances power most depends on the circumstances, that is, on what these religions have to offer in a given time at a certain place. As a result of the competition of the mesopotamic religions in the African subcontinent, Africans possess a remarkable fluidity in becoming converted and hence and so forth: what is the difference to them? The choice is between, for instance, only a single wife (Christians) or no drinking (Muslims). For leaders, it is a matter of which foreign cleric has the greatest power to add to his interests. Advantages depend on circumstances. Many Africans divide their children between the schools of all the imported faiths, much as prudent westerners do when investing on the stock market. Like Spinoza they do not worry about the specific type of foreign worship, but more about what Spinoza calls "utility".

What Happens to You Is Always Done by Someone

The real and to westerners astonishing anthropocentrism comes in as soon as questions are asked concerning the causes of increase or diminishing of one's own vital power. As a classical African, your vital power is derived from all kinds of forces: your name (your charging godfather-ancestor), your parents, your wife, your children, your hunting equipment (bows and arrows, as well as other forces you are wearing, such as vitally strong parts of hunting animals and other non-living objects charged by, say, a diviner) and all other animal, vegetable and non-living supplies you procure for yourself. In the system of transmission of power, your own power increases and diminishes.

A diviner can recharge objects that help you. In case, for instance, of hunting he charges not only your bow, but also something like a lion tooth hanging around your neck while hunting. When such objects start to "weaken" (lose power), you bring them to the diviner. Charging might take some days, during which time you, of course, will be careful. Nickel-cadmium batteries were amazing to westerners when they were introduced, but no surprise to Africans. Once I bought non-rechargeable batteries in a very small town. The seller claimed that they would auto recharge by simply giving them a rest for a while. "Will you pay me back if they don't?", I asked to test his conviction. He wouldn't. Inferring from this answer that I being tested by typical African "guile", and hence probably also was being asked a *muzungu* (western) price, I bid down on the batteries, starting from a wrong figure, erroneously offering him twice the money. "I cannot accept that" the man replied, "I want to be an honest trader". So the "rest-" or if you will "recovery-" theory was meant seriously after all.

The battery metaphor has helped me a lot. Mbiti (1969) uses the car battery as a metaphor. Think also of battery light: photons ("power") leaving an object ("force" in African terms) that has been charged. That is what you, as a force, do when you talk to someone (see Hamminga in this volume, p.). Every word is a photon (in Congo, the Mongo have a proverb saying: "ofonda nk' okaka, joi nta fondaka" [what rots away is a fallen tree, a word does not rot away]). And how can one survive alone? Who will charge you? The battery as an "individual" force, separate from charging devices, is doomed to dematerialize. Power transmission makes everything hang completely together, not only in the long run, but even on short notice. Consciousness is almost exclusively in use for "we"-considerations (as opposed to "I"-considerations). I have never heard an African speak about "my village". It is always "our village". Considering your African self as an individual comes closer than the western reader can be made to believe to asking a westerner to consider, say, his middle finger as an independent individual. And classical Africans would frown – at least as much as is often done in the West – on those males who treat their penis as an independent person.

The causes of these fluctuations of your power are *willful agents* (dead or living) *only*. Whatever happens to you, "somebody" is responsible. I87t is unthinkable that your vital power changed by a mere contingency. Even natural forces that change your vital power, like a torrential rain, are sent by people using power transmission procedures. Not even God is involved in the specifics of what happens to you. Some people may be identified as evil forces ("sorcerers"), but others may have been misused as evil force by others (they can be cured). Unfortunately this often makes certain people the scapegoats of a community, a danger to which the slightly deviant and childless are most prone.

Willful agents are living humans, dead humans (spirits) and other spirits that never have been living humans because they were born as spirits. The latter are known to reside in trees, rivers and assume bodies of certain types of animals.

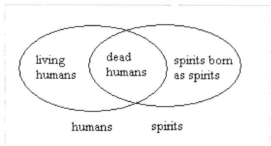

Hence, to acquire knowledge of the cause of decreases in ones vital power, one should find the force with evil intentions, *deliberately* triggering a chain of power transmissions that resulted in damage to your vital power. Analogously, knowledge concerning increases of your vital power should be acquired by research up the chain of power transmissions until you reach the living or dead person who *intended* this increase.

Elders and diviners will monitor these causes for everybody, since this knowledge is basic to the vital power of the community. Needless to say, the community is a force, and *knowledge itself is a force, transmitted by the ancestors to the living*.

Elders and diviners are concerned with the acquisition and updating of knowledge of vitality affecting forces. Such knowledge is not "produced" (a "labor" suggesting metaphor of knowledge acquisition acceptable to many westerners), but *given*. (Many great western scientists, however, talk about their brightest moments in similar ways, as seems to be reflected in Popper's distinction between discovery – think of the word "inspiration" that refers to *spirits* – and justification, which is depicted as a serious *labor* in the sense this concept acquired in the development of Christian tradition and is alien to African culture.) In general, any association of knowledge acquisition with *working* is just as alien to the classical African mind as it is to the classical Greek concept of knowledge. Just having respect, an open mind and readiness to receive is what counts.

Evil forces may have to be addressed with counterforces, and the identification of all such forces is fraught with a great deal of uncertainty, as any participant will readily admit. Against some force, you "try" another force (a herb, an arrow, a carefully charged stone, and many other means, some of them reported by westerners to be astonishingly effective on them). In the course of your life, you improve. Your knowledge grows. The older you get, the more you will be asked for advice, because the young depend on you.

Children coming from school with wisdom unknown to elders constitute a fundamental epistemological problem. A radical new chain of power transmission is to be accommodated. Sure, kids could do many things better than elders, like picking the jackfruit from the tree for breakfast, but by serving as a forces transferring knowledge they become like "elders". A clear tension.

Westerners are inclined to think there is an epistemological demarcation between "natural" knowledge about such things as forging iron, building a house, making pottery, hunting, fishing, harvesting on the one hand, and about "magic" on the other. That is a western problem. There is, from the African point of view, no difference here in epistemic status. Africans have their own demarcation lines between different types of epistemic status that, for the westerner, are not always easy to keep track of. There is *medicine*, *magic*, and *action of spirits*. *Medicine* is considered to be the most casual force: your bow is "loaded" by a medicine man, and also for instance the lion's tooth you wear around your neck. These forces enhance your hunting power. Other forms of medicine are: herbs against pimples, words spoken against sleeplessness etc. *Magic* for instance is what the diviner is doing for you when you fear theft or robbery: when at night you are sleeping in your hut, the diviner will make it look like a shrubbery, and the thief will miss it. I have been told that a flying saucer made of reed maintains a ten-minute service between Tanzania and New York (you travel naked without any luggage). Its fuel is human blood. You pay much more than you do on regular airlines. That's all *magic*. *Spirits*, finally, are not lightly to be manipulated by living humans in "sessions", like western believers in spirits tend to suggest. No: spirits make their own decisions. They come, usually because they are annoyed about something. Hamlet's dead father, however, appearing to his son to tell him how he had been killed and what he wants Hamlet to do, conforms to African spiritual etiquette. When a spirit comes it scares the hell out of you, but this has nothing to do with medicine or magic.

Many able African craftsmen combine medicine and magic, but after all, one can be both a good plumber and a meritorious water-polo player.

When I tried to construe a general demarcation between medicine and magic, on the basis of the many examples given to me, I had some success among Africans with the criterion that medicine is understandable, in principle, to everyone, and magic is only understandable to magicians. Medicine is a craft. Medicine men are not the only ones able to charge bows and lion's teeth, and use herbs to prevent, alleviate and cure all kinds of diseases. Those things are purely a matter of practice and experience, nothing special. But the magician who cures a painful knee at a distance of 100 kilometers (the son, who pays the visit to the magician, gets instructions on when and how to position his father to receive the magical forces) bewilders even the African.

To westerners, the difference between magic and medicine should be learned by understanding what is surprising, bewildering to an African and what isn't. The first thing to realize is that to an African *everything* is power transmission from one force going to another, and many forms of it that might bewilder westerners are casual to an African and hence not magic.

For the western understanding of epistemology from the African point of view the term "magic" threatens to mislead. I shall avoid it.

You might, it should finally be conceded, be the cause of your own decrease of power. That is when you yourself have done evil to someone (a member of the community, dead ancestor, or even a spirit). You could for instance have insulted someone, taken something, or have broken a rule in other ways. If you make good for it, by due apologies, maybe accompanied by gifts, you will be better. Others, who have acquired knowledge and experience, might help you to find the ones you have offended.

Secrets and Guile

Secrets and guile form a relevant part of a study of knowledge. After all, a secret is something somebody knows and does not want others to know. In western philosophy of science, the well known difference between "classified" and "unclassified" research receives little treatment even though it is well known that the former pays best.

Because of the extremely powerful African inter-human communication media, for normal westerners it would be impossible to have a secret while living in a classical African community.

I know this from being exposed several times in African environments (fortunately concerning secrets with not too evil intentions), despite the expertise I had acquired in my former marriage with a Russian. In Russia, due to a long cultural history of mental oppression both in public and in private, rooted far deeper than the communist cultural heritage, secret-creating and secret-detection capacities almost have the African finesse. "Tugonzáníá: gh'ámíra amátánta tákukóberá" ["We love each other", when he swallows the saliva he does not tell you] (Cultural Research Centre 1999a, proverb 934).

Africans themselves do much better in the field of secrets, because due to the "arms race" between secret detection and secret preservation, the African secret preservation techniques have attained stunning levels of sophistication. First of all, there are the social secrets, such as the secrets of the group of adult males. Secondly, no diviner will be ready to tell you the details of his trade, and this is accepted, as it is accepted for other types of specialized craft. This know-how passes from fathers to sons and nowhere else. But thirdly, every individual every now and then "misses the curves", taken by the community and at the outer side of the road finds something that he or she is not ready to share with others. This may be any kind of force. It may well be knowledge that others would immediately accept as true, but the spread of which would diminish the vital power of the inquisitive individual involved. Alternatively, it might be a conviction that would, if shared, be contested ferociously or might even lead to the banning of the individual.

Whatever the anomalous, unshared finding, its secret character blocks the advance of community knowledge. Since the conditions for something to be shared safely are very strong, the bulk of interesting findings die with single persons, as secrets, as a proverb of the Basoga says: " 'I'll tell you later' died without revealing its secret".

Before that, however, in his life, the person might have employed the secret well. To use secrets in a smart way is even a positive value in Africa, exemplified by smart animals like the tortoise. Of course, I am not going to publish the secrets of the tortoise, but once the tortoise boasted to both the hippopotamus and the elephant that he was a rope puller of matching caliber. On the day agreed for the contest he swam a rope across the river, at each end of which he connected one of his contestants. Thus he established the reputation he desired.

Time and Realism

"Future" is a word that both Europeans and Africans know. Mbiti (1969) explains brilliantly how the classic African concept "future", which he denotes "*sasa*", differs from the European one.

To westerners, time is a set of stripes drawn on the tarmac that is on the road on which they drive. They believe they are driving at exactly constant speed, so they think they know exactly when we all, not only westerners themselves, will cross these stripes. There are big stripes for years, smaller ones for months, days, hours, minutes, seconds, and so on. Westerners find it unwise to doubt whether the road is perfectly straight, regular, and goes on forever. Their journey stops when they die, but dying soon is not a real possibility to most of them, as it is to every African. Their agreements with each other about future deliveries and payments are very precisely drawn on this tarmac. If they fail to pay or deliver at the moment their *machine of time* has reached the agreed tarmac stripe they are in big trouble and probably lose their customer and all his friends. So, *agreements*, in Africa the cause of warm feelings of acquired or reinforced friendship, often cause westerners to be very nervous.

Africans have no such unshakeable belief in the future. Constant speed over regular tarmac might be possible, but the machine might just as easily break down, floods could remove the road, and a relative might be met. Africans do not like to waste much time speculating about the future.

> Bulí mbérí: tágúla bulí ínhúmá [What is forward cannot buy what is behind] (Cultural Research Centre 1999a, proverb 274).

The chance of the future being what we expect is considered low. Why lose energy on such hypothetical considerations! Instead of hours and numerical dates, Africans traditionally rely on *personal* emotional marks of time, like when you were born, when you married, when you had you first child, when there was a war. A typical westerners question is: "when was Museveni born?". The answer: 1944. The traditional African may ask: "1944? When was that?", and, if one is in or close to Museveni's family, one of the helpful answers may be: "That was when Museveni was born". As Karin Blixen's story about her cook shows ("the sauce of the grey horse that died", see Hamminga in this volume, p. 102), memory and memorizing is anchored in such emotionally appealing events in the past. *The time past* (Mbiti calls it *zamani*) *is personal, living*. But as far as the future is concerned, these personal. living marks are still to be made, and the African typically considers his or her influence on that as small. *The future is hypothetical, unreal and uninteresting to consider now.*

This view naturally entails that anticipation is generally unwise, and there is a second fundamental reason why anticipation is unwise: since all forces determining the future course of events are *personal*, anticipation is also *impolite*. In anticipating, you expect forces to do something, and that is a way forces, especially powerful forces – that is, the most important forces – do not want to be treated by you. You should not act in the expectation that they will co-operate, but you should modestly wait until they decide to do something for you. That is good behavior, that is: the behavior that optimizes your chances in nature. In short, you are taught to treat nature like you are taught to treat your father and mother: *an attentive and respectful waiting*. That is not only how you catch fish and deer, that is how you catch everything, including knowledge. The gestures of respect are sacrifice, speech, song and dance. They are, somewhat disrespectfully formulated, bait. Bait meant to encourage ancestors and other powers to exert the forces upon us that we need, that is, to give us forces that contribute to our survival.

From the traditional point of view, *power* and *past* hence are clearly two names for the same: power is the past. The past is the active power giving us forces every day. The past is real and living, referred to not in terms of the dead calendar-clock format but in terms of its main events (as Museveni explains on the issue of his date of birth, see Museveni in this volume, p. 11). The future is hypothetical, in the hands of powers surrounding us, far more powerful than we are.

As a result of its hypothetical nature, to Africans a certain future point in time seems further away than to a European. Waiting for the start of a play in Jinja, Uganda, I met a Ugandan sister who had just returned from her first visit to London. I asked her: one Ugandan week, how many London weeks would it be? She immediately understood my question, thought only for a second, looking over my head, and then said decidedly: six.

This would have tremendous consequences: it means that in one week's hard work, a Ugandan suffers six times as much as a Londoner. If he is free for one week, he enjoys it six times as much as a Londoner. That would make it very irrational for a Ugandan to work as hard as a Londoner, especially when you add that the Londoner feels sure about the future enjoyment of his working results and to the Ugandan the future is *unreal, unsure* and *hypothetical*.

Whether six or another number, to a Ugandan as compared to a European the present is larger and the future is smaller. Future enjoyment is more real to a European and he is willing to work now in order to fill his future with enjoyment. This future is "big" to him, and he likes it to be filled with enjoyment. To a Ugandan, the same work, requiring the same number of hours, occupies his present, which is something very large. The sacrifice is very high. The reward, filling his future with enjoyment, is low, because his future is small.

Making Causal Theories Is a Waste of Energy: Good Luck – Bad Luck

What will happen as a result of your actions is unsure, because your actions are like the waves a daffodil makes in the air. What does it do to the air? What does it do to yourself? Don't think of it too much. You'll waste your time. You float on forces you do not know much about, and you are not in control anyway. Though always and only persons, humans (living, but first and foremost dead humans and other spirits), are responsible for what happens to you, it is hard to know all of them and we invest in the acquisition of such knowledge only when we experience a persistent drag on our vitality. That is because you need to appease humans and spirits that somehow started to acquire the habit of always picking on you. For the rest, in your action, you "give" yourself to nature just as you give yourself to your community. So why, for instance, drive prudently? Burgman asks (1998, see p. 74). If you survive the wild ride, you had good luck; if you die, you had bad luck. Westerners, facing things neglected by Africans, "causing" (in western eyes) misfortunes, may ask why some preventive action (like regular brake and tyre control) has been neglected. Africans are likely to think that the waiving of the preventive action has little or nothing to do with the resulting misfortune, which is simply a matter of bad luck. Didn't others neglect to take the preventive action too, but without the unfortunate result? If big powers are against you, there is nothing you can do anyway, and you'll have to accept and comply. As Museveni writes about his efforts to educate the cattle keepers of Ankole: "If their cows died, they thought it was just bad luck" (Museveni in this volume, p. 16). Africans have remarkable capacities in their acceptance of suffering.

There is no way to study forces in isolation. Nature as a whole operates on nature as a whole. This implies that it makes no sense whatsoever to do controlled experiments in order to acquire knowledge of forces. In this view, western scientific method lacks every shred of meaning. Experimental isolation of forces is unthinkable. Wisdom does not reveal itself in repeated correct prediction or the persistent success in attaining certain practical aims. Museveni, on the cattle keepers of Ankole in his early days of teaching, writes: "Trust in a line of thought without having seen the predicted result was generally considered to be too precarious to base a change of method upon" (Museveni in this volume, p. 17).

On the contrary even, Karen Blixen suggests in *Out of Africa*, telling about her laywoman's effort to supply some medical help:

> If I had been able to guarantee recovery to every individual patient, who knows, their circle would have thinned. In that case I would have enjoyed the prestige of a medical doctor – apparently a highly able doctor from Volaia! – but would they still have been sure the Lord is with me? Because they know the Lord from the big years of drought, from the lions on the planes in the night, and the leopards near their houses when the children were there alone, and from the swarms of grasshoppers coming down on the land, nobody knew from where, and not a single blade would be left after they had passed. They knew him from the unimaginable moments full of happiness when a swarm had flown over the field without landing, or when in spring the rains came early and abundantly and let all the fields and planes bloom and yield a rich harvest. So, that highly able doctor from Volaia [Europe – B.H.] yet perhaps was an outsider when it came to the real big things in life (Blixen 1937, p.184)

Blixen's suggestion is here that for something to be real, good luck and bad luck should be part of it.

In a discussion on an exposition of techniques of rain-making by Dah-Lokonon (1997, p. 88), Jean-Marie Apovo describes an experiment where rain fails to fall.

> Then the rain-makers claim certain feelings were not quite right, or that a number of subjective conditions has not been met. One wonders why the workings of our ["our" refers here to African; Apove is a native African, though, apparent from his formulations, raised in the western concept of knowledge – B.H.] traditional intellectual practices are always subject to such psychological, individual and climatic conditions. What can we do to get rid of these subjective factors and achieve pure objectivity? (Apovo 1997, p. 123).

What Apovo wants to "get rid of", is the essence of the world, in the traditional African view.

On good luck and bad luck in Busoga (Uganda) there is a publication by the Cultural Research Centre (2000), Jinja.

Acquisition of Knowledge Relevant to the Principle of Minimum Investment

Burgman made a very important observation. We shall follow him here in detail (though not literally, see Burgman 1998). A basic rule that is generally honored is: keep out of the way of powerful forces unless you can handle them. In fact, it is considered wise to keep out of the way of any kind of forces that bother you. There is wisdom in reducing the number of things that have to be done. Here we have to *experiment*. Many things present themselves as being utterly necessary, but a little experimentation will show that they can often be omitted. Avoiding aggressive engagement is a wise thing to do, and very good for one's health. Burgman calls this the "Law of Minimum Investment" (Burgman 1998). Whenever nature devises a scheme, it invests a minimum amount of energy in it, so that it only just works. A lion can only just catch his prey, and often loses it; a kingfisher has more misses than strikes. Too much power in any particular place would upset the balance of nature. So people should also try to reach their goals with a minimum investment. What the minimum actually is should be established by experiment: how far can you reduce your input before the thing actually collapses? This explains why Africans tend to love to omit actions that seem indispensable to westerners. This has an immediate bearing on the level of maintenance of vehicles, houses and equipment. Taken on a much bigger scale this explains why technical progress is not a priority: interfering with nature in order to acquire knowledge about how to obtain more from it than one gets already, if this is already at least what one strictly needs, mans exposing oneself to unnecessary danger.

Africans feel that their "gentle approach" to nature is rewarded. If you do not make outrageous demands on nature, you will find out that nature responds with some degree of reliability and even generosity. It will answer your needs if you make your needs modest enough. So there is no need to preserve food on a big scale. This insight leads to the "feast or famine" attitude. Some outsiders may look down on this, but at least we have a feast every now and then. Feast is whenever there is a lot and we are allowed to finish it all. In the unreal, hypothetical and uninteresting future, nature may give something else again. Or not, in case we shall still have had a marvelous feast today. To illustrate: After a day of rioting in Kinshasa during which a supermarket was emptied by the mob, someone wrote on the wall of the supermarket: "merci pour la fête" (thank you for the feast).

In the context of the present 20th century technology and intense competition in the industrial world, this creates problems. For Africans know and desire some of the things that technology has produced. But the amount of work that goes into producing them or even procuring them may be more than what they find humanly desirable. Even when these articles are obtained, these very articles will demand a lot of care. Engines of all kinds all have their own laws of maintenance and safety. It is very dangerous to tamper with these laws. Yet all around us we see people trying to omit even the minimum demands that these artifacts make. Safety regulations are flouted with incredible ease. As a result calamitous breakdowns occur, and horrifying accidents. These will be ascribed to "bad luck". For behold: many people performed still worse maintenance and took even greater risks; so how come they did not have an accident, but got away with it? Thus the causal connection becomes obliterated, and the "good luck-bad luck" evaluation takes over.

We cherish such enormously powerful technical tools like guns and cars, but our principle of minimum investment makes us cherish mostly those technical objects that require neither further investment nor any maintenance: Africa is conquered by plastic bags, toe-slippers and jerry cans (that do not really need their screw top, as we quickly discovered).

On my second visit to Uganda, I brought a lot of jerry can screw tops, having seen them missing universally. They received little interest.

Conclusion I: Knowledge We Need

Our tribe consists of *persons* in a system (roots, trunk, branches, leaves, flowers, fruits, seed) like a tree. Persons are forces transmitting power to other forces (some of which are persons themselves, some are not). The power is the past. The roots. It is the ancestors. To stimulate the transmission of power to us by the ancestors, we have a variety of gestures of respect to them, mainly sacrifice, song and dance. These are small down-currents in the tree, called bait, running against the main, feeding and fertilizing (up-) stream of power. Time runs up with power. The power is the past. Power (past, until now) is what you can see, but, what is far more important: feel and hear. The past (until now) is real. The future is only hypothetical, determined beyond our control. We may have expectations about what the tree will look like in the future, but these are completely irrelevant. The future is wait-and-see (illustration: Hamminga 2005, Web Appendix).

What kinds of knowledge does the classical African need? The criterion is *survival, procreation,* the first requirement is considered to be *togetherness.* We should know how to achieve these goals.

Not wise to doubt or discuss

- God is the total of power.
- The world is the total of forces.
- The clan or tribe is the knowing subject.
- All knowledge is power.
- All knowledge is about forces and their powers.
- All our power, including that of knowledge, is procreationally transmitted. For ourselves this means: it comes from our ancestors.
- You don't go for knowledge, you do not acquire it by working or labor. You wait till it comes. It is being *given* to you by willful, powerful forces.

Things to keep an open mind about

These things are referred to in proverbs like: "Omúgeesi ekyámúzîmbyá ku ngírá: kulágíríwá" [Why a smith built his working place near the road, is to be corrected] (Cultural Research Centre 1999a, proverb 716).

- What are the powers of every different type of force? How best to employ those powers?
- Who transmits power in favor of my vital energy? How to deal with them?
- Who transmits power detrimental to my vital energy? How to deal with them? ("My" involves all mine, that is: ultimately the whole community.)
- What are the minimum conditions to keep something in operation?

Conclusion II: Why the Need for Science of Western Specification Is not Felt

In classical African culture, knowledge is not produced, but it comes, is given to you by tradition, the ancestors, as a heritage. So knowledge acquisition is a *purely social* matter, a matter of teaching, of being told, "uploaded" (by living, dead or spiritual powers) only. Like ancient Greek knowledge, it has nothing to do with sweating or working.

To Africans, knowledge is only relevant if it is directly about yourself, about today's vitality, today's concrete problems. About procreation. *The future is unreal.* You just wait for it to become present and then you act. There is no "pure curiosity". Any step towards satisfying pure curiosity is a step into the *unreal.* A waste of energy. *The possible and the future are not (yet) reality, hence irrelevant.*

One might well, in theory, imagine Africans trying, say, their different medicines on people or animals by way of test. But *there is no belief that causes can be isolated.* All forces involved are *living.* At the repetition of an experiment the forces involved might have acquired a different awareness and different intentions. Forces *learn.* Other forces may join the game next time. Thus *experiment in the western sense is void of meaning.* You can have experience, but that is not associated with the formally controlled comparison of similar events you have gone through.

Togetherness is the highest value. This entails agreement on what is and how it works. Such agreement is *required.* It is *not done, rude, misbehaviour* to challenge the consensus. *Everybody always agrees with everybody.*

Consensus is actively maintained. One of the consensus maintaining strategies is *prudent sloppiness* about our consensus. This requires prudent sloppiness of agreed *data*, like quantities and time. The force of prudent sloppiness is diminished by writing, recording, money and time measurement. Africans traditionally feel they should stay away from these forces

Once, as a student, I lived with 8 people in a Dutch house where cooking was done in turn, by a mechanism of collective deliberation based, I held, on irrational intuitions. I proposed to save 8 old tin cans for the 8 members. Each of us would start with 8 marbles in our own tin can, "paying" a marble each night to the tin can of the one who had done the cooking. This would grant everyone a credit of 8 meals after which he/she should prepare a meal for the others to "earn" a new set of marbles. The opposition was ferocious. I could not get my point across. One of the leading ladies claimed this would mean the immediate "death" of the community. I gradually learnt to "feel" when it was my turn. Later, I met a Norwegian girl teaching at an all-African primary school near Kampala who tried to learn to feel, at that moment still without much success, when she was supposed to go to which classroom, what children to expect, and what to do with them. She solved the problem by simply always being there, prepared for anything (other teachers simply did not show up or appeared suddenly). Like in the kitchen of my Dutch house, there was a "schedule" on the wall in this school which, like in my Dutch house, everybody would tell you was old. Like in my Dutch house, there was no clear leadership. Things were just "happening". Many questions can be asked: Do I start to "feel like" cooking when others don't? Or when I notice that other people's bad memories of my last turn start to fade? These are after the event questions. The western concept of rational strategy is the reverse: "reasons" are before the event and make you decide to do something. This is exemplified by the Lucky Luke cartoon in which the butler of an English lord touring through the Wild West starts to fight attacking Indians with his right hand, holding an encyclopedia, open at the entry "self defense" in his left. In the cartoon, of course, the butler wins. It is funny, but this butler's behavior bears a striking resemblance to the mode of operation of a western symphony orchestra sitting behind their multiple walls of paper, and to western poets reading from their own work. African musicians and poets do not work with paper. They concentrate fully on their Indians.

Watches and reading glasses are often considered to be desirable things, but whoever infers that they are used in the western fashion is in for a disappointment.

The minute recording of predictions, beliefs and the outcomes of events inconsistent with them, as is done in western science, but also in western performance analysis as used in business, does not rhyme with togetherness. It could, if thoughts could be treated as *independent* of the people who got them, but in a classical African community this is an unthinkable interpretation of the idea of a "thought". Like every force, *all thoughts have power coming from personal forces*. All thoughts are personal by definition (or, if you will, by "knowledge that is unwise to doubt").

No need is felt for inter-community pooling of knowledge. Every tribe has its own ancestors with the knowledge relevant to this particular tribe. Tribes have become genetically and culturally different during the past, *so did their knowledge*. Knowledge is not considered generally human, but community-specific. Nobody feels uncomfortable with the idea that Busoga truth is different from Asante truth. Nobody feels the need for *intertribal accommodation* of knowledge. Thus: *where there is communication, there is no pluralism, where there is pluralism there is no communication, at least not in order to settle for one truth.* (Of course, there is the kind of if-you-don't-do-this-we'll-do-that sort of communication.)

Many types of acquired knowledge are not even communicated within the group. People have secrets that they keep to gain power or not to lose power. Priests, diviners and specialized craftsmen especially, but in general everybody. This type of knowledge cannot advance and fortify the community as a whole. Often one uses it to strengthen oneself at the expense of others. *In abstracto* tricks based upon secrets make a person a hero, but don't get caught! Here, however, the difference from the West might not be so great. The western scientist, in considering whether to publish or not, also faces the payoff between the resulting fame and the loss of the lead in the research competition, and many good scientific results have the property of selling well as long as they are secrets (some even maintain that as a reason not to read too many academic journals).

A classical African can only change his view on what is if he can convince *all*, his entire community to join in. And he has to do so as soon as his alternative view occurs to him. Any view or thought is supposed to be immediately social. So there is no time for preliminary research. To start doing research on something is also supposed to be decided upon collectively. So, the act of convincing the rest should succeed at the very moment of the first occurrence of an alternative view. As we know from the history of western sciences, fundamentally new approaches at first usually do decisively worse in many fields than the conventional view with which they are competing. A new approach is carried on by enthusiasts who do not care to be generally considered to be "on the wrong track". Such enthusiasts usually concentrate on the success of an alternative view in solving particular problems, and optimistically believe that the "ocean of anomalies" will be accommodated in the future (Kuhn [1962] 1970; Lakatos 1970). In short, western science requires communities where there is no worry if for a *longer* while some believe this, others that. This runs counter the principles of the classical African community, where belief is directly linked to momentary survival.

Kagamé (1956) tells the following story: an old, illiterate Ruandan woman says with great confidence and emphasis: "These whites are really touchingly naïve; they have no intelligence" After being asked how she can say something like that, did we invent such miraculous things as these whites did, things beyond our power of imagination? She replies: "Listen well, my child. They have all simply learned that, but they have no intelligence whatsoever. They have no understanding of anything".

Conclusion III: The "Individual" *contra* the "Personal"

Appiah has devoted an entire section to "the individual versus the personal" (Appiah in this volume, p. 39). A basic way to phrase the astonishing dialectics of western versus classical African approaches is to say that in the West anonymous, free moving atomic individuality (*"every thing is individual"*) is the ideal self image, where the ideal self image of the classical African is holistic, community-dependent, power-connected personality (*"every force is personal"*). And, as should now be clear, this characterizes the difference between western and African "physics" (basic view on the working of the universe) as well! Needless to say, in neither culture can you fully attain nor be fully happy with the ideal self image that you have irreversibly been raised and grown up in, the one you've been taught, implicitly for by far the most part, as being *obvious*.

Many scholars, notably Tempels ([1945] 1959), Horton (1973, 1987) and Appiah (1992 and in this volume, p.), take pains to clarify the African idea of "personal", and its difference, yes, opposition to the western "individual". In a western factory you might have 50 identical "individual" machines operated by 50 "individual" workers. From the management point for view, neither are treated as personal. They are both costly production inputs capable of performing certain routines, nearly identical individuals liable to being counted and treated identically. Personal differences among the work force (like body size differences requiring different sizes of professional gear) are negatives: cost factors, reducing profit. In Africa even machines quickly acquire their own personal features, as repairs are not usually made in a standard way. In Africa, a machine (car, bus etc.) can usually be operated only by persons knowing this particular machine personally.

It is no accident that many parts of contributions to this book will strike many western academic readers as "personal" (as opposed to "objective"). By giving the personal the space it deserves (from the African point of view), we illustrate, we hope, how effective that is in creating the reader's awareness of the culture differences relevant to the acquisition and interpretation of knowledge.

Competitiveness and Romanticism

Whether things look essentially the same or different depends upon the distance of observation one chooses. Since it was my purpose to look at differences, I have chosen my "zoom factor" accordingly. I hope I came near enough to clearly display the differences between the African and the western strategy for acquiring and maintaining knowledge. The African one is very consistent, and should be so even to a westerner who comes to think about it. As far as it is "strange" to westerners, its consistency creates for them a window with an unexpected view on themselves.

An idea is a force that can gain and lose power. The ideas on which the western mind is based have achieved an "obviousness" to westerners, making them invisible, but permeating everything. But ideas can lose power too. And they do not have the same power everywhere. *The vicissitudes of "obvious" ideas that go on travelling, enhancing your power, as a muzungu, that is, as a human force coming from elsewhere.*

Western "dead" causal thinking has now found its way to the deepest places in Africa. The reason is simple. It gives you power: power to earn money as an engine repairman, and power to keep your car on the road, to get your product sold, to acquire your equipment. If you wish to update to the 21st century state of the art your (dead causal) knowledge on what cars do *not* need in order to stay on the road, you should definitely go to Africa: no western technician *knows* as *precisely* as a great many Africans what is the absolute minimum requirement for a road and a car to keep that car making progress on that road. That this knowledge seems less relevant to the westerner than it does to the African is a matter of priorities and circumstances, and quite obviously not one of difference in epistemic sophistication.

Finally: Both in the West and, as I have discovered personally, in Africa there are time-honored longings for the "happy life of the savage". It is well known that in the history of western thought the savage has been a venerated object of romanticism. But more than once my discussions with Ugandans about cultural change took, on their initiative, the path of the "spoiled society", and a longing for primitive tribal community life made impossible by the modern conditions in Africa. But there are also voices claiming the "superiority" of modern western culture. Here westerners take the lead, curiously enough showing an astonishing lack of scientific rationality in making observations. Moreover, Africans often are too impressed by western culture, as a result of erroneously considering it as the "force" that overpowered them. This partly explains the ease with which many "western" religious sects gain followers. They are erroneously identified as the forces behind the powerful western technical tools. Their leaders typically do not shy from keeping up that appearance. It should be stressed again that this paper makes no contribution to such sometimes romantic, sometimes competitive discussions. Their meaning is in itself quite unclear. In political debate, they can be, and are, misused by all sides. That is easy because they have no consequence for personal action, except to mislead people to cast their vote for one rather than another.

Doubts

Referring, as I frequently have, to literature concerning a tradition like the African that itself does not traditionally depend on writing, is a highly devious procedure. From the African viewpoint the genuine, optimal reference is to experience ("power exchange") in dealing with African people in life. That is why I have so frequently referred to personal experiences.

The big trap, or – Baconian – *forum*, stems from the *invisibility* at first sight of the ocean of cultural differences. It is difficult to see that there is something to explore. Once a small part is revealed, the rest remains as invisible as it ever was, and the inclination is to think that "the job is done" and there is nothing more to gain an understanding of. This will leave westerners stuck again, erroneously identifying what is out there with the dead circularity of western projections from western culture. Of course, projection is all one can do, but the *forum* consists of the treacherous signals one gets that, though our previous projections were ridiculous, one's present ones are "good".

Another problem is how to fix an identification of a "tradition" or "culture" in a constantly changing world. A frequently used method to deal with the changes is first to characterize "tradition", like a Weberian "ideal type", featuring the common properties of traditional African communities as they have almost disappeared now, and then deal with the historical road taken by Africans from that "traditional" state. Though notoriously dangerous in many circumstances, I have followed this procedure, referring to the "traditional" ideal type drawn as the *classical African community*. If no confusion is possible I have simply written *African*. If this has led to errors of excessive simplification, the least that could be harvested is a list of those errors and an agenda for correcting them.

In explaining the African point of view I often followed Burgman's (1998) habit of using the "we" form, quite inappropriate for me (I am a Dutch mix of Saxon and Friesian race and culture), but a highly pregnant and effective device.

The classical African community as it stands above should, as an ideal type of tradition, be one of pervasive African validity. If not, this paper is no good. Needless to say, it is restricted to the epistemologically relevant aspects.

It should finally be conceded that almost everything discussed has been observed and discussed before by others, in other contexts, often couched in other terms, so the chief merit of this paper, if any, is to reorder and rephrase matters in order to create what I hope is an African perspective yielding an instructive view of western knowledge acquisition, epistemology and philosophy of science.

Bert Hamminga
Cultural Research Centre
P.O. Box 673
Jinja
Uganda
e-mail: knowledgecultures@mindphiles.com

REFERENCES

Abraham, W. E. (1962). *The Mind of Africa*. Chicago: University of Chicago Press.

Apovo, J. (1997). Comment on Dah-Lokonon, Gbnoukpo Bodhou "Rain-makers': Myth and Knowledge in Traditional Artmospheric Management Techniques". In: Hountondji, P. (ed.), *Endogenous Knowledge: Research Trails*. Dakar: CODESRIA pp. 113-6.

Appiah, K. A. (1992). *In My Father's House: Africa in the Philosophy of Culture*. Oxford: Oxford University Press.

Bisasso, F. X. (1996). *Kleine Sprachkunde Luganda*. Bad Honnef: Zentralsstelle fuer Auslandkunde.

Blixen, K. (1937). *Out of Africa*. London: Putnam.

Burgman, H. (1998). Western Kenya: Ways Of Thinking. Jinja: http://mindphiles.com/knowledgecultures

Caesar, G. J. ([52BC] 1986). *The Gallic War*, with an English transl. by H.J. Edwards. Cambridge, Mass.: Harvard University Press.

Carothers, J. C. (1972). *The Mind of Man in Africa*. London: Tom Stacey.

Coetzee P. H. and A. P. J. Roux (eds.) (1998). *The African Philosophy Reader*. London, New York: Routledge.

Cultural Research Centre (1999a). *Ensambo edh' Abasoga* [Proverbs of the Basoga]. Jinja: CRC. http://mindphiles.com/CRC

Cultural Research Centre (1999b). *A Lusoga Grammar*. Jinja: CRC. http://mindphiles.com/CRC

Cultural Research Centre (1999c). *Reconciliation Among the Basoga*. Jinja: CRC. http://mindphiles.com/CRC

Cultural Research Centre (1999d). *Dictionary Lusoga-English, English-Lusoga*. Jinja: CRC. http://mindphiles.com/CRC

Cultural Research Centre (2000). *Good Luck, Bad Luck in Busoga*. Jinja: CRC. http://mindphiles.com/CRC

Dah-Lokonon, G. B. (1997). Rain-makers': Myth and Knowledge in Traditional Atmospheric Management Techniques. In: P. Hountondji (ed.), *Endogenous Knowledge: Research Trails*. Dakar: CODESRIA, pp. 83-112.

Griaule, M. (1948) *Dieu d'eau. Entretiens avec Ogotemmêli*. Paris: Editions du Chêne.

Griaule, M. (1965). *Conversations with Ogotemmêli. An Introduction to Dogon Religious Ideas*. London: Oxford University Press.

Hallen, B. (1981). *An African Epistemology: The Knowledge-Belief Distinction*. Ife: University of Ife.

Hallen, B. and J. O. Sodipo (1986). *Knowledge, Belief and Witchcraft: Analytic Experiments in African Philosophy*. London: Ethnographica.

Hamminga, B. (2003). *Ik heb een fiets in Jinja* [I've got a bike in Jinja]. Jinja, Naarden: MIND Foundation. http://mindphiles.com/bike

Hamminga, B. (ed.) (2005). *Knowledge Cultures, Comparative Western and African Epistemology* (*Poznań Studies in thePhilosophy of the Sciences and the Humanities*, vol. **88**). Amsterdam/New York, NY: Rodopi. Web Appendix: http://mindphiles.com/knowledgecultures.

Haumann, T. M. H. M. (1998). *Vrede langs het Oorlogspad. Ontmoetingen uit Zuid Soedan* [Peace Along the Path of War. Encounters in Southern Sudan]. Heeswijk, Utrecht: Dabar Luijten-Pax Christi.

Horton, R. (1973). *Modes of Thought: Essays on Thinking in Western and Non-Western Societies*. London: Faber and Faber.

Horton, R. (1987). African Traditional Thought and Western Science. *Journal of the International African Institute* **37** (2).

Hountondji, P. J. (1983). *African Philosophy: Myth and Reality*. London: Hutchinson University Library for Africa.

Hountondji, P. J. (ed.) (1997). *Endogenous knowledge: Research Trails*. Dakar: CODESRIA.

Ikuenobe, P. (1996). An Examination for the Universalist Trend Regarding the Nature of African Philosophy. *The Journal of Social Philosophy* **27** (2).

Jahn, J. (1961). *Muntu: An Outline of the New African Culture*. New York: Groove Press Inc.

Jahn, J. (1990). *African Culture and the Western World*. New York Grove Wiedenfeld.

Kagamé, A. (1956). *La philosophie Bantu Rwandaise de l'être*. Brussels: Academie Royale des Sciences Coloniales.

Kanyike, E. M. (1996). *The Power Factor in African Traditional Religions*. Jinja: Philosophy Centre Jinja (unpublished).

Kuhn, T.S. ([1962] 1970). *The Structure of Scientific Revolutions*. Chicago: Chicago University Press.

Lakatos, I. (1970). Falsification and the Methodology of Scientific Research Programmes. In: Lakatos, I. and A. Musgrave (eds.), *Criticism and the Growth of Knowledge*. Cambridge: Cambridge University Press.

Lamb, D. (1987). *The Africans*. New York, Toronto: Random House.

Liyong, Taban lo (ed.) (1972). *Popular Culture of East Africa*. Nairobi, Longman Kenia.

Masolo, D.A. (1986). Kwame Nkrumah, Socialism for Liberation: A Philosophical Review. *Praxis International* **6** (2).

Masolo, D.A. (1987). Alexis Kagamé and African Sociolinguistics. In: G. Floistad (ed.), *Contemporary Philosophy: A New Survey* 5. Dordrecht: Kluwer Academic Publishers.

Mbiti, J.S. (1969). *African Religions and Philosophy*. London: Heinemann.

Museveni Y. K. (1997). *Sowing the Mustard Seed*. London: Macmillan.

Ochieng'-Odhiambo, F. (1990). Foreword to *Trends in Contemporary African Philosophy* by H. Odera Oruka. Nairobi: Shirikon Publishers.

Ochieng'-Odhiambo, F. (1997). Philosophic Sagacity Revisited. In: A. Graness, and K. Kresse, K. (eds.), *Sagacious Reasoning: Henry Odera Oruka in Memoriam*. Frankfurt am Main: Peter Lang.

Plato ([380BC] 1977). *Plato's "Phaedo"* ed. with introduction and notes by J. Burnet. Oxford: Clarendon Press.

Plato ([355BC] 1973). *Phaedrus and The seventh and eighth letters* transl. from the Greek with introduction by W. Hamilton. Harmondsworth: Penguin Books.

Spinoza, B. de ([1677] 1977). *Ethica Ordine Geometrico demonstrata*. Stuttgart: Reclam.

Tempels, P. ([1945] 1959). *Bantu Philosophy*. Paris: Présence Africaine.

Bert Hamminga

LANGUAGE, REALITY AND TRUTH: THE AFRICAN POINT OF VIEW

> *Ofonda nk' okaka, joi nta fondaka*
> [What rots away is a fallen tree, a word does not rot away]
> Mongo proverb

Abstract. In the traditional African view, words and sentences are not viewed as being liable to objective reflective truth/falsehood-judgments. It is not a person-word-reality-view, but a person-word-person-view: the sender's words are units of orally produced energy that have the power to improve or degenerate the receiver's vitality. Words received can make you more powerful by increasing your confidence and your control over your environment. But they can equally well harm (parts of) you, by discouraging you in certain endeavors. From the traditional African point of view, words are not logical, but physical phenomena: words are forces affecting power.

Language as a Method of Power Transmission

After having studied the basic principles of logic and doctrines of philosophy of science, I felt very sure of their basic validity (at least much more than I do now). I considered it to be obvious that now I should be able to easily convince adherents to all kinds of irrational beliefs and methods of belief acquisition, such as astrologists, card readers, media, and especially their "clients" as you find them in modern western countries – at least as frequently as you find those upholding the officially acknowledged, full-sized western "rationality". I vividly remember the shock of my utter frustration when I experienced from my own conversations with such superstitious believers that philosophy of science did not, in my hands, turn out to have that power. And this was in contact with western people who had often grown up without such irrational beliefs, having acquired them individually in the course of their lives, often merely by reading some books, the words of which apparently appealed so much to them that my arguments taken from philosophy of science could not lure them back into rationality. I discovered myself unable to use philosophy of science as a "force".

The power of language. To Africans, language is a force. Its power is used by the speaker. For some people its power is greater than for others. Mbiti (1969) notes that the words of parents, for example, carry power, when spoken

In: Hamminga, B. (ed.), *Knowledge Cultures. Comparative Western and African Epistemology* (*Poznań Studies in the Philosophy of the Sciences and the Humanities*, vol. 88), pp. 85-115. Amsterdam/New York, NY: Rodopi, 2005.

to children, especially when spoken in moments of crisis: when they are blessings they "cause" good fortune, success, peace. When they are curses, they can cause all kinds of misery and sorrow. To explain this to westerners I like the metaphor of the photon: light is generally believed in the West to be an energy, transmitted in series of energy packets called photons. African speech is like western light, and its words are the photons. The speaker sends them to hit you, and they change your energy level. Sometimes upwards (for instance with messages of agreement, encouragement, good news, blessings), sometimes downward (bad news, criticism, insults, curses). The effect of words may be reasonably small, but they may also lift you in the air, your feet floundering, or knock you down. You can emit such packets too, and this leads you into an energy relation between communicating people. Many western artists find inspiration in the African idea of language as a force. Many western authors show awareness of this "photon" aspect of words.

An ironic but famous example is a passage in Thomas Mann's Zauberberg, where a charismatic heavyweight Dutch wheat-trader Peperkorn creates a thrill when at table in the dining room of a Swiss sanatorium. His (French) speech is astonishingly impressive, but absolutely void of semantic content (which goes completely unnoticed). It is accompanied with majestic gestures, and Mann describes in detail the regrets of the young Chinese tuberculosis patient at the far end of the table, who does not know French, but nevertheless applauds, shouting (in English) "well done!" (Mann [1924] 1992, pp. 752-3). Mann describes the predicament of the Chinese as "misimplication of the expression to the expressed" ("Fehlschluss vom Audruck aufs Ausgedrückte", Mann [1924] 1992, p. 753). From the African point of view, the reaction of the young Chinese is quite appropriate and Mann himself is the one who gets on the wrong track – by lapsing into western semantic fetishism.

In Africa, words can even save your life or kill you.

The Disadvantages of Writing

As Africans, we consider it a dignity to be able to write and calculate. Traditionally, writing was not a vital part of our modes of communication, and, according to western standards, we did not calculate very precisely. The western way of writing and calculating confronts us with a major and not often fully appreciated difficulty that requires some explanation.

If at some moment we are together orally on how things are or what should be done, then later on, if things change we shall still be together. That is easy when sun, moon and rain are the only objects in your mind if you think of time;, months and years might vary not so predictability in their number of days; debt, promises and agreements are seen as tokens of a relation of friendship more than as date/time anchored quantities of crops, animals or services. In such happy circumstances, it is not difficult to slightly change, if necessary, what we were about, together. Actually, nobody would even consider it a slight change (at least not publicly). *Prudent use of sloppiness serves our highest value of togetherness.* This useful instrument of sloppiness is beaten out of our hands by writing and calculating, by money, clock and calendar. Many of our national leaders try to keep money as sloppy as it can be; we ignore clocks as much as possible, although we now are proud to have them; and even the calendars issued by our most respected journals must, by western standards, be treated with suspicion, but this only reduces, not eliminates the damage done to the effectiveness of prudent sloppiness in maintaining togetherness. To us, it seems an insult to correct someone, let alone a powerful man, by referring to a piece of paper displaying an agreement or a calendar, or a ticking little engine on your wrist. This is not the way we traditionally interact. It is impolite.

Some examples: on the Uganda New Vision calendar of 1999, one month stopped a day short of the end, and the weekdays of the succeeding two months had to be renumbered by the user, though one month later weekdays and date matched again.

On New Years Day, January 1st, 1998, I was leaving an inn on Mount Elgon (Uganda, near the Kenya border), where I had stayed for the night. While writing the bill, the owner asked me: what is the date today?

After going through incredible efforts to collect twelve documents for my Ugandan motorcycle driving license I finally visited the Revenue Office to receive the license. I handed over all twelve documents and my passport. "What's your name?" I was asked. Of course all twelve documents carried it, many more than once. That is the very epitome of "oral" politeness.

The interesting volume Endogenous Knowledge, edited by Paul Hountondji (Hountondji 1997), known for defying the beliefs that African culture has a specific stance concerning literacy, has a table of contents that contains most of the articles of the book, but in different order and with different page numbers.

In the days before the Iraq war of 2003, United States intelligence produced a document proving that Iraqi leader Saddam Hussein had made an attempt to buy raw uranium in the form of yellow cake from Niger. The document was immediately generally dismissed as an obvious forgery: it was reported to bear a childish signature and a wrong date. Of course, it could have been a "forgery" in the western sense. African archives are not free of them. But many a genuine document bears a childish signature and a wrong date. Moreover, the African criteria for what is "genuine" are different from the western ones, "genuine" roughly being understood as: made by the powerful people in charge, "false" as: not endorsed by the powerful people in charge (where the question whether they previously signed it is deemed largely irrelevant and impolite, hence dangerous, to ask).

Any attempt to derive power from reminding you of the words you wrote, in the past, on some paper is not according to our etiquette. "You promised me…" is being rude. The other person is your friend; you should show trust in his memory of what has been agreed upon. If he does not come up with what is expected, forces have displaced him. It is impolite to confront him with this weakness, his inability to counter these adverse forces. And such adverse forces abound. Every day. Everywhere. To have your agreements on paper is potentially shameful to any of the parties who is to default. Usually both will default. It is normal. We have some power, but not much. Anything can interfere. So the paper may be there, as a solemn, modernistic sign of friendship, but we are not going to read it and ponder what it could mean if someone were to speak these words to us, let alone refer to what it exactly says when problems arise. When problems arise, you solve them as friends.

It is according to our etiquette to agree. Always. With everyone. To everything. If you claim that you saw the moon wavering on its course last night, we agree. If you ask whether it happens more often we'll say yes, even if we've never seen it or heard about it. That is a matter of respect and and expression of our readiness to be together with you. We always want to be very nice people – at least as long as we are not fully sure of having complete power over you, if you are lucky, which you could well be, even longer (see the good luck-bad luck issue, Hamminga in this volume, p. 72, and Burgman (1998) on "holding back" and on the concept of "Ng'uono" in Dholuo language). Classical Africans are not the only ones with reservations about writing. In his *Seventh Letter*, Plato argues against writing (at least about serious matters), with arguments coming near the prudent sloppiness view (Plato [355BC] 2001). Caesar ([52BC] 2001) reports similar reservations among Celtic druids.

Words should be heard if they are to have power. Put in western terms: from the traditional African point of view, strings of written symbols are *dead* words. Words that have ceased to be. They are scrapyard items. Africans themselves would say: strings of written symbols are no words in the first place, just as the print of my foot in the sand is not the power I generated to jump (neither is such a print my foot, nor even the sound it makes while jumping). Genuine words are forces exerted by someone, going into someone else or something else in nature. Packed in sound, words are sent off and received. It is the contents of the package that counts. That is: not what westerners would call the semantic content, but what it really contains, that is, a piece of the basic substance of the universe: *power*.

As a philosophy teacher in Jinja I was astonished by the ease and clarity of speech of the students. In carrying out an assignment to speak in class about a subject, they directed themselves in a lively and powerful way to the public. Most of them did not carry any notes, some had a tiny piece of paper. I have not observed any shyness. Their words seem to come right from their centre of gravity. The talks were way above the level of European students, very clear and very instructive for me as I was less acquainted with the subjects.

Also in Jinja, I was asked by a young student to help him finish a paper for another philosophy course on my computer. I agreed, being curious. The paper dealt with the history of skepticism. It briefly treated skeptical doctrines in the history of western philosophy. While typing, I found some statements about some philosophers that I did not properly understand. So I asked the student: what does this mean? His answer: "I did not have time to check the meaning of those words".

What the student transpired to have done was concocting his paper by copying sentences from philosophy textbooks and encyclopedias, like copying pictures. Now, in dealing with me, something surprising happened to him: I was not looking at his paper "as a picture", but directing myself to him personally, I spoke words he had written on the paper, starting an oral exchange using those words. He had not regarded it, and persevered in not regarding it as part of his assignment to check the meaning of the words: he was drawing – at least, that's what I made of it – his paper.

All this has little to do with ability to read. Let me just give you a stunning example of print reading I owe to a BBC TV documentary. Some Karamojong (a tribe in the North-East of Uganda) were suspected of having stolen cattle. They had not, but to refute the accusation they started a search for the stolen cattle. Two Karamojongs, K1 and K2, walk on a trail (followed by BBC TV). The trail is completely covered with prints of cows and other animals.

K1 to K2: "I count 28 cows".
K2 to K1: "Me too".

I have not wished to claim that a piece of paper with words can have no power. *Anything* can be used as a power package: a sound sequence, a bow, a leopard skin, a monkey bone. So too a piece of paper with words on it. But the *words written on the paper* will not transmit the power invested in the paper. You should bring the paper in the circumstances for which it is designed, by the person (*muntu*) who created it, to exert power upon something. Then you will experience the power that it has been loaded with. The power it has comes from the word *spoken* by the *muntu* while creating it, *not from what someone may have written on it*.

A good example of such powerful paper is *money*. The purchasing power of money, especially of paper money, has made many western nineteenth and even twentieth century economists ponder a lot and write thick books to "explain" it. This is generally considered, by economists, to be a project that failed. To Africans, this power is a completely standard natural phenomenon, just as it is completely natural that weak leaders create weak money and strong leaders create hard currency.

But 200 Uganda shilling (for an illustration, see Hamminga 2005, Web Appendix) is *not* 200 Uganda shilling because you can see, written on it, that number 200 and the Bank President's signature. It is 200 Uganda shilling because the leaders *stated it to be 200 Uganda shilling*. And its power is equal to the power of two chicken eggs.

The price of a chicken egg in Uganda was 100 USH (in 2000), no matter whether the egg was big or small, old or fresh, bought right from under the chicken's backside from a country farmer or in a town shop. From 1995 to 2000, inflation was about 5% annually but the chicken egg did not take part in it: in 2000 it still was worth 100 USH everywhere under all conditions. I did try to buy for less, but even considerably increasing the quantity demanded did not help. I tried to sell for more but never was able to strike such a deal. In 2004, after quite some inflation and depreciation of the Uganda Shilling, the egg still remains in the stable ratio of 1 egg for 100 Uganda Shilling.

If while employing the next piece of money you find it has less power, this informs you about the power of the word of its creators in the capital.

The Basic Structure of the Universe as Transpiring from the Grammar of Bantu Languages

Alexis Kagamé (1956) undertook the effort to explain the logic of the *bantu* world view from the basic classification of nouns in *bantu* languages. These are four: *muntu* (pl. *bantu*, person), *kintu* (pl. *bintu*, impersonal force), *hantu* (spacetime determining forces), *kuntu* (mode, way of being). Kagamé's taxonomy consists of subsuming all concepts in one of those categories. All entities are *forces* capable of exerting *power* on other *forces*. So, the world is a transforming sum total of forces exerting power on one another, thus increasing and decreasing each other's power. What follows is a mix of Kagamé's findings and my personal experience in Busoga, Uganda.

Bantu, "humans", includes every (for the following see the picture Hamminga in this volume, p. 66) person who lives *or ever lived*. It hence includes dead ancestors (*bazimu*), also called spirits. Dead humans continue to wilfully interfere with the affairs of the world.

Hence, who is dead, still is. To be dead is just one way of being. About Patrice Lumumba the Congolese often say: "Il a raison", which I heard one day erroneously corrected in translation on BBC world service by: "He was right". No, ancestor Lumumba, though dead, still is, hence, is right.

Besides the *muntu*, there is one other kind of willful agent: an *omuoyo* (pl. *emyoyo*). *Emyoyo* are spirits, but not spirits of ancestors (not *bazimu*). They are not born to have a human life before becoming a spirit, but are spirits right from "birth". The omu-emy class is a class of what could best be called "near humans". Their singular prefix is roughly identical (omu, omw-) to that of *muntu*, only in the plural they are different (*emy-* vs. *aba*). These near human spirits act in the world like *bazimu* (dead ancestors), and likewise have to be kept appeased. Usually they are more powerful. They may have bodies of some kinds of animals, like snakes and leopards, or alternatively use such animals by some kind of remote control, but also often are "seated" in in trees and rivers. Such rivers often have been given birth by human (*muntu*) mothers, hence have human ancestors. Animal-*emyoyo* are protected, even saved, with some peril, from precarious situations like being trapped in a 10 m deep latrine (as I was told concerning a leopard by a witness). The words "tree" and "river" are in this near human omu-emy class, as well as the words for different types of trees and rivers, and most things made of wood.

Though they are near humans, *emyoyo* (spirits born as spirits) are sharply distinguished from *bazimu* (spirits of dead ancestors) in one aspect: *bazimu* are always invisible, *emyoyo* always have a visible "body" or seat. Humans and near-humans together we shall denote as "willful forces". Quite logically, Lusoga language, for instance, has two words for "everyone": *buli muntu*, referring to *muntu*, humans only, and *buli omu*, referring to really everyone, that is, including *emyoyo*.

Bintu (impersonal forces) are for instance: utensils, plants, animals. These are forces created by a *muntu* (every non-muntu force is created by a *muntu*) and at their disposition for their survival.

Hantu is every force that has to do with the space-time coordinate. "Here", "there", "now" and "coming" are forces in themselves. When some force is "nowing", this means that the force "now" is exerting power on it. Hantu denotes that family of forces. *Hantu* is a good help for westerners in explaining modern string theory of physics to Africans.

Examples of *Kuntu* (mode, way of being) are forces like cold and beautiful. In Luo language for instance it is said that water "colds" and a woman "beautifuls" (Burgman 1998), meaning that the force "coldness" is exerting power on the water, and the force "beauty" is exerting power on the woman, which again is transmitted to the person feeling this coldness and seeing this beauty.

Another Kuntu is laughter. Amos Tutuola writes in *The Palm Wine Drinker*:

> In this night, we got acquainted with the laughter itself, because after every one of them had stopped laughing, laughter itself did not stop. It went on for two more hours. And because the laughter had to laugh about us this night, my wife and I forgot our suffering and we joined the laughter, because the laughter had an extraordinary voice that we never heard before in our lives. How much time we spent laughing with the laughter we do not know, but we only and exclusively laughed about the laughing of the laughter, and nobody who had heard it laughing, had been able to duck out of laughing, and somebody who would have continued to laugh with the laughter would have died of his own laughing or would have fainted, because laughing is the trade of laughter, because laughter feeds itself with laughter. Finally, we asked the laughter to stop laughing, but it couldn't (Tutuola [1952] 1962, p. 133; my transl. – B.H.).

Bintu *and* bantu

When a *muntu* makes a *kintu*, such as a bow, a hoe or a necklace, words (hereafter referred to as *nommo*, in Lomongo: *jói*, pl. *baói*; in Lingala: liloba, pl. *maloba*; in Lusoga: *ekíbonó*, pl. *ebíbonó*; in Luganda: *ekigámbo*, pl. *ebigámbo*) are spoken to charge the *kintu* with the power that it needs to perform its function.

Camara Laye writes about his father making a golden ornament. The diviner used to be present.

> During the process he [the diviner – B.H.] started speaking faster and faster, the rhythm became more and more possessive . . . he took part in the work in a special, almost direct and effective way. It seemed he enjoyed my father's happiness in creating something successful and beautiful and made no secret of it; enthusiastically he grabbed the snares, got excited as if he was my father, as if the work took shape under his own hands (Laye [1953] 1988, p. 36).

Karen Blixen:

> Once in Meroe I saw a girl wearing a five centimeter wide leather bracelet, completely covered with turquoise miniature beads, all of them of slightly different color and with a green, light blue and ultramarine reflection; it seemed to breathe on her arm, as a result of which I would like to have it and send Farah to her to buy it. After having put it on my arm it turned out to have died. It was nothing anymore, a cheap piece of trappings I had bought (Blixen 1937, p. 255).

The same kind of thing holds for plants and animals. They are creations, not made by God but by *bantu* and *emyoyo* using *nommo*, the "word". Nothing can be that has not been given a name by some *muntu* or *omuoyo*. Of course, making something like bougainvillea or elephant is not what an ordinary *muntu* deems himself capable of doing. But powerful spirits (ancestral spirits and *emyoyo* spirits) must be or have been capable of doing that, because only willful forces can create *bintu*. Bantu and *emyoyo*, together all "persons", living and dead, are the *only* willful forces, using the other three types of forces as instruments by organized release of their powers for their purposes, sometimes good, sometimes bad. Other forces (*kintu, hantu, kuntu*) will neither start to exert power by themselves *nor even by accident*. Hence, when something happens, *always* some *bantu or emyoyo* have "done" it.

The verbs "making" and "creating" should not be taken in a very technical sense. With things like DNA, technology is only related as far, for instance, as *making a baby*, free of *in vitro* fertilization doctors in white coats and test tubes, just by making love, centers around a DNA process. But if people can make children without much effort in pleasurable conditions, which should be conceded by everyone, making rivers, elephants, bougainvillea and the other things you see around you must be a piece of cake (at least for ancestors and *emyoyo*).

Everything, *bantu* included, comes from *bantu* and *emyoyo*. This complete reduction of causality to the intentions of willful forces is an astonishing deed of abstraction.

Everything results, and only results from the intentions willful agents.

This does *not* mean that

Every event that happens has been intended by some willful agent

because, first, events often are unintended results of "fighting" agents none of whom gets exactly what he wants. And, second, events often are unintended side effects of actions of agents whose intentions have no reference whatsoever to the event. Many African tribes have a saying roughly like "Where elephants walk the grass is crushed". "Elephants" then stands for willful agents, crushed grass being the unintended side effect of their willful actions.

Bantu know the difference between living (trunc: *zima*) and being dead (trunc: *zimu*). Persons, animals, and plants plans can be alive, but they can also be dead. Other forces are dead by their nature, like stones, clay and other materials. A living animal or plant (a *kizima*: impersonal, non-willful, living force) is a body unified with a shadow. When it dies, body and shadow separate and disappear by natural decay. On death, the *kizima* stops both to *live* and to *be*.

Not so with a living human (*muzima*)! When a *muntu* stops *living* this *muntu* does not stop *being*. Before death a *muntu* is a *muzima* (living human), after death he is a *muzimu* (dead human). When a baby is born, it is not yet a *muntu* (person), but a living *kintu* (*kizima*, impersonal living force). It becomes a living person (*muzima*) only after its father uses *nommo* to call the child's name. If the baby dies before the father has spoken its name, there will be no mourning because no *person* (*muzima*) has died but only a *kizima*. In naming, fathers use their power to *make* persons of their little, newborn, impersonal forces by using language as a force acting on the baby. The name of the baby is an energy packet containing *magara*, the power inherited by the baby from the ancestor whose name it got. "Calling the name" hence should be understood as asking the name (that is the ancestor's power) to come. On "arrival" of the name, the baby becomes *muntu*. Magara is not soul, let alone the soul of the ancestor, but a "starter's pack" of the specific *muntu* power of this ancestor. If an ancestor is known to be very powerful, you can be sure many babies will receive his name.

This *nommo*-idea is also supported by Tristram Shandy's father in Laurence Sterne (1760, vol. I, ch. XIX). Treatment here would lead us to far, but the intelligent reader's understanding of the matter can benefit from thrice fully and carefully reading this subtly composed chapter.

Nommo makes your baby a *muntu*, but it also makes a king. The tribe of Mepe (Ghana) found that the visiting unemployed Dutchman Henk Otte is "inhabited" by their late king Ferdinand Gakpetor, the grandfather of his Ghanaian wife. He was crowned, and during the Dutchman's crowning ceremony the priests suddenly called the name Ferdinand Gakpetor. Otte: "When I was called by this name, people got hysterical, they started to scream and cry in excitement. This name caused outright ecstasy" (Valk 2000, p. 3). This ecstasy was – the report does not confirm to me whether Henk fully understood this himself – aroused by the actual arrival of the spirit (at the request of the priests calling his name) of the late great Ferdinand Gakpetor, "fertilizing" Henk with his huge ancestral power.

As a *muntu* you were created by your father, who was created by his father etc. That means that by yourself you are nothing. You are just a cluster of ancestral power. If you speak, some of that power is radiated. Your words are packages containing ancestral power.

Matip, asking Cameroon children what is a blackboard, was told: "that is the black wall on which you talk with the dead" (Matip 1956, p. 11).

There is no thought of a law of conservation of ancestral power, that is, if somewhere power is gained by a *muntu* of *kintu*, then it does not follow that somewhere else power is lost. You do not necessarily yourself lose the amount of power you transmit. There seems to be unlimited power in nature – at least from the limited human perspective – but it can only be obtained by power transmission to you from other *bantu* and *emyoyo*.

If a *muzima* (a living *muntu*) dies, the *muntu* becomes a dead *muntu*, a *muzimu*. The *muntu* died like a *kintu* does, but unlike the *kintu does not cease to be* (as *bintu* do). Bazimu lie buried on the family plot, not far from the house. They stay around, give advice, quarrel, get angry with people, have to be appeased, they behave just as they did while living (so the *muzima* who were close to them in life know very well how to deal with them). They remain an integral part of the clan, deserving respect just as they did while still living, now even more because death elevates your status. As a *muntu*, you will never eat or drink something before having dropped something on the ground. That is a *libation* to the ancestors. Choking is generally regarded as a sign that you forgot to drop your libation. So: the dead ancestors are there, directly around you. Every day, always. Just like your living family members.

The *kintu-muntu* distinction as a language classification of nouns has some pecularities and seeming exceptions. One type of plant is in many *bantu* languages not in the *kintu* class but in the same class as *emyoyo*: the tree. And one type of complex object also is often an exception: the river. Trees and rivers have bodies that move and whisper. Trees even have a shadow. Rivers fertilize, which is a typical feature of a willful agent. Trees and rivers may become the seat (*hantu*, the time-place force) of a *muzimu* or an *omuoyo*. Hence, in *bantu* languages, trees and rivers typically are found in the same grammatical noun class as *omuoyo*. In Lusoga for instance, tree is *omuti* (pl. *emiti*) and river – omugga (pl. *emygga*). But, to be fair, the Lusoga version of this omu-emi noun class contains some items of which I have not yet obtained a satisfactory explanation, such as rope, latrine and, genuinely puzzling, even a word seemingly denoting "time" (Cultural Research Centre 1999a).

This is one of the features that created the western misunderstanding of Africans as "animists" believing "everything has a soul". In fact Africans do not have the questionable western belief in "souls" at all.

The Conjuring Mode

The whole system of forces is kept in motion by power transmission. The means of power exertion is *nommo*, the word. Nommo, the word, is an "energy packet", willfully sent by a *muntu* or *emyoyo*. All the power that a *muntu* disposes of comes from *nommo* sent to him from other *bantu* and *emyoyo*, either directly or through the medium of other forces (*kintu, hantu, kuntu*). You have no means to create power by yourself. The only way to obtain power is "heritage", gift, from *bantu* of your genealogical tree: father, grandfather and all ancestors to any degree or from an *omuoyo*. To make your ancestors feel you deserve the power they can give you, you observe taboos, you obey rules, you obey powerful *bantu*, you pray, you clap, you sing, you dance and you sacrifice.

I know of no better way to explain the idea of *nommo* than Janheinz Jahn's (1961). He selected and explained words from Ogotommêli (featured in Griaule 1965). We shall follow Jahn literally for a while:

> "Nommo", Ogotommêli says, "is water and glow. The power of life that charges the word, flows out of the mouth in vapor which is water and word". Nommo hence is water, glow and semen in one word. Nommo, the power of life, is the liquid as such, is a unity of mental-physical liquidity that gives life to everything, permeates and affects everything. "The power of life of the earth", Ogotommêli speaks, "is water. Equally, the blood is coming from water. Even in stones you find this power, because humidity is in everything". And since man is master of the art of the word, he is the director of the power of life. He is receiving this power through the word, speaks it to other people and thus implements the meaning of life. That is why Ogotommêli says: "The word is for all in this world; one should exchange it to make it coming and going, because it is good to give and take the powers of life". Even engendering a person, resulting, as it does, not only in a physically, but at the same time in a spiritually living being – *muzima* – is not merely an engendering by semen, but at the same time an engendering by the word. In his plastic language Ogotommêli puts it thus: "The good word goes, also if received by the ear [and genitals too, as Ogotommêli states elsewhere, because it receives the fertile semen of the word], directly to the genitals and turns around the womb like the copper spiral does around the sun. This water-word yields the humidity necessary for procreation and keeps it level, and by means of this humidity *nommo* lets a water-semen cell penetrate in the womb. It changes the water of the word into semen and shapes it like a human, incited with *nommo*...". All efforts of mankind, every movement in nature rests upon the word, upon the life-creating power of the word, that is water and glow and semen and *nommo*, that therefore is the power of life itself. The word liberates the "clotted" powers of the minerals, prompts plants and animals into action, hence stimulates *bintu*, the things, into meaningful behavior. The word of the *muntu* – and *muntu* comprises living humans, the dead the spirits and the gods – is the effective power causing the movement of "things" [his quotation marks suggest that Jahn is not too happy with the expression "things". "Impersonal powers" are the subject here – B.H.] and the continuation of that movement. All the other action is only addition. Amma, "the big progenitor", created the world by the semen of the word.
>
> For everything happening in the world, for fertility and drought, for disease and recovery, for good luck and bad luck therefore, some *muntu* is responsible; a human, a dead person, an *orisja*. The diviner tells you where the word causing the misfortune came from, the diviner knows the counter-word that is stronger and thus can avert the misfortune, the disease. All such vehemently defamed magic practices rest upon the practice of *nommo*.
>
> No "medicine", "talisman", "magic horn", not even the poisons work without the word. If they have not been given words, they have no meaning. Just by themselves they are capable of no activity whatsoever. Only the intelligence of the word releases the forces and make them work. Substances, minerals, juices are nothing but the "vessels" of the word, of *nommo*. Nommo is the *concretum* by which the abstract principle *magara*

realizes itself. . . . The word as such is not charged with feeling, it does not contain ideas, neither is it an idea, nor an image in the European sense. It is only the vocal representation of an object and has no cultural value as such. It is the *muntu* who gives the word a cultural meaning, by turning it into word-semen or image. If an African replaces one word with another and makes an image of this word in the same way he did in his original language, he retains the essence of his original language, the creative transformation of the spoken. Not the vocabulary, but the way in which the language is treated is essential to the language of his land of origin. Kuntu, the way in which, is an independent force. The character of the African culture finds its expression in *kuntu* (Jahn 1961, pp. 142-4; my transl. – B.H.).

That means that what makes language to an African language is its use in the African way. There is no restriction on the sound sequences employed; they could be taken from any language, English included. It is the power transmission that that counts. They come from the speaker who controls the art of African speaking. Language is a force. But that is *only* because *muntu* supplies power to the language. The *muntu* is the source of the power. Thus the word, the medium of speech, is interpreted as the "packet" or "container" or "(blood) vessel" that persons employ to send the energy around that keeps the universe moving. And it is the *only* way power in the universe is transmitted. And transmission of power is actually *all* that is happening in the universe. Compared to that, what westerners call language obviously pales into insignificance.

Ogotommêli (Griaule 1965) explains why water is not *kintu*, not in this class where you find animals, plants and stone. All watery forces, like rivers, channels, brooks, are, in Lusoga at least, the omu emy class. Compare this to Herakleitos (Ephesios [500BC] 1962): ". . . water becomes soul" (phrase 36). "For the soul, it is passion [or death], to become humid . . ." (phrase 77).

In Catholic liturgy, priests throw "holy" water over the believers, and water is used to baptize. Modern biology characterizes terrestrial life as "water-based".

All this does not mean that according to Africans, whites do not use language as a force. Quite contrarily, Africans normally assume that whites do use language as a force, like they do themselves. This gives rise to a host of misunderstandings: the technical power of the West is lightly assumed to come your way in the word of some white crook of some western Christian sect.

Language fertilizes, Ogotommêli says. That humid fertilizing semen of language is not the kind of thing that you allow to dry on paper! And being fertilized is a thing you want to be done to you by your loved ones from nearby, in this splendid sexual organ, the ear, and not a thing you allow to be done to you by someone you do not know, someone far away or even long dead. In the West we nowadays do *in vitro* fertilization in cases of unavoidable medical necessity. Likewise, the African nowadays sometimes reads written words (say, the manual of his new TV). Born out of necessity. To be avoided as much as possible.

Language. Speaking. Every *muntu* speaks roughly the way the God of Jews, Christians and Muslims spoke when creating the earth: "Let there be...". That is, your words transmit *power that you use to realize your intentions*. This "Let there be..." mode of speaking might be called the *conjuring mode*. The only difference between African *bantu* and the idea of God in religions originating from the Jewish is that the amount of power you have as a *muntu* is considered to be little. It is what your ancestors have been able and willing to give you. As a *muntu*, your speech is essentially conjuring. God, as conceived by *bantu*, is not a person (*muntu*) and hence does not conjure, does not transmit power, does not use the word (*nommo*). In most tribes, a *muntu* does not pray to God. He prays to *bazimu* and *emyoyo*: ancestors and other spirits.

Every father can, as we have seen, put the force of *magara* in his *kintu* baby, turning his baby into a *muntu* by giving it its name.

Westerners hearing from a CD, a song like the rain song on display on Hamminga (2005; Web Appendix) will not easily hear the power of the words. That is because it is sung in a recording studio. The words are not given power by the singers. Hence the song is meaningless in the African sense (it has meaning only in the western sense: the "dictionary meaning" of the words). But when you hear it in a local language, standing with the singers in the burning sun when the rain is late, it will be different. If you have not lost all your feelings in your western upbringing, you will feel the punch the words give you. You will easily understand that often the rain does indeed come...

When you are on the road and ask how to get somewhere, and how far it is, you will always hear: "it's not far". That is meant to be a service: saying this will make it not far. If, nevertheless, it is, they still use the little power they have available in your interest, which is very kind. And surely they have given you courage (power), at least until you discover you'll not be there before dark. It is wrong to infer from its still being far that people were lying. What they did is try to help you by saying "it's not far" in the conjuring mode.

Non-verbal Language

"Will you do it?"
"I'll do it."
And when it's not done, westerners often complain about Africans.

Though word, as *nommo*, is central to African physics, to properly feel what specific force is in the words spoken by an African one cannot limit oneself to merely being open to the semantic content, the "dictionary meaning" of the words that are spoken. In receiving power from a *muntu*, you should open yourself to the *muntu* in his entirety, not only to the semantic content to which the knowledge of vocabulary resident in your brains map the words spoken by the *muntu*. If you shake a *muntu*'s hand, you should feel this hand carefully. The hand speaks. You should "hear" it. And one might need pages of words to write what some hand sometimes said. The body speaks. In Africa, learning to speak with your body is *at least* as demanding as learning to speak with your mouth and vocal cords. The dance is a method of expression that everybody is supposed to master, just like speech. So African communication primarily involves feeling (in the sense of *Hear*ing – capital H – to be explained below p. 101), and in addition to that watching, too.

If *muntu* I'll-Do-It makes a relaxed and balanced impression, you can trust it will be done. But he may radiate some lack of determination. That means he may sincerely hope he will be able to do it, but he is not sure. The phrase "I'll do it" is conjuring mode: he shows his willingness to use the power of his words to influence the circumstances in favor of the job being done. But he is not sure whether his power will suffice for it being done. There are stronger forces around, the power of which might displace our path. Thirdly, *muntu* I'll-Do-It may radiate outright despair. He may feel almost sure he will be unable to do it. But you never know, good luck for both of you might be around the corner and unexpectedly or even miraculously allow the job to be done. So he uses the force of his words to say "I'll do it", even though at the same moment he feels almost sure that the force of his words will be insufficient for the "wish" ("conjured event") to be realized. Thus, he still does for you what he can! In such a case, a westerner will normally misinterpret the gesture and defame the speaking of the sentence "I'll-do-it" as lack of sincerity where actually it is an act of extreme solidarity against the odds.

As is well known from psychology, an important aspect of the development of children is the refinement of motor control. At first a baby does not seem to have a lot of detail in its body movement: it moves arms and legs almost as entire wholes, it has no control over individual fingers, and the repertoire of sounds is more controlled by pressure of the breathing muscles then those muscles it will later use to speak words. Yet, everybody knows, babies talk.

And mothers understand them very clearly. At this stage, you can move a baby to any culture and there will be no problem.

In the next stage, long before words, let alone meaning of words, become controlled, facial language starts to develop.

Little children rely so much on facial expression that I can be with *bantu* children for hours without realizing we control only a few common words. Our bodies and faces do the talking. Then we play, they bring me fruit, take me to the cows. Western children do the same: they do not rely heavily on the semantics of language. White adults, though, if they are from the southern tribes of Europe, often simply neglect you if they judge your control of their language to be insufficient. White adults from the northern European tribes tend to feel highly embarrassed when having to deal with someone whose language is not controlled by them. Adult *bantu*, having alternatives to words, are usually much less embarrassed and both ready and able to find a way through

An African community is a togetherness that is very tense and close, densely connected by streams of energy packets. When they clap as a group of one hundred, you hear one single clap, as if they are connected by the kind of nerve system that within a human or animal body perfectly harmonizes the movements of the body's muscles. The perfectly regular clap sequence is the "basic sentence" of power transmission medium in Africa.

In the basic clap, the hands meet as perfect mirror images, not skewed in the western way (for an illustration, see Hamminga 2005, Web Appendix). The function of the basic clap comes close to the lines or squares on western jotting pads, or the units of a western graph, or the pixel of a computer screen. Westerners know a weak version of it as the "count" used in playing written music. Westerners clap at the end of a performance. The public is charged by the performance and through clapping, they discharge themselves: "Bfff, bfff, bfff . . ." The skewed clap is power-consuming. "Applause" dies out, after a duration determined by the energy the public needs to get rid of. This is unknown in traditional Africa, for the simple reason that *African clapping* (with the symmetrical clap) *is self charging*: "Pa!, pa!, pa!...". Needless to say, the hand is a voice that speaks just like mouth and vocal cords. As a voice, the clap fertilizes the ear. And the ear feeds again the clapping hands with power. African clapping starts a resonating, standing oscillation (see below p. 106) and is not, like it is in the West, the changeover to a relaxed, after-concert dinner.

If you watch dance in Africa, even the bodies as a whole seem to be interconnected by ultrasophisticated wireless communication media. These media all are forces. The movements of the body in the dance are ultimately defined on the basic clap. What in the West is called "language" is not the conjuring power transmission but the mere exchange of semantic information. In Africa, that is only one subsidiary aspect of language, and of communication generally.

For whites the other aspects could best, for a start, be called "non-verbal modes of expression": music, dance, theatre, sculpture, painting. In Africa, these forces do the same as verbal language: transmission of power from one *muntu* to another, directly or indirectly over *bintu*, *hantu* and *kuntu*. Just as language is not "art", dance, theatre, sculpture, painting is not "art" in the western sense: amusement for some who have money and think they have "taste". It has nothing to do with such kinds of artificialities; in Africa, it is the *real* thing: the channelling of power, the fundamental physics of the universe. It is the *sole* condition for survival and vitality of every *muntu*. It is through these channels that power reaches you that ultimately determines how successful you will be in life. That means: how successful you will be in acquiring a rich and steady supply of food, shelter, wives and children. This is illustrated by the fact that almost all African languages denote "good" and "beautiful" with the one and the same word, a word that usually really should be translated with "of quality" or "effective" – in Lusoga and Luganda: *obulungi* (Jahn 1961, p. 165; Kagamé 1956, p. 385).

Seeing and Hearing

In attempting to understand what whites could best call "non-verbal" communication, we at the same time find another reason why letters written on paper have no power almost anywhere in Africa: *feeling*, *smelling* and *hearing* fall under one general category of sensing, for which almost invariably the same word is used as for hearing proper (like *ndoka* in Lomongo, *okuwulira* in Lusoga and Luganda). This general African category of non-visual sensing we shall denote as *Hearing* (capital H). The other category is pretty much what whites call seeing. The power mainly comes to you by *Hearing*. And you transmit power mainly by making it *Heard*. The visual, though important, is secondary. So, for instance, the visual representations of words have no power for a *muntu* who just receives a paper on which the words are represented by symbolic drawing. But if a word is spoken it penetrates the ear, a sexual organ, as we have seen above (Hamminga in this volume, p. 97). The Hearer gains power by being fertilized.

Lamb (1987), among the first group of journalists entering Uganda president Idi Amin's house after his escape to Libya in 1979, found huge stockpiles of unopened letters from foreign ambassadors, ministers and presidents.

Karen Blixen (1937) about her young Kikuju cook:

> His memory for recipes was awesome. He could not read and did not know English, so cookbooks had no value to him, but he piled up everything ever taught to him, with the help of his own system that I never got a hold on, in his unattractive head. He named the diverse dishes after some event on the day he had learned to make them, so he spoke of the sauce of the "lightning that struck in the tree", and the sauce of "the grey horse that died" (Blixen 1937, p. 165).

A blackboard's signs can get *nommo*, meaning, though written: by the words the teacher speaks when the signs are written, and by the sounds the chalk makes while being used to write on the blackboard.

Only one thing is purely visual: the shadow joining the body of some force when it starts its life, and leaves it again on death. Both a *muzima* and a *kizima* are unifications of body (*Hear*able and visible) and shadow (only visible).

Bazima get, in addition, that third force *magara* when their fathers name them with *nommo*.

In the West, you have seers, visionaries. Not in Africa. Diviners are Hearers (that is feelers, smellers, ear-hearers).

Once I consulted a diviner to ask what I should do about the nine year old daughter of my sister who was afraid to go to sleep alone. His research procedure consisted of grabbing around in a heap of shells, his staring, not-seeing eyes only stressing his concentration on his feeling.

At Christmas, huts and houses have paper hanging on walls and from ceilings, cut in beautiful forms by folding, cutting and then unfolding it again. The paper used is from old school notebooks. Thus I had the opportunity to read a lot of math-work done by the children. They learn a lot even deep in the bush. Up to differentiation and integration at high school. But I saw no graphs, no pictures at all. Only formulas.

Basoga (South Eastern Uganda) do not count days, they count nights. Asked whether this means that to Basoga nights are more important than days, the answer given is unambiguously yes, the reason being that when it is dark you procreate, the most important thing in life. This is another angle from which the visible is considered secondary.

Most important rituals take place in complete darkness. Visiting spirits make themselves heard and felt to nightly visitors to pitch-dark shrines. Light, that is vision, disturbs

In African dance, *Hear*ing and making *Hear*d is the most powerful engine of power generation, you *Hear* the rhythm of drums, *you Hear your own body moving with the rhythm of the drums, you Hear the dead and the spirits coming; you Hear it by the way your body unifies with the rhythms.*

The primary explanation of the western stress on *seeing* as opposed to *Hearing* (big H) is the western tradition of discouraging bodily interaction. The result is a widespread pathological substitution among adolescents of feeling with vision, creating an undue overconcentration on how people *look* (overconcentration on fashion and body shape, eating disorders) and a primacy of *visual stimulation* in the rituals of sexual attraction (sexual disorders). Once such habits are acquired in adolescence they become part of someone's basic character, and once such characters dominate a society, its culture becomes a culture one-sidedly leaning on the visual.

"Having the music", to many western people means having the piece of paper on which symbols are written that allow those who are capable of motorically processing these visible symbols to produce the sounds intended by the composer. Also, in the West there is frequent talk of the "color" of a sound (e.g. in orchestration), while to the African the "sound" (or "feeling") of a color is a more powerful expression.

The worrying shift, in the West, of stress towards the visual at the expense of the Hearable is being aggravated by the developments in communication techniques: literacy, especially the stress in early education on learning to read, has a clear role in this, but once relations (far from only working relations!) are maintained over the internet, the visual – pace all amusing sounds a computer can make – has finally conquered the exclusive right to steer the compass of the western mind.

All this amounts to a primacy, in African culture, of what in the West is called intuitive understanding of fellow humans (and animals). In the West, this is often considered to be a "female" virtue. After some good exercise one can experience, in a mixed group of westerners and Africans, astonishing examples of inferiority of the former as compared to the latter in intuitive understanding.

No wonder, then, the African dominance of *Hear*ing as the means of inquiry contrasts in quite a remarkable way to the western paradigm ideas of science, distorted as they are by the idolatry of the visual: western scientific observation is typically illustrated with *visual* examples like seeing some liquid turn red or blue, seeing a pointer at some number, seeing at which mark of a measuring rod some object ends. If what one observes is actually a *sound* (animal studies) or *rhythm* (heart rhythm), things seems to get seriously scientific only after such non-visual observations are *visualized* in oscilloscopes, heart scans, pictures of frequency statistics etc. This leaning upon visual impressions can be found even in western "scientific" research on human beings: strong western currents in human science like behaviorism attribute primary importance to what one can *see*. The main type of observations one can do on humans – *feelings* and *intentions* – are thought to lack sufficient "objectivity". As a result, at western universities the study of the human being is usually left to those who neither have a lot of understanding of it nor wish to gain any.

Be this as it may, it should be clear that in a type of society like the classical African where the willful agents (humans and spirits) are *the* movers of the world, *Hear*ing (big H) is the main thing you should be able to do, and seeing is decidedly secondary. As a result there is no idea, like in many other cultures, of "religious" phenomena being "transcendental". The "transcendental" features only in answers to questions of those who regard "invisibility" as a primary problem. Where one relies on the "*Hear*able" rather than the visible, everything is simply here in this world, a dream as much as an ancestor, and there is no need for a borderline between this world and the "transcendental". Neither is there any African notion resembling the modern western scientific remnant of the problem of the transcendental, the problem of "theoretical terms".

Music

If we pass over the border of verbal and non-verbal expressions as whites conceive it, one can think of going from speech to music. In Africa, however, there is no distinction between speech and music. A *muntu* can speak on a drum, a snare or a horn just as well as when he uses his mouth and vocal cords (or, for that matter, his hands). And when he uses his mouth and vocal cords, he *always* makes music. Bantu languages are rhythmical and tonal. *White frames of speech are made of consonants*: you usually still understand the sentence if you only have the consonants: *Wht frms f spch r md f cnsnnts*. You will not get away with the vowels only: *ie ae o ee ae ae o ooa*. In *bantu* languages, this is the other way around: the vowels make up the frame. Obviously, *bantu* distinguish many more vowels than are distinguished in western languages. Learning to speak a *bantu* language is a *musical* education.

When I first met one of my brothers in Uganda, he introduced himself to me as "Stsjúrtsjie Man". That is what they called him. "Stsjúrtsjie" turns out to be derived from "security". It is the vowels of the word that count to this brother of mine, and the "e" and "i" of "security" are not even considered to be real vowels. Left with a damaged card, whites would rather be stuck with

s c r t m n

than

e u i y a

But a Musamia (*muntu* from Samia tribe) like Stsjúrtsjie Man would no doubt prefer *ú* ie *a*.

He went through all this trouble of learning to say "stsj" only to be counted as a member of the English speaking community. To himself, it means little.

When a *muntu* sings, he does the same as when he speaks: power generation. Singing just adds to the power. Platoons of running African soldiers sing: singing words is more important fuel for running than unhindered breathing!

All African traditions know the drum language, though less and less people speak it. Whites often erroneously consider this as a type of "Morse code". But the drum tones really consist of rhythmic sequences of timbres closely related to the ones you would hear when the *muntu* uses his mouth and vocal chords instead. Drum makers and players acquire esteem according to the degree they can make the drum sound like a *muntu*. Whites tend to think drums have "no tone". But it is tone, all the different tones that you can play on one and the same drum that makes a drum do what it is designed to be: a word generating and reinforcing power. A mouth.

At Hamminga (2005, Web Appendix) a photo is on display on which the author joins the drums with his self-designed "recoprano" (European recorder with reed powered soprano saxophone mouthpiece).

Dance

I have done some dancing with Africans and it is my clear impression that to them, dance starts as a reinforcement of a tonal rhythmical movement created by clapping and voice. Drums are the next item to add.

At Hamminga (2005, Web Appendix) a photo is on display showing the author learning some dancing from experienced drum artisans in Bufulubi (Busoga, Uganda). There is no teaching by slow motion rehearsal of steps while counting and other "brainy things you find in western dancing schools. You just start and are "loaded" by the other dancers.

Clapping makes you at the same time both *feel* your own clap in your arm muscles and hands, and hear it with your ear. Those two types of *Hear*ing reinforce each other in the course of events that will follow.

For this reinforcement the symmetric clap is far more effective than the western skewed clap (Hamminga in this volume, p. 100).

Drumming and singing likewise makes you sense *both* the sound producing movements of your body *and* the vibration of your ears that results from the sound you make. You are together with people. There is mutual fertilization and self-fertilization. Bodies synchronize. The medium of synchronization is not the visual but the *Hear*able: your own body, and the rhythmical power it receives through sounds. To enforce this process of synchronization and fertilization, people start dancing. Dancing creates internal body signals: you feel the rhythm of your own movement, you feel how your body starts not only to resonate rhythmical power entering it, but also *to resonate its own movements*.

What finally comes about can best be compared to what engineers call a "standing oscillation", the kind of forces that can destroy a bridge when a platoon of soldiers passes if marching synchronically (that is why before crossing a bridge the command "out of step" should be given). At a certain moment in this process the complete standing oscillation is attained but the bridge of the African dance is designed to endure. It will not collapse. It will keep on vibrating with oscillation of increasing amplitude. The dancing radiates an enormous energy, yet neither players nor clappers nor singers nor dancers feel they expend any. It seems to them they finished their work by lighting the fire, it spreads and deepens by itself. Their bodies seem to move automatically, they no longer feel like their own, their bodies are "used" by the dance. *The dance itself has become a force* that makes people float around effortlessly.

Needless to say these powers radiated by the force "dance" must come from *bantu* and *emyoyo*. Usually the dancing is thought to be a complex of many powers, coming from many rhythms and even many metrics (polyrhythmics, polymetrics), and every rhythm is a force sent by a spirit who makes you move according to that rhythm. In polyrhythmic dance different dancers are "possessed" by different rhythms, they are conceived to be "mounted" by different spirits.

There is no better way to become convinced of the completely literal truth of the basic *bantu* language structure and basic *bantu* power and force philosophy relative to *bantu* reality than to join them in clapping, singing, drumming and dancing.

It made early missionaries very afraid (of the hidden power in themselves that their God makes them fear to bring out), so in liturgy, every move in the direction of the standing oscillation is abhorred. In the beginning they were afraid of any drumming whatsoever. Nowadays, drumming is being more commonly accepted by foreign Christian zealots in their temples, but only regularly on quarter notes, sometimes eighths, sometimes even daringly skipping one note in the measure, but you will never hear the really powerful skips, such as, for a start, on the one or the three. If Modern African Christian church music were to be taken seriously by Africans it would transmit a disastrous weakness and destroy vital power so much that it would take its visiting believers the whole rest of the week to recover from. But for this and other reasons traditional *bantu* power allows the Mesopotamic religions to be resident in the outward bounds of *bantu* consciousness only. Bantu vital roots span dimensions that are completely absent in every type of Mesopotamic religious consciousness. The two can relate to each other only due to the Machiavellism Africans feature as soon as it come to practical and superficial things like in what temple to worship, and what rules to follow in worship, dress, and other matters relevant to the Mesopotamic cultural outsiders.

Westerners know the party dance where two people feel each other's movements and move together (and where the typical western man feels clumsy and shy) and the art-dance on stage, where a group of trained professionals worked hard to memorize a choreography and others *watch* its performance. African dance has little to do with art dance: if as a *muntu* you do not join the dancing, you sing and the least you do is clap. You are always part of it. Dancing is intended to generate and call power with the help of everyone around, and the least of purposes is to drag everybody in. There is no strict dividing line between performers and watchers. As far as there is, it changes position continuously. You might be "public" at one moment. In terms of ancient Greek theatre this "public" is more choir than public; there is not really a concept of "public". A few seconds later you might be the "main actor". The basic thing is being together and allowing some moments for everybody to be in the centre. Everybody! Power reveals itself to you through your *Hear*ing senses (that is feeling, smelling and ear-hearing), not visually. These *Hear*ing senses also signal when you clap, sing, drum and dance, simply different stages of essentially the same activity of power generation and reception.

In stepping from speech to music and then to dance, nothing essential changes in the nature of communication: it remains by nature a process of power transmission from *bantu*, living and dead, to any other force, increasing or decreasing the addressee's power and vitality. What increases, roughly speaking, are the power loads transmitted. On average, music carries more and dance carries most. Music and dance add power to an act of power transmission.

Visual Design

With visual design we enter a part of African communication that is far less important than visual design in the West. Though you can *Hear* a mask or an image by touching it, and you see people doing that a lot, this is not what it is made for. It is made to be seen. Vision, though very important for finding your way and catching an animal, is not a medium of power transmission.

In the dance, a *muntu* dancing a rhythm is "mounted by" the spirit of that rhythm. Without a mask that would be clear enough; nevertheless masks representing this spirit are often made by a woodcarver and worn by the dancer specialized in that spirit. It adds to the impact of the spirit's power. Moeover, the spirit might feel insulted if no trouble is taken to prepare a beautiful mask for him. He may stay away or restrict himself to a weak show.

This is not merely a disappointment from an amusement point of view. The spirit may protect against negative forces that are a threat to life itself. We do not deal with trifles here, these are often matters of life and death.

There are four basic types of (mask) dances:

- Where the spirits come and ride dancers.
- Where the dancers please spirits by performing for them.
- Where the dancers are performing actors representing a spirit who does not come.
- Comedy, entertainment and satire.

The next step is that you may wish a spirit to be near you. You might decide to promote that by ordering a sculpture of it to put into your house. This brings us close to writing, because writing is just one type of visual design. A sculpture is nothing if nobody gives it power. Janheinz Jahn explains this with great clarity:

> It is the word . . . that makes something a different power from what is was before, to what it should be: an image. The name giving determines what is expressed. The woodcarver makes a little sculpture while he says: "This piece of wood is Erinle". . . . Next, he makes a second sculpture while he says: "This piece of wood is the king of Ondo". It could well be that the two sculptures are indistinguishable. Yet, the first is Erinle and the second is the king of Ondo, because not the shape, but name giving through *nommo* determines what the sculpture represents. African sculpture does not display individual expression or psychology because those individual aspects are not attributed by the chisel but by the word. . . . Now suppose the woodcarver made and named a series of indistinguishable sculptures and named them, but they got mixed up. The sculptures have lost their force and can regain force only by renaming . . . The user can also deprive an image of its "face" by saying: "You do not mean anything to me anymore". . . . This explains why Africans treat sculptures deprived of their faces without care (Jahn 1961, p. 152; I freely followed Janheinz Jahn).

Now consider such a thing as a business contract. As a piece of paper shaped by a writer it is in the category of *kintu*. It can be *named*: "this is my friendship with by brother *X*". But it can be deprived of its face. Who is its user? If both parties are user, they should agree on the name. Anyway, its shape does not matter, *visual shape is not individual in Africa*, or, stated differently: *naming can never be done visually*, so the paper representing the contract could just as well be blank!

Papers with written words are *bintu* that can represent individuality only by virtue of name giving: *nommo*. But the *nommo* is the *exclusive* force attributing the individuality, so the paper has no individuality in itself. Its individual representation is "granted" ("given") and can be withdrawn.

The same holds for *amulets*, objects carrying powers against different kinds of evils and misfortunes as a result of being charged by a diviner. The amulet, a stone, bone, piece of skin, tooth or whatever, is by itself *kintu*. The diviner loads it with power by means of ancestral and spiritual *nommo*. If you fail to pay, he'll remove it and your amulet is the same old worthless *kintu* again.

There frequently is an exception to the rule that the dead forces of nature, such as stone, water, minerals, animal skin are *kintu* if unnamed. The exception is wood. A spirit can have named some tree as its "seat". Because it is named already, special procedures may be needed to make a mask or sculpture that is to represent a *muntu*.

Digression on Sad Developments

As a result of the technical power emanating from western culture, nowadays one finds some very worrying developments in Africa: adopting the tokens of western culture is a fashion in the elite: pretending to be a visual reader of meaning, one likes to wear glasses.

In some African circles power is no longer generated by dance. Once, in an organized school festivity that I attended, a woman chief inspector came in, being handed over several tens of sheets of paper by her assistant, taking her glasses (with 0 diopter glasses due to her completely healthy eyes), and started to read: "Kampala, the twenty second of . . . nineteen . . . It is my task to . . . " and so on and so forth, this lasted for almost an hour. Bantu are very good in quietly sitting, and waiting till something they do not understand is over, especially when the people going through the ceremony are thought to be powerful. This time however, after some forty minutes, the hall started to mutter a little.

Nowadays, you can find the richer *bantu* (with western suits, mobile phones and private cars) in churches clapping skewed (!), the way they see the westerners do (for an illustration, see Hamminga 2005, Web Appendix).

Conclusion: Language, Reality and Truth

From the African point of view God, or the Universe, is Power. The Universe consists of forces. They are classified as

- Willful forces, here denoted by *omu* (pl. *aba* or *emy*). There are two kinds: a) *bantu* (humans, alive and dead, the dead are spirits), and b) *emyoyo* (non human spirits).
- *Kintu* (non-person forces), including animals, plants and chemical substances (but water and trees – wood generally – are in the omu emy class).
- *Kuntu* (how forces). If some force finds itself in the modality *standing, living, being dead*, the respective how-force has acted on it.
- *Hantu* (where forces). If some force is at a certain place at a certain time, the where-force of this place-time has been acting on it.

Language from an African point of view is power transmission. Words are power packets sent to an addressee. Though power can be transmitted from any kind of force to any other kind of force in any of the four categories, only *bantu* and *emyoyo* can be ultimate intentional causes ("starting points") of power transmission process. Reality might not perfectly meet the intentions of any of the willful agents who *make* reality in the struggle for life. But reality is entirely the – partly unintended – result of *actions with intentions* by willful agents. Truth is not a "passive" correspondence of statement with fact, but

> *All truth is actively realized by willful agents using their power in vital competition.*

The more powerful you are, the bigger will be your share of truth. A power transmission process can be complicated and work highly indirectly though many, even uncountable mediating forces of any of the four categories. An ordinary *muntu* should not expect to be able to keep track of more than a very tiny part of it, even diviners often have to confess their actions have been impeded by unexpected, unknown forces.

In this universe of power transmission *muntu* feels *completely* dependent of what others are willing to give him. He constantly directs himself to forces where he is likely to be the benefactor, appeases them, shows respect by sacrifice, song and dance. That is all he can do: he is using the little power he has to get some more by stimulating the benevolent powers, like bait might help you catch a fish.

One of the frequently used methods of "bait producing" power generation is resonance: creating a standing oscillation, in the way a platoon of marching soldiers can destroy a bridge. This is done by enforcing speech with the help of clapping, singing, drumming and dancing (in roughly that order of intensity).

There is no law of conservation of power. A *muntu* has no such thing as a stock of power that necessarily diminishes when he transmits some to others. When you transmit, this might cost you power, you may afterward just want to sit and to sleep, you may be hungry (eating refuels you with power of course), but it may even make you feel good, satisfied about what you have done, make you feel strong and increase your vitality.

Most acts of power transmission are quite understandable to westerners, who are used to doing the same in their lives, only naming them less appropriately; some others the white can get used to without much effort. In most "magic" there is little magic.

Power transmitted enters the ear of the addressee. Or rather the Ear, including ear, smelling sense and feeling sense. The Ear is a genital. The eye is useful but not a genital. The only essential task of the eye is seeing whether a body has a shadow. If it has, it lives. Any visual design will only represent something after being *told* by the *spoken word* (*nommo*) of a *muntu* what it is. Nothing can have an "objective" meaning of its own. Letters written on paper, the way bazungu (foreign humans) use them, naturally fall in that category: visual designs that get meaning only after the user has told to the visual design what it represents. Like any visual design, written words can have no meaning in themselves.

Since the visual is, in classical African culture, decisively secondary to the "Hearable" (hearable, feelable, sensable), the idolatry of visual observation as the empirical basis of science as practiced in the West is fundamentally alien to it.

In essence, speech, music, dance and imagery all serve the same purpose. Power is the thing you need in life. There are many types of power you need: knowledge of: health, energy, agility, shrewdness, rain, food, children and so on. You get it from other *bantu* and *emyoyo* by power transmission: speech, song, music, dance. So, African poetry, music and dance are closer to western *knowledge*, transmission of knowledge (science, schooling and training) and application of knowledge (engineering) than to western *art* (in much the same way as Appiah has been at pains to explain (Appiah in this volume, p. 36) that it is more knowledge, science, than what westerners call "religion").

And that is the reason why I have had to devote so much attention to what is often erroneously called African "art". By far the most things thought by westerners to be "art" in Africa certainly are not. It is westerners who have pushed their most talented communicators – singers, musicians, dancers, actors, painters, sculptors, writers – to the sidelines of their own society by calling them "artists" and putting them and their work in special places outside the main roads of society, paying attention to them only in the less serious part of their time, called "leisure time". In traditional Africa, talented communicators are at the centre of society. They are in charge of perpetuating the power transmission to where it is needed: those who still have to gain vitality and power, the young, those who for some reason lost power (like the sick) and in general to anyone who could use some more, and who could not?

"Musicians" like Bob Marley, Fela Kuti and Lucky Dube, no African will tire of explaining to the westerner, are, to the African, much more than musicians in the western sense of the word. To call them "musicians" is to focus on the vehicle of communication rather than on what is transmitted.

It is often noticed that beautiful pieces of "Art", made by Africans with great effort, can get treated without any care, say to fill a roof hole or to burn. That visual design *kintu* has been someone, but lost its face, hence its value. Only one who cherishes the visual as meaningful in itself, on its own, without name giving by *nommo*, could hang such a thing on the wall and enjoy looking at it. To the African, it simply is no one and hence of no other value than the *kintu* value of its materials.

The question can finally be asked whether not even the *word as a sound* must be given a name by *nommo*, before it can carry power. It might even be that the *word, seen as a concept with an established meaning in a language* might be considered *kintu* as long as it is not given a name by *nommo*. I have thus far not been able to find ways to conclusively test these hypotheses, probably because the basic principles of the African use of language are as obvious to Africans as the western principles are to westerners, and hence just as little reflected upon.

Bert Hamminga
Cultural Research Centre
P.O. Box 673
Jinja
Uganda
e-mail: knowledgecultures@mindphiles.com

REFERENCES

Abraham, W. E. (1962). *The Mind of Africa*. Chicago: University of Chicago Press.
Akoha, A. B. (1997). Graphical Representational Systems in Precolonial Africa. In: P. Houtondji (ed.), *Endogenous Knowledge, Research Trails*. Wiltshire, Chippenham: CODESRIA series.
Appiah, K. A. (1992). *In My Father's House: Africa in the Philosophy of Culture*. Oxford: Oxford University Press.
Bisasso, F. X. (1996). *Kleine Sprachkunde Luganda*. Bad Honnef: Zentralsstelle fuer Auslandkunde.
Blixen, K. (1937). *Out of Africa*. London: Putnam.
Burgman, H. (1998). Western Kenya: Ways Of Thinking. Jinja: http://mindphiles.com/knowledgecultures
Caesar, G. J. ([52BC] (1986). *The Gallic War*. With an English transl. by H. J. Edwards. Cambridge, Mass.: Harvard University Press.
Caesar, G .J. ([52BC] (2001). Bello Gallico on Celtic Druids and Writing. In: http://mindphiles.com/knowledgecultures
Carothers, J. C. (1972). *The Mind of Man in Africa*. London: Tom Stacey.
Chukwudi, E. E. (ed.) (1997). *Postcolonial African Philosophy, A Critical Reader*. Malden, MA, Oxford: Blackwell.
Coetzee P. H. and A. P. J. Roux (eds.) (1998). *The African Philosophy Reader*. London, New York: Routledge.
Cultural Research Centre (1999a). *Ensambo edh' Abasoga* [Proverbs of the Basoga]. Jinja: CRC. http://mindphiles.com/CRC
Cultural Research Centre (1999b). *A Lusoga Grammar*. Jinja: CRC. http://mindphiles.com/CRC
Cultural Research Centre (1999c). *Reconciliation among the Basoga*. Jinja: CRC. http://mindphiles.com/CRC
Cultural Research Centre (1999d). *Dictionary Lusoga English, English Lusoga*. Jinja: CRC. http://mindphiles.com/CRC
Diagne, S. B. and H. Kimmerle (eds.) (1998). *Time and Development*. Amsterdam, Atlanta GA: Rodopi
Ephesios, H. ([500BC] 1962). *Heraclitus Ephesius* edited by Geoffrey Stephen Kirk. Cambridge: Cambridge University Press.
Griaule, M. (1948) *Dieu d'eau. Entretiens avec Ogotemmeli*. Paris: Editions du Chêne.
Griaule, M. (1965). *Conversations with Ogotemmêli, An Introduction to Dogon Religious Ideas*. London: Oxford University Press.
Hallen, B. (1981). *An African Epistemology: The Knowledge-Belief Distinction*. Ife: University of Ife.
Hallen, B. and J. O. Sodipo, (1986). *Knowledge, Belief and Witchcraft: Analytic Experiments in African Philosophy*. London: Ethnographica.
Hamminga, B. (2003). *Ik heb een fiets in Jinja* [I've got a bike in Jinja]. Jinja, Naarden: MIND Foundation. http://mindphiles.com/bike

Haumann, T. M. H. M. (1998). *Vrede langs het Oorlogspad. Ontmoetingen uit Zuid Soedan* [Peace along the Path of War. Encounters in Southern Sudan]. Heeswijk, Utrecht: Dabar Luijten-Pax Christi.

Horton, R. (1973). *Modes of Thought: Essays on Thinking in Western and Non-Western Societies.* London: Faber and Faber.

Horton, R. (1987). African Traditional Thought and Western Science. *Journal of the International African Institute* **37** (2).

Hountondji, P. J. (1983). *African Philosophy: Myth and Reality.* London: Hutchinson University Library for Africa.

Hountondji, P. J. (ed.) (1997). *Endogenous Knowledge: Research Trails.* Dakar: CODESRIA.

Ikuenobe, P. (1996). An Examination for the Universalist Trend Regarding the Nature of African Philosophy. *The Journal of Social Philosophy* **27** (2).

Jahn, J. (1961). *Muntu: An Outline of the New African Culture.* New York: Groove Press Inc.

Jahn, J. (1990). *African Culture and the Western World.* New York Grove Wiedenfeld.

Kagamé, A. (1956). *La philosophie Bantu Rwandaise de l'être.* Brussels: Academie Royale des Sciences Coloniales.

Kanyike, E. M. (1996). *The Power Factor in African Traditional Religions.* Jinja: Philosophy Centre Jinja (unpublished).

Lamb, D. (1987). *The Africans.* New York, Toronto: Random House.

Laye, C. ([1953] 1988). *L' enfant noir.* Paris: Plon.

Liyong, Taban lo (ed.) (1972). *Popular Culture of East Africa.* Nairobi, Longman Kenia.

Mann, T. ([1924] 1992). *Der Zauberberg.* Frankfurt am Main: Fischer Taschenbuch Verlag

Masolo, D. A. (1986). Kwame Nkrumah, Socialism for Liberation: A Philosophical Review. *Praxis International* **6** (2).

Masolo, D. A. (1987). Alexis Kagamé and African Sociolinguistics. In: G. Floistad (ed.), *Contemporary Philosophy: A New Survey* 5. Dordrecht: Kluwer Academic Publishers.

Matip, B. (1956). *Afrique, nous t'ignorons.* Paris: La Nef de Paris éditions.

Mbiti, J. S. (1969). *African Religions and Philosophy.* London: Heinemann.

Museveni Y. K. (1997). *Sowing the Mustard Seed.* London: Macmillan.

Ochieng'-Odhiambo, F. (1990). Foreword to *Trends in Contemporary African Philosophy* by H. Odera Oruka. Nairobi: Shirikon Publishers.

Ochieng'-Odhiambo, F. (1997). Philosophic Sagacity Revisited. In: A. Graness, and K. Kresse (eds.), *Sagacious Reasoning: Henry Odera Oruka in Memoriam.* Frankfurt am Main: Peter Lang.

Plato ([355BC] 1973). *Phaedrus and The Seventh and Eighth Letters.* transl. from the Greek with introd. by W. Hamilton. Harmondsworth: Penguin Books.

Plato ([355BC] 2001). *The Seventh Letter.* http://mindphiles.com/knowledgecultures

Sterne, L. (1760). *The Life and Opinions of Tristram Shandy, Gentleman.* York: Published by the author.

Tempels, P. ([1945] 1959). *Bantu Philosophy.* Paris: Présence Africaine.

Tutuola, A. ([1952] 1962). *Der Palmweintrinker: ein Märchen von der Goldküste.* München: List

Valk, G. (2000). Nederlandse werkloze koning van stam in Ghana [Dutch Unemployed King of Tribe in Ghana]. *NRC Handelsblad*, 01-18-2000, p. 3.

Leszek Nowak

ON THE COLLECTIVE SUBJECTS IN EPISTEMOLOGY: THE MARXIST CASE AND A PROBLEM FOR THE AFRICAN VIEWPOINT

Abstract. The idea of a collective, but not necessarily universal epistemological subject is not only inherent in African tradition but also in the sciences and humanities as understood in the western tradition. In this paper I propose to delineate this collective subject by means of the construction of the Marxian concept of a *theoretical representative of a social class*. This allows for avoiding a trap that is necessarily faced by any collectivist viewpoint.

Problem with the Collective Thinking Subject

To western thought one of the most surprising properties of African thought is the idea of ascribing knowledge to certain kinds of collective subjects – such as family lines. The idea that it is not John or Mary who are the thinking subject but the family line is totally incomprehensible to western philosophy, still dominated as it is by individualism. Especially as African thought includes one of the presuppositions of the "heathen" beliefs in the spirits of forefathers and their watching over us, it is as much to be ignored as "metaphysics" is in the negative meaning of the word.

But let us look at three facts that require some attention. First, the historical one. It is hardly true that epistemological collectivism is the peculiarity of African thought. It first became apparent in the European thought with Hegel, and manifests itself wherever the Hegelian influence is or was discernible, e.g. in 19th century British idealism (Bradley [1967] 1883, [1893] 1999) or Marxism (Brzozowski 1910; Lukács 1923; Gramsci [1947] 1975). Its presence in the latter is not only a "historical" fact but also a present-day one.

This concept, at the same time, has not been fabricated but is clearly borne out by a methodological analysis of science. Who is the epistemic subject related to quantum mechanics? Apparently it is not individual people of our era in general, because most of them simply do not know this branch of knowledge, and even if they happen to have read some of the literature they still may not understand it. Only a handful of theoreticians of physics remain. The straightforward answer seems to be as follows: that quantum mechanics (QM) is accepted means that it is accepted by every physics theoretician. However, one of the basic principles of methodology is that, regardless of our

In: Hamminga, B. (ed.), *Knowledge Cultures. Comparative Western and African Epistemology* (*Poznań Studies in the Philosophy of the Sciences and the Humanities*, vol. 88), pp. 117-128. Amsterdam/New York, NY: Rodopi, 2005.

understanding of the concept of theory, *theory is a system*, which implies logical consequences (Cn). Therefore, the requirement that *if X accepts QM and t is a consequence of some proposition T* from the set of QM, therefore X accepts t* should also hold true for quantum mechanics. The problem consists in the dilemma that the set of consequences of the QM theory is infinite, and the larger part (probably infinite as well) of the propositions of this theory remains unknown to anyone, let alone accepted. Thus, as to the question who accepts quantum mechanics, only one answer is possible: nobody living.

This kind of answer can be avoided by using the meaning postulate introduced in the logic of beliefs which describes the following concept of acceptance: *if X accepts p and q is a consequence of p, then X accepts q*. X fulfilling conditions of the kind presented above is referred to as the "ideal believer". To each scientific theory an ideal believer can be ascribed and the individualist terminology may be kept up – that is the terminology, but not individualist concepts. For does the ideal believer differ that much from the supragenerational family line? He is not more empirical, but less so: the family line is composed of forefathers, that is: people who once were real. The ideal believer, on the other hand, has never existed nor ever will exist in a human form.

Indeed: there are reasons with all due respect to treat the African concept of the family line as a collective subject. They are, however, reasons against epistemic individualism, but not necessarily for epistemic collectivism. We have, namely, to distinguish two viewpoints with regard to the subjects of beliefs:

(I) if X believes p, then X is an empirical human being; thus the primary subjects of beliefs are individual people – and the beliefs of other subjects (scientific circles, the society of a given era, etc.) can be reduced as secondary to the individualist;

(C) if X believes p, then X is a human collective, understood in any way as a being separate from individuals x_1, ..., or the x_n it is composed of; with the primary subjects of beliefs being then collectives, and the beliefs of the individuals it consists of (family lines, classes, nations, civilization etc.) being discussed in a sense secondary to collectivism.

Let us notice that the foregoing argument (no individual can reasonably claim to accept any scientific theory) speaks against the individual thesis (I), but not necessarily in favor of the collectivist thesis (C) either. In the area of scientific beliefs, the counterpart of the family line would be the society of physicists understood as a supra-individual being. But what is this collective? How can any beliefs be ascribed to it? And what should it mean that this Platonian idea believes in something or rejects something?

It is clear that not only the individualist western epistemology, but also the collective African one have fallen into a trap. As I have mentioned at the beginning, there are trends in European thought that strive to overcome the problem of going beyond this opposition. One of them is Marxism. So, an insight into how apt intuitions of individualism are reconciled with felicitous intuitions of collectivism in Marxist epistemology may prove useful to people believing in or dealing with African epistemology.

The problem of the Thinking Subject in Marxist Epistemology

The belief that the *collective point of view* is inherent in the epistemic perspective of Marxism is very frequent among Marxists; Marxism then concentrates not on individuals' characteristics, but on larger wholes: classes, strata, entire societies. The epistemic subject then is not this or that individual, but a *collective subject*, equal to the sets of all societies of a given historical era.

Raising the question of the peculiarity of the Marxist epistemology is very valuable, as far as an understanding of the epistemic subject is concerned, and so is making a supposition that this peculiarity is connected with the collective point of view. But the deliberations on this point are, I believe, often encumbered with the same erroneous assumption that, in order to speak about a collective, one must necessarily use collective concepts pertaining to many individuals at the same time. For example – for the Marxist point of view a considered object in economics needs to be identified with a set of all the members of a given social class; in order to take into account the Marxist point of view in epistemology, a business entity has to be identified with a collection of all the societies of a given historical era; etc., which leads to an acceptance of the collectivist thesis (C). In this way, however, the *collective point of view*, which forms an important peculiarity of Marxism, turns into a *collective complex,* thus giving rise to severe theoretical difficulties.

Let us think: what actually is an entity understood as a collection of all members of a given social class? In what sense can we say that this creation aims at maximizing profits or providing for social needs to the maximum? The meaning of the expression "X aims at p" becomes completely obscure when by X is meant a collection of individuals in the sense of set theory. Can this set, in the ordinary meaning of the word, take any decisions? We can say that an activity was performed by this or that person or a team of persons in the case of complex activities, consisting of many components, but what does it mean that an activity was performed by a set of individuals (in the distributive sense)?

A similar problem arises in connection with the viewpoint identifying the epistemic subject with a collection of all the societies of a given era. For what does it literally mean that a statement is accepted by a collective subject understood as a set of societies? It certainly does not mean that each person, or the majority of people, from these societies accept this statement as true. This is easy to understand once we realize that the "quantum mechanics argument", discussed above, presents serious difficulties for the collectivist thesis (C). Once the foregoing mistaken assumption is accepted, there seems to be no escape from the Scylla of individualism and the Charybdis of Durkheimism.

But let us reject this misleading assumption, according to which, in order to express the *collective point of view* accepted by Marxism, concepts referring to many individuals simultaneously have to be used, and we will see that these difficulties can not only be avoided, but also that the Marxist epistemology, which will be discussed below, presents a different, neither collectivist nor individualist epistemic perspective.

The Collective Point of View in the Marxian Theory

Let us take a closer look at how the collective point of view is expressed in the Marxian economic theory. Thus, the *Contribution to the Critique of Political Economy* opens with the following remark:

> To begin with, the question under discussion is *material production*. Individuals producing in a society, and hence the socially determined production of individuals, is of course the point of departure. The solitary and isolated hunter or fisherman, who serves Adam Smith and Ricardo as a starting point, is one of the unimaginative fantasies of eighteenth-century romances à la Robinson Crusoe (Marx [1859] 1968, p. 41).

This comment clearly includes a *collective point of view* which is juxtaposed with the individualist assumptions of the classic political economy. But does this point of view really consist in considering a number of individuals instead of one only? What if Ricardo considered three or four individuals? This is where some Marxists are confronted with a peculiar "baldness problem": how many persons does one have to refer to before the individualist point of view can be rejected? The absurdity of this problem pinpoints clearly that it was presented incorrectly.

Marx, in his research practice in Volume I of the *Capital* (Marx [1867] 1983) discusses two persons: the industrial capitalist and the industrial laborer. And the *collective point of view* in Marx is expressed not through the number of persons considered, but through qualities, the characteristics they are vested with. The classicists of political economy equip their individuals with the supra-historical properties of manufacturers and consumers who express their relationship through the world of things. The construction of these individuals departs from anything which would not be a perpetually repetitive characteristic of individual people of all times regarded in isolation. Marx acts to the contrary. The individuals regarded by him are the laborer and the capitalist, who are equipped, on the one hand, with properties which are historically relativized (in accordance with the historicism principle), and yet on the other hand they stand in peculiar relational characteristics which express their relations to other people. Hence, the theoretical constructs of industrial capitalist and industrial laborer from Vol. I of the *Capital* are vested with historical and social properties. If the industrial laborer is someone who produces surplus value for the capitalist, then this expression includes certain relational (social) characteristics – the laborer is defined by way of reference to the capitalist; and the other way round. However, the producer of the surplus value of which we speak has historically relativised properties which did not become apparent at every stage of historical development – he is, for example, separated from his workshop, sells his labor power, etc. Therefore, the Marxian constructs are characterized historically and socially, whilst the constructs of classic English economics (as well as the contemporary subjectivist economics) are characterized ahistorically and individualistically (i.e. they are composed of properties possessed by man regardless of the stage of historical development and his relationship with other people).

The dialectics of our cognition is such that reality is best and deepest learnt when no real objects are discussed. And that is because these objects are subjected to all sorts of influences, both main and secondary. Therefore, for the essence of reality to be viewed without the distracting peripheral influence, the latter have to be ignored. In this way certain possible (because not conflicting) objects are constructed which include only properties crucial to real objects. They are, however, not real objects – since these, according to the assumption, also have peripheral properties, as well as the main ones. This does not imply that reality is departed from – they are its key properties that are discussed, its essence. The only objects having solely the essence of reality are not ordinary physical bodies but theoretical constructs devised by the researcher for reasons analogous to those for his inventing points or geometrical straight lines.

The case under discussion can be treated analogously. The Marxian capitalist and laborer are only theoretical constructs (ideal types) and possess only those properties which Marx considered as the main ones in real capitalists and real laborers. They are constructed according to the *historicism principle*: only those values can be assessed as main – i.e. essential to social values – which are specific to a given formation, i.e. social structure in a given phase of technical economic history. Also, according to the rule of sociological relationism: only relational values (i.e. characteristics expressing certain human relationships) may be assessed as main to social values. Both rules taken together express the *collective point of view*. I am led to believe that it is included in the following remark made by Marx in the preface to the first German edition of Vol. I of the *Capital*:

> I paint the capitalist and the landlord in no sense *couleur de rose*. But here individuals are dealt with only in so far as they are the personifications of economic categories, embodiments of particular class-relations and class-interests (Marx, Engels [1867] 1983, p. 16).

These *collective subjects* are constructed based on the assumption that the main properties, which cannot be disregarded while constructing the subjects, are relational properties connected with belonging to certain social classes (rule of sociological relationism) forming a society at a certain stage of historical development (historicism principle).

By way of summary, the Marxian *collective point of view* is expressed in the directive to construct subjects (economic, epistemological, etc.) according to the rules of historicism and sociological relationism. These subjects may be referred to as collective subjects, but it has to be remembered that they are theoretical constructs of some kind and not simply sets of individuals or groups of individuals.

Construction of the Collective Subject

Let us now present the concept of the collective subject in more detail. It will be at the same time an attempt at defining the difference between the individualist and Marxian points of view of the humanities. The point is that both rules for the construction of a collective subject formulated above function in Marxism on the basis of well-defined theoretical assumptions and it is only after these two formal rules have been combined with these assumptions that one can answer the question why these and not other collective subjects are constructed in Marxism, i.e. collective subjects having characteristics of this and this type. Why, for example, does the construct referred to as the industrial capitalist (and henceforth the meaning of the term *Industrial capitalist)* include the appropriation of the surplus value produced by the laborer, and not any other relational property (expressing inter-human relationships) relativized historically?

The idea that I would like to defend is such. Thus, Marxist epistemology allows for constructing such collective subjects only who

- possess exclusively relational properties (sociological relationism) relativized historically, but
- only those properties which are to be found in relations determined by the theory of historical materialism with firm foundation properties.

In order to explain the concept of foundation property, the structure of a socio-economic formation has to be presented. It is a relational system constructed in the following way:

$$(U;\ P;\ W;\ M;\ C_I;\ C_{II},\ L,\ Pr,\ O)$$

where:
U - universe composed of individual objects,
P - set of people (society of a given formation),
W - set of work products,
M - means of production,
C_I - class of owners of means of production,
C_{II} - class of immediate manufacturers,
L - relations of labor division and organization,
Pr - production relation,
O - ownership relation,

and fulfills at the same time the following conditions:

- immediate manufacturers of C_{II} produce goods from the set of W using the means of production from M,
- persons from the set of C_I, while owning the means of production, also appropriate the surplus value produced by manufacturers from C_{II},
- in order for the surplus value to be sufficiently high, the persons from C_{II} need to be in relations of labor division and organization L.

A foundation property is any property which can be formulated using the terms of a theory of a socio-economic formation understood as above. Thus, we see how collective subjects are constructed in the Marxist theory – they are ascribed only those relational and historical characteristics which are either foundation characteristics or are related to the foundation properties determined by historical materialism.

Problem Constructing an Epistemological Subject

Until now we have mainly talked about the methodological directives according to which collective subjects are constructed in the Marxist theory. Discussion of the construction of specific collective subjects (e.g. economic, legal, etc.) would require taking up different issues each time. The characteristics ascribed to these subjects depend on the relations of these characteristics with foundation properties (i.e. with properties consisting in one person being an immediate manufacturer, owner of the means of production, appropriating the surplus value, etc.). At the same time, these relations are sometimes difficult to ascertain, since a full and systematic reconstruction of the theory of historical materialism is still to be completed. Nevertheless, it is known that the relations discussed are more or less close. In the case of economic subjects they are easily tangible, because their defining properties are directly included in the characteristics of the relational system i.e. a socio-economic formation. In the case of other subjects (e.g. legislator) one would have to indicate an "intermediate link" connecting the foundation properties (referring to the characteristics of a socio-economic formation) with properties defining those subjects.

It is especially difficult to establish – in the light of the Marxist theory – what properties are to define the epistemological subject to which the knowledge of a given era is attributed. It certainly is not any epistemic individual. According to the point of view presented above, it will be a theoretical construct of a certain kind, namely a collective subject. But how should such a subject be constructed?

A reference to a certain important concept, which had been used by the inventors of Marxism since at least *The German Ideology* (Marx and Engels [1932] 1953), may be helpful in settling this question – the concept of a theoretical – or literary – class representative. And this is how this concept is explained:

> Little must one imagine that the democratic representatives are indeed all shopkeepers or enthusiastic champions of shopkeepers. According to their education and their individual position, they may be as far apart as heaven and earth. What makes them representatives of the petty bourgeoisie is the fact that in their minds they do not get beyond the limits which the latter do not get beyond in life, that they are consequently driven, theoretically, to the same problems and solutions to which material interest and social position drive the latter, practically. This is, in general, the relationship between the *political* and *literary representatives* of a class and the class they represent (Marx, Engels [1932] 1953, p. 50).

This statement seems absurd on the face of it. For what can be the connection between theoretical problems posed and solved by a bourgeois sociologist or economist and the problems and solutions of a capitalist? In what sense can we say that this sociologist or economist arrives at the same solutions in theory that are achieved by the capitalist represented by them in practice? Still less comprehensible is how the capitalist is to arrive in practice at the same ontological or epistemological doctrines (e.g. individualism) that are put forward by a bourgeois philosopher.

Theoretical Social Class Representative

It seems that the concept of the theoretical class representative can be interpreted in a way which allows the foregoing questions to be answered, since this interpretation testifies to the deep, yet concealed connections between the social position of a class and the theoretical creativity of its representatives. This calls, however, for an explanation of certain principles of the Marxist philosophy of science, which can be done only in severely abridged form.

The cornerstone of each scientific theory is formed by a differentiation of the investigated set of factors into main and secondary ones. A theory is, namely, a sequence of models, the first one of which contains the basic laws determining how variables depend on factors which are main to them; at this abstraction level all peripheral variables are ignored, that is, it is counterfactually accepted that these do not occur. A second model contains a concretization of the initial laws, namely statements which describe how the investigated variables depend on factors which are main to them, as well as on the peripheral factors introduced in this more realistic model. This practice is followed when building even more realistic models (and less abstract ones, i.e. based on a smaller number of idealizing assumptions), until a model which is thought to approximate reality is arrived at. As we can see, it is with reference to the accepted main factors and to peripheral factors that the structure of a scientific theory is created. Thus, what drives a researcher to assume some factors are main and other peripheral? The researcher's philosophical assumptions, expressed in these rules of essential stratification that he unspokenly and often unconsciously accepts, seem to play a major role. The rule of essential stratification determines what types of factors are main to factors of a given kind. We have already encountered examples of the rule of essential stratification – both the historicism principle and the rule of social relationism are general rules of essential stratification which set down what type of factors are main to social phenomena.

The (E, T) system, where T is a scientific theory (i.e. a sequence of increasingly concretized models of a given area of reality) and E is the epistemic perspective of this theory (i.e. a system of rules of essential stratification) is that which I refer to as the theoretical orientation. Let us notice that since the rules of essential stratification do not determine a specific factor main to another one, but decide on the type of variables main to phenomena of some kind, the epistemic perspective does not unambiguously point at a theory, but permits an entire class of theories concordant with it. The choice between these possible variants is a matter of the researcher's imagination and decision – whether the choice was right is verified by experience, thus deciding on the aptness of the rules composing the epistemic perspective of this theory.

We can now say that a theoretical representative of a given class is that researcher whose theory assumes the same epistemic perspective as that of the theory assumed in the practice of the class he represents. Or, to put it differently – a supporter of a theoretical orientation which assumes the same epistemic perspective as the practical orientation assumed in the actions of a member of a given class is a theoretical representative of this social class.

Therefore, a theoretical representative of a given class can be someone who originates from an opposing class, or even – from the point of view of economic criteria – is its member (e.g. Engels). Thus we see that – as postulated by Marx in the excerpt quoted above – a theoretical representative may be, in terms of their education, personal situation, etc., as far removed from the represented class as heaven is from earth. The only thing that is important is that in his mind he does not get beyond the limits which the given class does not get beyond in life., i.e. that he accepts the same way of essential structuralization of reality which is assumed in the practice of the class represented by him. For example, the characteristic feature of the practical activity of the bourgeoisie is comprehending the social world as a collection of individuals which take decisions, create – by way of a contract or voting – all social communities, etc. It is then no coincidence that individualism is the most characteristic feature of bourgeois thought. It is clearly evident (e.g. in social contract theories) or more or less concealed (e.g. psychologism in the humanities), but it is all-important that it invariably assumes the following rule of essential stratification: for all social values the main variables are those that characterize individuals (e.g. individual people). And this is a rule that, it is assumed, is eagerly embraced by each member of the bourgeoisie in their practical activities.

Epistemological Subject

The foregoing findings allow us to answer the question who this epistemological subject is. He may simply be equated with the theoretical representative of a given social class. This of course leads us to the conclusion that in the case of those sciences where the differentiation of epistemic perspectives is possible due to their relations with the practice of given social classes (it is so, for example, in the humanities), we are faced with various epistemological subjects corresponding to different classes. Where these sciences whose epistemic perspectives are independent of the class structure are concerned, we deal with only one epistemological subject (it is so, for example, in environmental studies).

Needless to say the above picture is simplified. First of all, it draws on the idealized concept of a socio-economic formation consisting of only two basic social classes, outlined in one of the paragraphs presented above; while, to put the matter more realistically, the formation actually consists of a multitude of classes, with class divisions that are so clear at first (i.e. on the very abstract level) becoming blurred and overlapping. The image of theoretical class representation by researchers presented above would have to be adjusted accordingly, too.

Leszek Nowak
Adam Mickiewicz University
ul. Szamarzewskiego 89c
60-569 Poznań
Poland
email: epistemo@main.amu.edu.pl

REFERENCES

Bradley, F. H. ([1967] 1883). *The Principles of Logic*. London: Oxford University Press.
Bradley, F. H. ([1893] 1999). *Appearance and Reality: A Metaphysical Essay*. Bristol: Thoemmes.
Brzozowski, S. L. (1910). *Legenda Młodej Polski* [The Legend of Young Poland]. Lwów.
Gramsci, A. ([1947] 1975). *Letters From Prison* selected, translated from the Italian, and introduced by L. Lawner. London: Cape.
Lukács, G. (1923). *Geschichte und Klassenbewusstsein: Studien über marxistische Dialektik* [History and Class Consciousness: Studies in Marxian Dialectic]. Berlin: Malik.
Marx, K. H. ([1859] 1968). *Zur Kritik der politischen Ökonomie* [A Contribution to the Critique of Political Economy]. Berlin: Dietz.

Marx, K. H. and F. Engels ([1867] 1983). *Das Kapital*, Erster Band. *Marx Werke* Bd. 23. Berlin: Dietz.

Marx, K. H. and F. Engels ([1932] 1953). *Die deutsche Ideologie: Kritik der neuesten deutschen Philosophie in ihren Repräsentanten, Feuerbach, B. Bauer und Stirner, und des deutschen Sozialismus in seinen verschiedenen Propheten* [German Ideology]. Berlin: Dietz.

Bert Hamminga

THE POZNAŃ VIEW: HOW TO MEAN WHAT YOU SAY

Abstract. The Poznań view is about the logical structure of theories, about what such theories claim and how rationally to judge and improve them. In the context of this volume it is relevant to explore what the Poznań view and the African ideas about knowledge have to say about one another.

The Poznań view, as will be explained below, is about the logical structure of theories, what such theories claim and how rationally to judge and improve them. In the context of this volume it is relevant to explore what the Poznań view and the African ideas about knowledge have to say about one another.

Throughout history, scientists and philosophers of science reflecting on knowledge acquisition in their own culture have molded the western ideas of what constitutes scientific rationality. For what follows below, as Appiah (Appiah in this volume, p. 50-55) has made clear in his contribution to this volume, the profound impact of the invention, refinement and spreading over all classes of western societies of *the arts of writing and reading* is crucial: since the development of writing, the need for the physical presence of the proponent of a theory was removed. Western-style "theories" became things that could stand on their own, they became impersonal objects of scrutiny. The introduction of printing enhanced this literal procedure. The power of writing has boosted the development of western ideas and the progress of western science. Finally, "theories" could become objects of study like all other things, like physical processes and chemical substances etc., thought to be impersonal. Writing became to western ideas what gravity is to what lives on the dry part of the earth's surface: something so familiar and self-evident from the earliest days of anyone's awareness that only the greatest mind can realize that it is a justified object of systematic questioning and scrutiny.

By studying a traditionally oral culture like the African, one can gain new insights in the impact of writing and printing on western science and knowledge. This is not merely a matter of being able to work with, or having to do without a technique like any other. What is gained, and what is lost, by making such a transition? Answers to such questions are likely to unearth now long-hidden conditions of western scientific rationality. It involves profoundly different ways of perceiving and dealing with yourself and the world, too

In: Hamminga, B. (ed.), *Knowledge Cultures. Comparative Western and African Epistemology* (*Poznań Studies in the Philosophy of the Sciences and the Humanities*, vol. 88), pp. 129-139. Amsterdam/New York, NY: Rodopi, 2005.

profound even for criteria to exist that could determine who is on the "better" side.

The Question: Is the Primacy of Seeing (as Opposed to Other Ways of Sensing) to Scientific Observation a Precondition of Idealization?

Leaving aside for a moment all differences of opinion on what science is, how it works, and how it works properly, the western idea of science, though in different wordings and definitions, crucially involves some kind of distinction between a theory and what it is about, and the notion of a theory conforming or not conforming what the theory is about. The paradigm example of tests, leaving aside differences in opinions on how they are to be performed and what is the proper reaction to the different kinds of their results in the framework of a sound scientific strategy, is to check to what extent observations conform to how these observations should be if the theory were correct. Etymologically, and in natural language, the term "observation" refers specifically to *visual* sensing. As I claimed elsewhere in this volume (see Hamminga in this volume, p. 101), this is far from accidental. Indeed, the bulk of testing material adduced to evaluate scientific theories reports not on what people heard, tasted, smelled or felt, but on what they have *seen*. What is primarily felt (like temperature, pressure, sound, time) is subjected to procedures mapping the phenomenon felt by a spatial function to a *visual* scale (in these cases: a thermometer, a barometer, an oscilloscope, a clock). That is because the visual is the western paradigm of objective sensing and measurement. We find it already in the work of Herakleitos: "The eyes are more reliable witnesses than the ears" (Ephesios, H. [500BC] 1962, phrase 101a) and "About important matters one should not judge blindly" (Ephesios, H. [500BC] 1962, phrase 47).

The seeable allows considerations of *distance and angle*, hence *quantification* and hence ultimately the introduction of *mathematics* in the theories. Mathematics, in its turn, works with the seeable (graphs) as its most important tool, and also allows one to quantify the degree to which a theory is "off the mark", hence to judge whether some theory is a better approximation to reality than another. This in turn enabled scientists to treat theories as *idealizations*, claims that are strictly true only under ideal (non-real) conditions, and to accept such an ideal theory only because it is a better approximation than any rival theory or it is believed to be suitable to be made so by taking properly into consideration some more forces and factors involved.

This, basically, is the Poznań view of scientific theories as it emerges from the works of Leszek Nowak and Isabella Nowakowa. An impressive part of the statements of this paper can be found in the works of Leszek Nowak and Isabella Nowakowa. The reader is primarily and generally referred to the most recent comprehensive exposition: Nowak and Nowakowa (2000).

The idea is that idealization rests on approximation, approximation rests on mathematics, mathematics rests on quantification, and quantification rests on observation. The relative priority given to non-visual sensing in African culture, and, viewed from the other side, the relative poverty of non-visual sensing in western culture, as I stressed (Hamminga in this volume, p. 101), clearly raises a question which may concern a hidden condition for western-style science. That question is: does scientific observation presuppose such a priority for visual sensing, as opposed to other types of sensing, like hearing, tasting, smelling or feeling? In hearing, tasting, smelling and feeling there seems little one can quantify, except some transitive relations like "louder", "saltier", "harder", "smoother", "warmer", that are hard to make into an objective basis of scientific taxonomy. Western culture may have turned its weakness of one-sidedly relying on the visual into an advantage, as far as the growth of scientific knowledge is concerned.

Literacy: The Visual Sentence and What It Is About

Let me first deal in some more detail with the preconditions of western thinking in terms of the abovementioned distinction between a theory and what it is about, and the notion of a theory conforming or not conforming what it is about. As can be seen from Professor Appiah's contribution to this volume, especially his section "Literacy prompts generalization" (Appiah in this volume, p. 52), an author of written words tends to shun the use of indexicals like *here, now, you* and *me*, because to a reader, unlike a listener, these may be unclear. Professor Appiah phrases the problem as the need, when you write, to "fill in much of what context provides when we speak" (Appiah in this volume, p. 53). In contrast to a speaker, an author is wise to refrain from such indexicals and thus to *generalize*. An important part of what happens in such a process is the inclusion in the language of specifications of what our assertions are *about*. In oral interaction, most of that is obvious, hence no object of worry. The process of abstraction may hinge crucially on the process of making our assertion literal, hence non-indexical, for after this is done, a reader can study a *sentence* lying visibly before him. Attempts to understand such a sentence or statement crucially involve the distinction between the general assertion made and what in an oral context would have been indexicals, that is, what the assertion is about. This gives logical birth to the theory-object distinction, indispensable to the rest of the development to viewing the theory as an "image" of something, necessarily imperfect, that should be handled as an idealization.

According to what I hope is a fair depiction of the traditional African idea of the visible, all visible things, whether written words and sentences, paintings, carvings, things chiseled or formed by nature, derive their meaning from spoken language (*nommo*). A little statue, for instance, is considered meaningless in itself. The act of saying to such a statue: "You are Erinle" (see Hamminga in this volume, p. 108), thus *making* it (an act of "fertilization") Erinle, is hence an astonishing one-blow transition from the completely abstract to the completely concrete. On a (dead) empty stage the director has called the (living) actor in.

This, I hold, should be compared to the more gradual road to the concrete used by western scientists. Their culture, the "little statues" are *sentences*, written, visible sentences, containing "objective" meaning in themselves, irrespective of their authors or "owners". By taking this road, you are able to turn the transition from the abstract to the concrete into one consisting of many large and small steps. A basic law, like Galileo's law, is very abstract, but nevertheless already contains some meaning in itself that is independent of which person proposes or believes the law. There is a lot to be done before such a law can suitably approximate a real-world process. A whole sequence of secondary, tertiary etc. factors causing deviations from the law in a particular type of case under scrutiny should still be taken into account. But how this should be done is not *completely* arbitrary once you accept Galileo's law as a basic law. Once certain such layers of concretization are added, the whole theory becomes more and more concrete, without ever definitively arriving at that final stage of Janheinz Jahn's example: "You are Erinle". Thus it seems that the treatment of written language as something containing an independent, objective meaning ultimately allows the conquest of the vast middle ground between the absolutely abstract of the visible thing and the absolutely concrete truth created by the spoken word that seems to form pretty much a classical African dichotomy. And it should be no surprise that teachers of explicitly idealizational structures like abstract economic theory, as President Museveni reports in the context of University of Dar es Salaam – teachers "mainly from Europe and America" (Museveni in this volume, p. 14) – run into the trouble of having to answer the question: "But why do you assume? Why don't you study reality? Why do you waste so much time constructing models when you have reality?"

Idealization, Symbolization: How to Mean What You Say

I would suggest that the considerations above concerning gradualness versus absoluteness of the transition from the abstract to the concrete sheds some interesting light on Appiah's objections ("The nature of belief', Appiah in this volume, p. 23) against symbolist interpretations of traditional African claims. Appiah stresses a distinction between, on the one hand, elements of procedures known to be symbolic by the agents involved (like offering gold dust to the ancestors), and, on the other, traditional views believed by members of that tradition to be true (like the existence of – dead – ancestors and their interference in the daily life of the living). Some onlookers, identified by Appiah as anthropologists and sociologists of the "symbolist" creed (he refers to Skorupski's (1976) analysis of Durkheim and he believes Lévi-Strauss thinks similarly, Appiah in this volume, p. 28), tend to treat the latter as symbolic too. Such symbolists, Appiah writes, "are able to treat traditional believers as reassuringly rational only because they deny that traditional people mean what they say" (Appiah in this volume, p. 34).

According to Appiah, traditional people do mean what they say, but they can of course be wrong. Discussing the process of what he calls "demythologization" of western traditional religious beliefs in the course of the progress of western science, Appiah observes: "the effect of it has been to treat doctrines that were once taken literally as metaphorical or ... symbolic" (Appiah in this volume, p. 31).

The relegation of some claim believed to be true to the realm of the symbolic, an act of progress of scientific knowledge, does not, Appiah holds, show that the claim *always* has been symbolic, but that in the light of new knowledge a correction had to be made. There had been a genuine belief, but it turned out to be false. Having a false belief is a matter, Appiah writes, of bad luck. Your chances are turning once you dispose of new knowledge that allows you to correct yourself. In this context Appiah writes: "It is a familiar theme in the history of theology that Christianity has followed in some measure Oscar Wilde's epigram: 'Religions die when they are proved true. Science is the record of dead religions'" (Appiah in this volume, p. 31).

I would add that tendencies to reassuringly treat something as "symbolic" relate to treating it as "religious": when a method of a culture remote in time or space is not understood by western research workers, you often find it interpreted as a "ritual" or a "religion". Somehow in such cases this labeling is considered to be more helpful than it would be in the case of western methods of knowledge acquisition and employment. This is to be doubted, not because the "religious" and "scientific" rituals are necessarily equal under all criteria but because it prevents the research worker from realizing that the performer of a non-western and/or ancient ritual has the same aims as a modern western scientist or engineer. Priests may not be in every way be comparable to modern scientists, but in their own culture they are *consistently* seen as engineers, that is, experts (as far as expertise goes) in controlling the power of the forces in the universe to achieve certain desired aims.

Similar problems occur when western scientists and western onlookers, like philosophers of science, try to make sense of modern western scientific beliefs and their change over time. Scientific laws never hold perfectly in the world whose description they are supposed to be. Sometimes this is evident from the name of the law, for example the "law of ideal gases". Sometimes it follows from the very formulation thereof, if it contains conditions like "the earth is a point-mass". Sometimes it results only from the comments of scientists saying, for instance, that such and such a fact does not negate the law because it refers to the circumstances that are abstracted from in the law in question. The world that a western-style scientific theory is about is not the world we live in, that is, not exactly. The world of basic physics (classical mechanics) is one of bodies devoid of geometrical dimensions, submerged in inertial systems, moving in a frictionless manner, etc. The world of basic economics is one of balanced economies where the supply of commodity equals exactly the social demand for it, where there is a uniform growth of technology, etc. The world of many theories in the humanities is one in which there are only people who consistently follow their values or who do not at the any given point of time entertain two contradictory beliefs. And so on and so forth. Indeed, all western science simplifies, it is about ideal worlds and the real empirical contexts in which the theories are tried out is nothing but more or less distant from its scientific idealizations. "Symbolism?"

The problem arises of how the ideal worlds of scientific theories are related to what is real. The answer common in western science is: the ideal worlds of science are deformations, that is, they preserve the essential traits of our world but they are not equipped with the remaining, hopefully less decisive ones. A physicist who assumes that a fall takes place in the frictionless medium deforms the actual phenomenon of falling bodies. The ideal fall is therefore considered under the condition of zero friction. Hence the law is about free fall. Freely falling bodies are far from really falling bodies.

The method of idealization is basically a method of deformation. It transforms as it were our world into ideal worlds. That is why idealization does not resemble what is sometimes erroneously considered to be a paradigmatic example of science, namely a chronicle. It would be false to think that the theoretician observes facts, notices their appearances, looks for repetitions and similarities in order to find some general rules. As Leszek Nowak has pointed out, (Nowak 1977, pp. 344ff), it is rather the *caricature* that seems to be the paradigmatic example of science. A cartoonist leaves out some details of the object presented, thus stressing what is thought to be to be characteristic of it.

The method of idealization consists basically of three steps: the adoption of idealizing conditions, the forming of idealizational hypotheses, and their concretization. Idealizing conditions are assumptions (e.g.. "the resistance of air does not occur", "demand equals supply", "man does not accept contradictions") which are made in order to simplify the empirical subject matter. By introducing them – what is thought to be – the pure idea of a given type of phenomena is formed. It is deprived – consciously and explicitly, but often also implicitly and without due notice – of the empirical features which are considered to be secondary. What remains in the idea contains merely the principal properties of the empirical original.

Thus, a theory starts as in ideal law K claimed to hold under, say, an number k of ideal conditions. The claim is not testable because it is not possible to find a case where all k conditions are met, at least not strictly, to the full 100%. Indeed this most abstract version K is usually thought to be quite remote from any realistic case. Attempts to close the gap between the ideal world in which the k conditions hold and the more realistic worlds in which less, or even none of the conditions hold and the law would be testable are called *concretizations*. A concretization consists of considering how the law K should be modified to incorporate, say, the complications of dropping ideal condition k. This leads to a modified law K-1, claimed to hold under conditions k-1 to 1. It it hoped that the more concrete law K-1 is a better approximation of the real processes the theory is designed to be about than the more abstract law K. The intricacies of the method of idealization and concretization are dealt with in Nowak, L and I. Nowakowa (2000). It is not only many philosophers of science who have got used to analyzing scientific theories this way. Nowak and Nowakowa also quote working scientists expressing themselves in strikingly similar terms:

> We get the understanding of the laws of nature by considering the simplest cases and neglecting at first all the possible complications . . . [However,] as long as we are concerned with rectilinear motion, we are far from understanding the motions which are observed in nature . . . [T]herefore, our next step will consist in determining the laws governing such [curvilinear motions] . . . [with the aid of] the method of generalisation. The method of generalisation is not determined univocally . . . one condition must be, however, strictly satisfied: the generalised concept should reduce to the initial one, if the same initially adopted conditions are met (Einstein and Infeld 1942, pp. 22-3, 28).

> If it is adopted that everything is tied with everything and that there are no more significant things but everything is significant, then science disappears. Science is based on the assumption that it is possible to find in the chaos of phenomena some significant things and to isolate them from the less important ones and to say – at least with growing approximation – that such and such course of phenomena is evoked by such and such

causes and the other causes are less important and are therefore negligible. If we do not succeed in doing this, we must end with scientific research (Werle 1975, p. 5).

[W]e look upon economic theory as a sequence of conceptual *models* that seek to express in simplified form different aspects of an always more complicated reality. At first these aspects are formalized as much as feasible in isolation, then in combinations of increasing realism. . . . The study of the simpler models is protected from the reproach of unreality by the consideration that these models may be prototypes of more realistic, but also more complicated, subsequent models (Koopmans 1957, pp. 142-3).

[In geography] most research begins with a relatively simple hypothesis . . . whose aim is to show the way to find other factors which are to be accounted for in order to explain more comprehensively the problem under investigation. Due to this, the first hypothesis leads to constructing more complicated hypotheses (MacCarthy and Lindberg 1966, p. 91).
etc. etc.

But, of course, apart from the spontaneous methodology, found wherever scientists raise the discussion to the level of how to do science in their own field, there is the modern explicit philosophical methodology as proposed by philosophers of science who make a science of studying how scientific theories are structured, how they are construed, how they are improved. Here we come at the analogue of the problematic relation between traditional African believers and anthropologists as analyzed by Appiah (Appiah in this volume, p. 34): a philosopher of science studying quantum mechanics, though he may believe the theory, is, professionally, not committed to that belief. He may have outright disbelief or a type of belief not shared by his objects of study, namely the scientists working at quantum mechanics.

That has only lately been realized in philosophy of science and even today not everywhere, I dare say, fully. Until late in the 20th century, many philosophers of science thought one should study rationality by inspecting theory structure and methodological procedures of the Great Reputed Theories, such as relativity theory or quantum mechanics. Studying out-of-date western theories would make you a mere historian, capable of finding interesting facts in how at least imperfectly rational scientists of the past dealt with their now superseded defective theories. Studying contemporary theories of non-western cultures would make you an anthropologist. In this idea of philosophy of science as the quest for rationality of the Great Reputed Theories, philosophers of science not seldom claim that, though scientists are right to believe in their modern reputed theory, they could use some professional scientific philosophical advice on what is the best logical formulation of their theory and on the proper justifications for their beliefs associated with their theory. But there are limits: it is still generally, and probably correctly, felt that claiming, for instance, that a belief in quarks and electric fields is symbolical, threatens to disqualify you for decent academic jobs at western universities.

Appiah's "symbolist" anthropologists are in a similar epistemic position: they study the beliefs of others. Traditional believers and their beliefs are their objects of study. He claims "symbolist" anthropologists are "able to treat traditional believers as reassuringly rational only because they deny that traditional people mean what they say" (Appiah in this volume, p. 34). This symbolist approach should evoke in every philosopher of science memories of the discussion in which the concept of the "rational reconstruction" of a theory (Lakatos 1971) arose: according to Lakatos, a rational reconstruction should be an account, not of the real theory and its real process of coming to be accepted, but a rationally acceptable version of that theory. He required this acceptable version to be vindicated by a rational reconstruction of the theory's process of coming to be accepted, not necessarily identical to the process as it actually occurred. Appiah points out that the traditional actors under scrutiny themselves have, in what we in the philosophy of science context would call their spontaneous methodology, a concept of "symbolic", with the help of which they form their own clear opinions of what is symbolic and what isn't. And he also points out that what is, according to the actors, not symbolic, may be false and require – according to themselves, according to onlookers, or both – a correction of their belief system.

Appiah's call for a healthy distance between the actor and the onlooker has two sides. On the one hand, he seems to call for limiting anthropological efforts to recording carefully what in the context of philosophy of science would be called the spontaneous methodology. Preconceived modern western philosophical concepts indeed are likely to hinder fruitful interpretation of what traditional believers think, do, and think they are doing. Particularly confusing is the employment of a concept of "symbolical" different from ideas concerning symbolism prevalent in the traditional belief systems themselves. Nevertheless, western theories and beliefs can rightly be said to be caricatures, and often are denoted by their adherents in maybe not such strong but nevertheless similar terms like "abstract representations", "simplified models", "idealizations" etc. The question whether or not this is the same in the African context is legitimate. It is an empirical question. The idealizational approach in the philosophy of science claims that an account of western theories and beliefs as held to be true in our real world is too simple, at least too simple an account of how scientists deal with their beliefs in practice (that is, when it comes, for example, to resolving inconsistencies, dealing with counterexamples and unexplained observations, and finding a new basic theoretical approach when the old one is thought to be in irreparable trouble). In different cultures, different vehicles may travel the road from the ideal, general, abstract law to the concrete case, as I have suggested above with the example of how a person's word (*nommo*) turns an abstract African statue into the concrete Erinle (Hamminga in this volume, p. 108). But whether or not that is so, is not a matter of philosophical debate but of empirical research.

Bert Hamminga
Cultural Research Centre
P.O. Box 673
Jinja
Uganda
e-mail: knowledgecultures@mindphiles.com

REFERENCES

Appiah, K. A. (1992). *In My Father's House: Africa in the Philosophy of Culture*. Oxford: Oxford University Press.

Brzeziński, J., F. Coniglione, T.A.F. Kuipers, and L. Nowak (eds.) (1990). *Idealization I: General Problems* (*Poznań Studies in the Philosophy of the Sciences and the Humanities*, vol. **16**). Amsterdam: Rodopi.

Einstein, A. and L. Infeld (1942). *The Evolution of Physics*. New York: Simon and Schuster.

Ephesios, H. ([500BC] 1962). *Heraclitus Ephesius* edited by Geoffrey Stephen Kirk. Cambridge: Cambridge University Press.

Jahn, J. (1961). *Muntu: An Outline of the New African Culture*. New York: Groove Press Inc.

Jahn, J. (1990). *African Culture and the Western World*. New York Grove Wiedenfeld.

Kmita, J. (ed.) (1973). *Elementy marksistowskiej metodologii humanistyki* [Elements of the Marxist Methodology of the Humanities]. Poznań: Wydawnictwo Poznańskie.

Koopmans, T. C. (1957). *Three Essays on the State of Economic Science*. New York: McGraw-Hill.

Lakatos, I. (1971). History of Science and Its Rational Reconstructions. In: Buck and Cohen (eds.), *Boston Studies in the Philosophy of Science*, vol. **8**. Dordrecht: Reidel, pp. 91-136.

MacCarty, H. H. and J. B. Lindberg (1966). *A Preface to Economic Geography*. Englewood Cliffs, NJ: Prentice Hall.

May, M., R. de Pinxten, M. Poriau and F. Vandamme (eds.) (1977). *The Cognitive Viewpoint*. Ghent: Ghent University Press.

Nowak, L. (1971). *U podstaw Marksowskiej metodologii nauk* [Foundations of the Marxian Methodology of Science]. Warszawa: PWN.

Nowak, L. (1972). Theories, Idealization and Measurement. *Philosophy of Science* **39**, 533-47.

Nowak, L. (1973). Popperowska koncepcja praw i sprawdzania [Poppers Conception of Laws and Testing]. In: Kmita (1973), pp. 303-24.

Nowak, L. (1977). The Classical and the Essentialist Concept of Truth. In: May et al. (1977), pp. 344-53.

Nowak, L. (1980). *The Structure of Idealization. Towards a Systematic Interpretation of the Marxian Idea of Science* (*Synthese Library*, vol. **139**). Dordrecht, Boston, London: Reidel.

Nowak, L. and I. Nowakowa (2000). *Idealization X: The Richness of Idealization* (*Poznań Studies in the Philosophy of the Sciences and the Humanities*, vol. **69**). Amsterdam: Rodopi.

Nowakowa, I. (1972). *Idealizacja i problem korespondencji praw fizyki* [Idealization and the Problem of Correspondence of Laws of Physics], PhD thesis. Poznań: Adam Mickiewicz University.

Nowakowa, I. (1975). Idealization and the Problem of Correspondence. *Poznań Studies in the Philosophy of the Sciences and the Humanities* **1** (1), 65-70.

Nowakowa, I. (1975). *Dialektyczna korespondencja a rozwój nauki* [Dialectical Correspondence and the Development of Science]. Warszawa-Poznań: PWN.

Nowakowa, I. (1994). *Idealization V: The Dynamics of Idealizations*. Amsterdam-Atlanta: Rodopi.

Skorupski, J. (1976). *Symbol and Theory*. Cambridge: Cambridge University Press.

Werle, J. (1975). Fizyk o materii [A Physicist on the Matter]. *Argumenty* **22**, 5-6.

Wilde, O. (1982). Phrases and Philosophies for the Use of the Young. In: Montgomery Hyde H. (ed.), *The Annotated Oscar Wilde*. New York: Clarkeston N. Potter Inc.

CONTRIBUTORS

Kwame Anthony Appiah

Kwame Anthony Appiah is professor of Afro-American Studies and Philosophy, Harvard University, Cambridge, USA. He is the author, with Amy Gutmann, of *Color Conscious: The Political Morality of Race* (Princeton University Press, 1996), winner of the Annual Book Award of the North American Society for Social Philosophy for the book making the most significant contribution to social philosophy. This book was also the recipient of the Ralph J. Bunche Award of the American Political Science Association for the best scholarly work in political science that explores the phenomenon of ethnic and cultural pluralism. His other books include *In My Father's House: Africa in the Philosophy of Culture* (Oxford University Press, 1992), winner of the Annisfield-Wolf Book Award and the Herskovits Award of the African Studies Association for the best work published in English on Africa, and of *Necessary Questions* (Prentice-Hall, 1989), an introduction to analytic philosophy. He has also published two monographs on the philosophy of language, and three novels: *Another Death in Venice* (Constable, 1995), *Nobody Likes Letitia* (Constable, 1994), and *Avenging Angel* (Constable, 1990). He is co-editor with Henry Louis Gate, Jr. of *The Dictionary of Global Culture* (Knopf, 1996) and he and Professor Gate are now co-editing the *Perseus Africana Encyclopedia*.

In addition, he has published many articles and reviews on topics ranging from post-modernism to the collapse of the African state. His philosophical work has largely been in the philosophy of language and of mind; his work in African and African-American Studies focuses on questions of race, ethnicity, culture, and identity. Professor Appiah's current projects include *Bu Me Bé: Proverbs of the Akan* (of which his mother is the major author), an annotated edition of 7,500 proverbs in Twi, the language of Asante, in Ghana, where he grew up. He is an editor of *Transition* magazine and of the *Microsoft Encarta Encyclopedia Africana*. He has been President of the Society for African Philosophy in North America, and Chair of the Joint Committee on African Studies of the Social Science Research Council and the American Council of Learned Societies.

Bert Hamminga

Bert Hamminga, Cultural Research Centre, Jinja, Uganda, is by origin a Dutch economist and philosopher of science (Ph.D. Amsterdam University). He is the author of *Neoclassical Theory Structure and Theory Development, Studies in Contemporary Economics,* vol. 4 (Springer Verlag, 1983). With W. Balzer he edited *Philosophy of Economics, Erkenntnis,* vol. 30, nr. 1-2, 1989, reprinted in book form as: Balzer, W. and Hamminga, B. *Philosophy of Economics* (Kluwer, 1989). His main contribution to the *Poznań Studies* discussions on idealizations is "The Structure of Six Transformations in Marx's Capital" in Brzeziński, J. et al. (eds.) *Idealization I: General Problems* (*PSPS&H*, vol. 16; Rodopi, 1990), pp. 89-111. With N.B. de Marchi he edited *Idealization VI: Idealization in Economics* (*PSPS&H,* vol. 38; Rodopi, 1994). His publications on the foundations of labor market theories include "Demoralizing the Labor Market: Could Jobs be like Cars and Concerts?", *Journal of Political Philosophy,* vol. 3, no. 1, March 1995, 23-35. He is chief editor of *PHiLES* (http://mindphiles.com).

Yoweri Kaguta Museveni

Yoweri Kaguta Museveni has been president of Uganda since January 29, 1986. In the years before this his party, the National Resistance Movement, gradually built up the socio-political structure of his country from the bottom up, starting by creating Local Committees. This work and his economic achievements since, an unprecedented success story, form the subject of his book *Sowing the Mustard Seed* (Macmillan, 1997).

Leszek Nowak

Professor Leszek Nowak is one of the founders of the philosophy of idealization and concretization as it has been developed in the past three decades. Its main discussion forum is the book series of which this book is a part, the *Poznań Studies in the Philosophy of the Sciences and the Humanities.* Nowak is its editor-in-chief. His latest comprehensive statement of the present state of the theory is: Izabella Nowakowa and Leszek Nowak, *Idealization X: The Richness of Idealization* (*PSPS&H*, vol. 69; Rodopi, 2000).

INDEX AND GLOSSARY

aba, 110
abashomeire (the educated), 16
Abraham, W.E., 82, 113
abstract, -ion, 8, 42, 53, 54, 93, 96, 125, 127, 131, 132, 133, 135, 137
Achebe, C., 31, 55
agreements, promises, -ing, contracts, 58, 59, 61, 62, 70, 76, 77, 86, 87, 88, 108, 126
Akoha, A.B., 113
alphabet, literate, -cy, -ary, writing, 11, 12, 13, 15, 16, 21, 31, 33, 51, 52, 53, 54, 55, 77, 81, 86, 87, 88, 89, 90, 97, 100, 101, 108, 109, 111, 129, 131, 132
ancestors, dead but still around, source of all power, including knowledge, see also dead, 8, 16, 20, 23, 26, 27, 29, 30, 38, 45, 50, 51, 52, 54, 57, 59, 61, 63, 64, 65, 66, 68, 71, 75, 76, 78, 91, 93, 94, 95, 96, 98, 104, 133
anthropology, 7, 25, 27, 33, 36, 133, 136, 137
anticipation, 71
Apovo, J., 73, 82
Appiah, K.A., 23, 55, 79, 82, 111, 113, 129, 131, 133, 136, 137, 138, 141
arguments, 7, 15, 17, 18, 51, 61
art, 15, 33, 60, 101, 107, 111
Augustine, 44

bad luck, 16, 36, 52, 72, 74, 88, 96, 133
bait, 71, 75, 110, 111
bantu, pl. of *muntu* (human person, see also personal), 89, 90, 91, 92, 93, 94, 95, 96, 97, 98, 99, 101, 104, 105, 106, 107, 108, 110, 111
Barth, K., 44
Bazima, 102
bazima, pl. of *muzima* (living *muntu*), 94, 95, 96, 102
bazimu, pl. of *muzimu* (dead *muntu*, *muntu*-spirit), 91, 94, 95, 98
Beattie, J., 33
belief, 23, 25, 26, 28, 29, 30, 31, 32, 33, 34, 35, 36, 37, 38, 39, 40, 41, 42, 43, 45, 46, 47, 48, 49, 50, 55, 58, 59, 117, 118, 119, 130, 133, 134, 136, 137
bintu, pl. of kintu (impersonal force), 90, 92, 93, 94, 95, 97, 108, 109, 112
birth, 11, 71, 91
Bisasso, F.X., 82, 113
Blixen, K., 82, 113
Bradley, F.H., 117, 127
Brzeziński, J., 138
Brzozowski, S.L., 117, 127
Buber, M., 32
Burgman, H., 63, 73, 82, 88, 91, 113

Caesar, G.J., 82, 88, 113
Carothers, J.C., 82, 113
cause, explanation, 26, 27, 36, 37, 39, 40, 41, 42, 43, 44, 45, 46, 47, 52, 65, 66, 68, 76, 80, 86, 90, 93, 110, 136
ceremony, method, ritual, 8, 16, 17, 18, 23, 24, 25, 26, 27, 29, 30, 31, 33, 35, 38, 40, 48, 50, 72, 85, 99, 103, 111, 117, 133, 134, 135, 136, 137
Christianity, 31, 32, 33, 38, 43, 44, 46, 58, 63, 64, 67, 98, 133
Chukwudi, E.E., 113
clapping, 96, 100, 105, 106, 107, 111
class (social c.), 13, 110, 119, 122, 123, 124, 125, 126, 127
Coetzee, P.H., 82, 113
collective epistemological subject, 57, 58, 59, 75, 117, 118, 119, 122, 123, 124, 127
collective, -ity, togetherness, 11, 12, 24, 31, 35, 38, 58, 59, 60, 75, 77, 78, 86, 88, 100, 105, 107, 117, 118, 119, 120, 122, 123, 124
Coniglione, F., 138
consistency, 34, 35, 50, 51, 52, 54, 80
contracts, agreements, promises, -ing, 58, 59, 61, 62, 70, 76, 77, 87, 88, 108, 126
Coquery-Vidrovitch, C., 46, 55
Cultural Research Centre, 59, 62, 70, 76, 82, 83, 112, 113, 138, 142

Dah-Lokonon, G.B., 83
dance, 24, 26, 27, 43, 58, 60, 71, 75, 96, 99, 100, 101, 102, 105, 106, 107, 108, 110, 111
dead, see also ancestors, 8, 12, 29, 59, 61, 62, 63, 66, 68, 72, 76, 91, 93, 94, 95, 96, 97, 102, 107, 110, 132, 133
Dennett, D., 42, 55
Diagne, S.B., 113
diviner, engineer, priest, 8, 24, 25, 26, 27, 30, 35, 36, 38, 40, 45, 47, 50, 51, 52, 63, 65, 66, 67, 69, 78, 96, 106, 109, 110, 111, 134
drumming, 24, 60, 104, 105, 106, 107, 111

Ebyetaaga, 19
education, teaching, school, 11, 12, 13, 14, 15, 16, 18, 19, 20, 58, 61, 64, 71, 72, 76, 126, 132
Einstein, A., 135, 138
emiti, 95
emy, 110
emygga, 95
Emyooga, 20
emyoyo, pl. of *omuoyo* (non-human spirit), 91, 92, 93, 95, 98, 106, 110, 111
energy, 57, 59, 72, 76, 86, 94, 95, 97, 100, 106, 111
Engels, F., 124, 126, 128
engineer, priest, diviner, 8, 24, 25, 26, 27, 30, 35, 36, 38, 40, 45, 47, 50, 51, 52, 63, 65, 66, 67, 69, 78, 96, 106, 109, 110, 111, 134
Ephesios, Herakleitos, 113, 130, 138
epistemic, -ology, ological, 7, 23, 35, 57, 64, 67, 68, 80, 82, 117, 118, 119, 120, 122, 124, 125, 126, 127, 137
epistemological subject, collective, 57, 58, 59, 75, 117, 118, 119, 122, 123, 124, 127
essence, 26, 27, 29, 38, 97, 107, 111, 121, 125, 126, 134
Evans-Pritchard, E.E., 35, 36, 37, 43, 44, 48, 55
experiment, 16, 17, 37, 49, 72, 73, 76
explanation, cause, 26, 27, 36, 37, 39, 40, 41, 42, 43, 44, 45, 46, 47, 52, 65, 66, 68, 76, 80, 86, 90, 93, 110, 136
expression, 28, 31, 63, 88, 121, 122, 136

family (-line), tribe, village, 12, 19, 20, 24, 29, 38, 59, 60, 61, 70, 75, 95, 117, 118
feeling, 59, 61, 74, 75, 92, 97, 99, 101, 103, 105, 106, 107, 111, 130, 131
fertilization, 75, 93, 97, 101, 105, 132

forces, 37, 39, 40, 41, 42, 57, 59, 61, 62, 63, 64, 65, 66, 67, 68, 69, 71, 72, 73, 75, 76, 77, 78, 79, 80, 81, 85, 88, 90, 91, 93, 94, 95, 96, 97, 99, 100, 101, 102, 106, 107, 108, 109, 110, 134
future, 70, 71, 74, 75, 76, 78

Geertz, C., 29, 55
generalize, -ation, 52, 62, 131
giving, the general way of acquiring anything, including knowledge (see also sacrifice, libation, song, dance, oscillation), 15, 24, 27, 28, 29, 57, 61, 62, 71, 72, 74, 75, 93, 95, 96, 98, 108, 109, 110, 112
gods, 24, 96
good luck, 16, 36, 52, 72, 74, 88, 96, 133
Goody, J., 51, 55
Gramsci, A., 117, 127
Griaule, M., 46, 47, 55, 83, 96, 97, 113
guile, 68

Hallen, B., 46, 47, 48, 55, 56, 83, 113
Hamminga, B., 57, 82, 83, 85, 112, 113, 129, 138, 142
hantu (spacetime force, there-then-force), 90, 93, 95, 101
Hantu, 110
Haumann, T.M.H.M., 83, 114
hearing, 60, 75, 101, 131
Hearing (capital H) all non-visual sensing, 60, 75, 101, 102, 105, 107, 111, 130, 131
Hegba, M. P., 33, 34, 39, 56
heritage, 76, 95
Herodotus, 45
history, -ical, 13, 25, 31, 35, 44, 49, 81, 117, 119, 121, 122, 123, 124, 129
Horton, R., 33, 34, 39, 40, 41, 42, 43, 45, 46, 47, 48, 52, 55, 56, 83, 114
Hountondji, P. J., 83, 114

idea, thought, think, -ing, 17, 25, 26, 31, 33, 47, 48, 50, 54, 57, 58, 59, 60, 64, 72, 78, 80, 97, 117, 119, 126, 131, 137
ideal, 34, 48, 79, 118, 130
ideal type, 81, 82, 121
idealization, 125, 127, 134, 135, 137
Ikuenobe, P., 83, 114
indexicals, 53, 54, 131

Index and Glossary

individual (v. collective, see also collective), 14, 46, 48, 57, 58, 59, 69, 117, 118, 119, 120, 121, 122, 123, 124, 126, 132, 137
individual (v. personal), 30, 40, 41, 61, 70, 75, 79
Infeld, L., 135, 138
intention, 26, 28, 42, 63, 66, 76, 93, 98, 103, 110
Irenaeus, 44
Islam, 31, 46, 64

Jahn, J., 83, 96, 101, 108, 114, 138

Kanyike, E.M., 84, 114
Kimmerle, H., 113
Kintu, 110
kintu, pl. *bintu* (impersonal force), 90, 92, 93, 94, 95, 97, 108, 109, 112
kizima (living impersonal force), 93, 94, 102
Kmita, J., 138
knowledge, 7, 11, 12, 16, 17, 18, 20, 21, 22, 23, 25, 26, 27, 28, 34, 48, 50, 55, 57, 58, 59, 63, 66, 67, 68, 69, 70, 71, 72, 73, 74, 75, 76, 78, 80, 82, 110, 117, 129, 131, 133
Koopmans, T.C., 136, 138
Kuhn, T.S., 37, 49, 56, 78, 84
Kuipers, T.A.F., 138
kuntu (modality force, how-force), 90, 93, 95, 97, 101
Kuntu, 110
labor, 59, 67, 71, 74, 75, 76, 106, 121, 123

Lakatos, I., 56, 78, 84, 137, 138
Lamb, D., 84, 114
language, 8, 12, 19, 21, 28, 31, 33, 37, 38, 53, 54, 60, 63, 85, 90, 91, 94, 95, 97, 99, 100, 101, 104, 105, 106, 110, 112, 131, 132
Luyui, G., 114
Lévi-Strauss, C., 28, 133
libation, sacrifice, 24, 29, 38, 71, 75, 95, 96, 110
Lindberg, J.B., 136, 138
literate, -cy, -ary, writing, alphabet, 11, 12, 13, 15, 16, 21, 31, 33, 51, 52, 53, 54, 55, 77, 81, 86, 87, 88, 89, 90, 97, 100, 101, 108, 109, 111, 129, 131, 132
living, 21, 24, 30, 57, 62, 63, 65, 66, 67, 70, 71, 72, 76, 90, 91, 93, 94, 95, 96, 101, 102, 107, 108, 110, 111, 132, 133
Liyong, T. I., 84, 114
luck, good l., bad l., 16, 36, 52, 72, 74, 88, 96, 133
Lukács, G., 117, 127

MacCarty, H.H., 138
magara (ancestral power), 94, 96
magic, 32, 33, 36, 37, 38, 39, 48, 67, 68, 96, 111
Mann, T., 114
Marx, K.H., 5, 117, 119, 120, 121, 124, 126, 127, 128, 142
Masolo, D.A., 84, 114
Matip, B., 114
May, M., 138
Mbiti, J.S., 70, 84, 85, 114
medicine, 48, 67, 68, 76
mesopotamic, 64
method, ritual, ceremony, 8, 16, 17, 18, 23, 24, 25, 26, 27, 29, 30, 31, 33, 35, 38, 40, 48, 50, 72, 85, 99, 103, 111, 117, 133, 134, 135, 136, 137
Miller, R., 35, 56
minimum investment, law of, 73, 74, 75
muntu, pl. *bantu*, (human person, see also personal), 89, 90, 91, 92, 93, 94, 95, 96, 97, 98, 99, 101, 104, 105, 106, 107, 108, 110, 111
Museveni, Y.K., 11, 60, 71, 72, 84, 114, 132, 142
music, 59, 60, 100, 101, 104, 107, 111
Muslim, 31, 46, 64
muzima, pl. *bazima* (living human person), 94, 95, 96, 102
muzimu, pl. *bazimu* (dead human person, *muntu*-spirit), 91, 94, 95, 98

nommo (name, word), 12, 21, 24, 28, 51, 52, 57, 65, 67, 85, 86, 90, 92, 94, 95, 96, 97, 98, 99, 105, 108, 109, 111, 112, 132, 134, 137
Nowak, L., 117, 131, 134, 135, 138, 139, 142
Nowakowa, I., 131, 135, 139, 142

observation, 37, 103, 111, 130, 131, 135, 137
Obugaaga, 19
obuso, 21
Ochieng'-Odhiambo, F., 84, 114
oftarama (evening sessions), 12
ogrugyezi, 19
okugana (storytelling), 12
okulembeka, 19
okuterama, see *okugana*, 12
olubimbi, 19
omu, 110
omugga, 95

omuoyo, pl. *emyoyo* (non-human spirit), 91, 92, 93, 95, 98, 106, 110, 111
omuti, 95
oscillation (standing), 100, 106, 111

past, *zamani*, 12, 20, 24, 70, 71, 75, 78, 136
personal (v. individual), see also *muntu*, 11, 12, 27, 30, 39, 40, 41, 61, 64, 70, 71, 75, 78, 79, 81, 89, 93, 94, 96, 97, 98
philosophy, 7, 8, 11, 23, 25, 33, 37, 39, 42, 43, 45, 47, 49, 58, 60, 64, 68, 82, 106, 117, 125, 129, 134, 135, 136, 137
Pinxten, R. de, 138
Plato, 84, 88, 114
polite, im- , -ness, 51, 71, 87, 88
Popper, K.R., 37, 47, 56, 67
Poriau, M., 138
power, the universe consists of forces exchanging power, 5, 11, 17, 21, 27, 28, 30, 32, 36, 39, 57, 59, 61, 62, 63, 64, 65, 66, 67, 68, 69, 71, 72, 74, 75, 76, 78, 79, 80, 81, 85, 87, 88, 89, 90, 91, 92, 93, 94, 95, 96, 97, 98, 99, 100, 101, 102, 105, 106, 107, 108, 109, 110, 111, 112, 129, 134
present, 24, 71, 76
priest, diviner, engineer, 8, 24, 25, 26, 27, 30, 35, 36, 38, 40, 45, 47, 50, 51, 52, 63, 65, 66, 67, 69, 78, 96, 106, 109, 110, 111, 134
promises, -ing, contracts, agreements, 58, 59, 61, 62, 70, 76, 77, 87, 88, 108, 126

rational, 20, 25, 30, 34, 35, 39, 133, 136, 137
rational reconstruction, 137
Rattray, R.S., 24, 30, 38, 56
reading, 11, 12, 13, 51, 52, 53, 54, 60, 88, 109, 129, 131
real, reality, 14, 28, 42, 71, 75, 76, 101, 106, 110, 118, 121, 125, 126, 130, 132, 134, 135, 136, 137
reasoning, reason(s) to believe (see also belief) 17, 25, 26, 28, 36, 44, 45, 46, 58
religion, 23, 25, 26, 28, 29, 30, 31, 32, 33, 34, 36, 37, 38, 39, 40, 41, 42, 44, 45, 46, 48, 50, 52, 64, 81, 98, 104, 111, 133
ritual, ceremony, method, 8, 16, 17, 18, 23, 24, 25, 26, 27, 29, 30, 31, 33, 35, 38, 40, 48, 50, 72, 85, 99, 103, 111, 117, 133, 134, 135, 136, 137
Roux, A.P.J., 82, 113

sacrifice, libation, 24, 29, 38, 71, 75, 95, 96, 110
sasa (future), 70, 71, 74, 75, 76, 78
school, education, teaching, 11, 12, 13, 14, 15, 16, 18, 19, 20, 58, 61, 64, 71, 72, 76, 126, 132
science, 7, 8, 13, 15, 16, 17, 23, 25, 31, 32, 33, 35, 37, 38, 39, 40, 41, 42, 43, 44, 45, 47, 48, 49, 50, 51, 52, 54, 58, 59, 60, 62, 68, 76, 77, 78, 103, 111, 117, 125, 127, 129, 130, 131, 133, 134, 135, 136, 137
secrets, 68, 69, 78
seeing, visual, 75, 92, 101, 102, 103, 104, 106, 107, 108, 109, 111, 130, 131
sensing, Hearing (capital H), 60, 75, 101, 102, 105, 107, 111, 130, 131
Shakespeare, W., 13
singing, 24, 58, 60, 71, 75, 96, 105, 106, 107, 110, 111, 112
Skorupski, J., 28, 34, 56, 133, 139
sloppiness (prudent s.), 77, 87
Sodipo, J.O., 47, 48, 56, 83, 113
song, 24, 58, 60, 71, 75, 96, 105, 106, 107, 110, 111, 112
Soyinka, W., 48, 56
speech, 53, 58, 60, 71, 86, 97, 98, 99, 104, 107, 111
Spinoza, B. de, 63, 64, 65, 84
spirit, 72
spirits, 24, 25, 26, 27, 29, 30, 31, 32, 36, 39, 40, 53, 63, 67, 68, 72, 76, 91, 93, 96, 98, 102, 104, 106, 108, 109, 110, 117
Sterne, L., 114
subject, 57, 58, 59, 75, 117, 118, 119, 120, 122, 123, 124, 127
subject, collective epistemological, 57, 58, 59, 75, 117, 118, 119, 122, 123, 124, 127
symbolic, -ism, 27, 28, 29, 30, 31, 32, 33, 34, 38, 39, 133, 136, 137

Ta Kwesi, 26
teaching, school, education, 11, 12, 13, 14, 15, 16, 18, 19, 20, 58, 61, 64, 71, 72, 76, 126, 132
Tempels, P, 84, 114
Tennyson, A., 13
Thales, 47
theory, 7, 21, 23, 26, 31, 34, 36, 37, 38, 39, 40, 41, 42, 45, 47, 48, 49, 50, 51, 52, 54, 57, 62, 72, 73, 75, 82, 104, 110, 118, 121,

Index and Glossary 147

122, 123, 124, 125, 126, 127, 129, 130, 131, 132, 133, 134, 135, 136, 137
think, -ing, thought, idea, 17, 25, 26, 31, 33, 47, 48, 50, 54, 57, 58, 59, 60, 64, 72, 78, 80, 117, 119, 126, 131, 137
Thomas, K., 31, 32, 37, 49, 56
thought, think, -ing, idea, 17, 25, 26, 31, 33, 47, 48, 50, 54, 58, 59, 60, 64, 72, 78, 117, 126, 137
Tillich, P., 32
time, 11, 12, 20, 24, 53, 64, 70, 71, 74, 75, 76, 77, 78, 86, 90, 91, 95, 101, 110, 136
togetherness, collective, -ity, 11, 12, 24, 31, 35, 38, 58, 59, 60, 75, 77, 78, 86, 88, 100, 105, 107, 117, 118, 119, 120, 122, 123, 124
tree, 24, 57, 58, 59, 61, 66, 75, 85, 91, 95, 110
tribe, family (-line), village, 12, 16, 24, 59, 60, 61, 70, 75, 78, 93, 98, 117, 118
truth, 7, 17, 23, 24, 25, 31, 33, 34, 35, 37, 48, 57, 60, 61, 64, 72, 73, 75, 82, 110, 120, 129, 131, 133, 134, 139
Tutuola, A., 114
Tylor, E.B., 30

universe, world, the universe consists of forces exchanging power, 29, 34, 35, 36, 39, 40, 42, 43, 44, 45, 50, 61, 62, 63, 75, 79, 89, 90, 91, 96, 97, 101, 104, 110, 121, 123, 126, 129, 132, 134, 137
utility, 34, 35, 64, 65

Valk, G., 115
values (main v. peripheral), 121, 125, 126
Vandamme, F., 138
village, tribe, family (-line), 12, 19, 24, 27, 59, 60, 61, 70, 75
visual, seeing, 75, 92, 101, 102, 103, 104, 106, 107, 108, 109, 111, 130, 131
vitalism, vitality, 21, 57, 59, 60, 61, 65, 66, 69, 72, 76, 86, 101, 107, 110, 111, 112

water, 19, 63, 91, 96, 97, 110
Weber, M., 44
Werle, J., 136, 139
Wilde, O., 31, 56, 133, 139
willful (force, agent), 66, 75, 91, 93, 95, 104, 110
Wilson, B., 45, 56
Wiredu, K., 29, 40, 46, 56
witchcraft, 35, 36, 37, 43, 47, 53

word, name, *nommo*, 12, 19, 21, 24, 28, 51, 52, 57, 65, 67, 85, 86, 90, 92, 94, 95, 96, 97, 98, 99, 105, 108, 109, 111, 112, 131, 132, 134, 137
work, 59, 67, 71, 74, 75, 76, 106, 121, 123
world, universe, the world consists of forces exchanging power, 29, 34, 35, 36, 39, 40, 42, 43, 44, 45, 50, 61, 62, 63, 75, 79, 89, 90, 91, 96, 97, 101, 104, 110, 121, 123, 126, 129, 132, 134, 137
writing, alphabet, literate, -cy, -ary, 11, 12, 13, 15, 16, 21, 31, 33, 51, 52, 53, 54, 55, 77, 81, 86, 87, 88, 89, 90, 97, 100, 101, 108, 109, 111, 129, 131, 132

Yeats, W.B., 13

zamani (past), 12, 20, 24, 70, 71, 75, 78, 136

POZNAŃ STUDIES IN THE PHILOSOPHY OF THE SCIENCES AND THE HUMANITIES

Contents of back issues

VOLUME 1 (1975)

Main topics:
The Method of Humanistic Interpretation; The Method of Idealization; The Reconstruction of Some Marxist Theories.
(sold out)

VOLUME 2 (1976)

Main topics:
Idealizational Concept of Science; Categorial Interpretation of Dialectics.
(sold out)

VOLUME 3 (1977)

Main topic:
Aspects of the Production of Scientific Knowledge.
(sold out)

VOLUME 4 (1978)

Main topic:
Aspects of the Growth of Science.
(sold out)

VOLUME 5 (1979)

Main topic:
Methodological Problems of Historical Research.
(sold out)

VOLUME 6 (1982)

SOCIAL CLASSES ACTION & HISTORICAL MATERIALISM

Main topics:
On Classes; On Action; The Adaptive Interpretation of Historical Materialism; Contributions to Historical Materialism.
(sold out)

VOLUME 7 (1982)

DIALECTICAL LOGICS FOR THE POLITICAL SCIENCE
(Edited by Hayward R. Alker, Jr.)

VOLUME 8 (1985)

CONSCIOUSNESS: METHODOLOGICAL AND PSYCHOLOGICAL APPROACHES
(Edited by Jerzy Brzeziński)

VOLUME 9 (1986)

THEORIES OF IDEOLOGY AND IDEOLOGY OF THEORIES
(Edited by Piotr Buczkowski and Andrzej Klawiter)

VOLUME 10 (1987)

WHAT IS CLOSER-TO-THE-TRUTH?
A PARADE OF APPROACHES TO TRUTHLIKENESS
(Edited by Theo A.F. Kuipers)

VOLUME 11 (1988)

NORMATIVE STRUCTURES OF THE SOCIAL WORLD
(Edited by Giuliano di Bernardo)

VOLUME 12 (1987)

POLISH CONTRIBUTIONS TO THE THEORY AND PHILOSOPHY OF LAW
(Edited by Zygmunt Ziembiński)

VOLUME 13 (1988)

DIMENSIONS OF THE HISTORICAL PROCESS
(Edited by Leszek Nowak)

VOLUME 14 (1990)

ACTION AND PERFORMANCE: MODELS AND TESTS.
CONTRIBUTIONS TO THE QUANTITATIVE PSYCHOLOGY
AND ITS METHODOLOGY
(Edited by Jerzy Brzeziński and Tadeusz Marek)

VOLUME 15 (1989)

VISIONS OF CULTURE AND THE MODELS OF CULTURAL SCIENCES
(Edited by Jerzy Kmita and Krystyna Zamiara)

VOLUME 16 (1990)

IDEALIZATION I: GENERAL PROBLEMS
(Edited by Jerzy Brzeziński, Francesco Coniglione, Theo A.F. Kuipers and
Leszek Nowak)

VOLUME 17 (1990)

IDEALIZATION II: FORMS AND APPLICATIONS
(Edited by Jerzy Brzeziński, Francesco Coniglione, Theo A.F. Kuipers and
Leszek Nowak)

VOLUME 18 (1990)

STUDIES ON MARIO BUNGE'S *TREATISE*
(Edited by Paul Weingartner and Georg J.W. Dorn)

VOLUME 19 (1990)

NARRATION AND EXPLANATION.
CONTRIBUTION TO THE METHODOLOGY OF THE HISTORICAL RESEARCH
(Edited by Jerzy Topolski)

VOLUME 20 (1990)

Jürgen Ritsert
MODELS AND CONCEPTS OF IDEOLOGY

VOLUME 21 (1991)

PROBABILITY AND RATIONALITY
STUDIES ON L. JONATHAN COHEN'S PHILOSOPHY OF SCIENCE
(Edited by Ellery Eells and Tomasz Maruszewski)

VOLUME 22 (1991)

THE SOCIAL HORIZON OF KNOWLEDGE
(Edited by Piotr Buczkowski)

VOLUME 23 (1991)

ETHICAL DIMENSIONS OF LEGAL THEORY
(Edited by Wojciech Sadurski)

VOLUME 24 (1991)

ADVANCES IN SCIENTIFIC PHILOSOPHY
ESSAYS IN HONOUR OF PAUL WEINGARTNER ON THE OCCASION OF
THE 60TH ANNIVERSARY OF HIS BIRTHDAY
(Edited by Gerhard Schurz and Georg J.W. Dorn)

VOLUME 25 (1992)

IDEALIZATION III: APPROXIMATION AND TRUTH
(Edited by Jerzy Brzeziński and Leszek Nowak)

VOLUME 26 (1992)

IDEALIZATION IV: INTELLIGIBILITY IN SCIENCE
(Edited by Craig Dilworth)

VOLUME 27 (1992)

Ryszard Stachowski

THE MATHEMATICAL SOUL.
AN ANTIQUE PROTOTYPE OF THE MODERN MATEMATISATION OF
PSYCHOLOGY

VOLUME 28 (1993)

POLISH SCIENTIFIC PHILOSOPHY:
THE LVOV-WARSAW SCHOOL
(Edited by Francesco Coniglione, Roberto Poli and Jan Woleński)

VOLUME 29 (1993)

Zdzisław Augustynek and Jacek J. Jadacki

POSSIBLE ONTOLOGIES

VOLUME 30 (1993)

GOVERNMENT: SERVANT OR MASTER?
(Edited by Gerard Radnitzky and Hardy Bouillon)

VOLUME 31 (1993)

CREATIVITY AND CONSCIOUSNESS.
PHILOSOPHICAL AND PSYCHOLOGICAL DIMENSIONS
(Edited by Jerzy Brzeziński, Santo Di Nuovo, Tadeusz Marek and Tomasz Maruszewski)

VOLUME 32 (1993)

FROM ONE-PARTY-SYSTEM TO DEMOCRACY
(Edited by Janina Frentzel-Zagórska)

VOLUME 33 (1993)

SOCIAL SYSTEM, RATIONALITY, AND REVOLUTION
(Edited by Marcin Paprzycki and Leszek Nowak)

VOLUME 34 (1994)

Izabella Nowakowa

IDEALIZATION V: THE DYNAMICS OF IDEALIZATIONS

VOLUME 35 (1993)

EMPIRICAL LOGIC AND PUBLIC DEBATE.
ESSAYS IN HONOUR OF ELSE M. BARTH
(Edited by E.C.W. Krabbe, R.J. Dalitz, and P.A. Smit)

VOLUME 36 (1994)

MARXISM AND COMMUNISM: POSTHUMOUS REFLECTIONS ON
POLITICS, SOCIETY, AND LAW
(Edited by Martin Krygier)

VOLUME 37 (1994)

THE SOCIAL PHILOSOPHY OF AGNES HELLER
(Edited by John Burnheim)

VOLUME 38 (1994)

IDEALIZATION VI: IDEALIZATION IN ECONOMICS
(Edited by Bert Hamminga and Neil B. De Marchi)

VOLUME 39 (1994)

PROBABILITY IN THEORY-BUILDING.
EXPERIMENTAL AND NON-EXPERIMENTAL APPROACHES
TO SCIENTIFIC RESEARCH IN PSYCHOLOGY
(Edited by Jerzy Brzeziński)

VOLUME 40 (1995)

THE HERITAGE OF KAZIMIERZ AJDUKIEWICZ
(Edited by Vito Sinisi and Jan Woleński)

VOLUME 41 (1994)

HISTORIOGRAPHY BETWEEN MODERNISM AND POSTMODERNISM.
CONTRIBUTIONS TO THE METHODOLOGY OF
THE HISTORICAL RESEARCH
(Edited by Jerzy Topolski)

VOLUME 42 (1995)

IDEALIZATION VII: IDEALIZATION, STRUCTURALISM,
AND APPROXIMATION
(Edited by Martti Kuokkanen)

Idealization, Approximation and Counterfactuals in the Structuralist Framework – T.A.F. Kuipers, *The Refined Structure of Theories*; C.U. Moulines and R. Straub, *Approximation and Idealization from the Structuralist Point of View*; I.A. Kieseppä, *A Note on the Structuralist Account of Approximation*; C.U. Moulines and R. Straub, *A Reply to Kieseppä*; W. Balzer and G. Zoubek, *Structuralist Aspects of Idealization*; A. Ibarra and T. Mormann, *Counterfactual Deformation and Idealization in a Structuralist Framework*; I.A. Kieseppä, *Assessing the Structuralist Theory of Verisimilitude*. **Idealization, Approxima-tion and Theory Formation** – L. Nowak, *Remarks on the Nature of Galileo's Methodological Revolution*; I. Niiniluoto, *Approximation in Applied Science*; E. Heise, P. Gerjets and R. Westermann, *Idealized Action Phases. A Concise Rubicon Theory*; K.G. Troitzsch, *Modelling, Simulation, and Structuralism*; V. Rantala and T. Vadén, *Idealization in Cognitive Science. A Study in Counterfactual Correspondence*; M. Sintonen and M. Kiikeri, *Idealization in Evolutionary Biology*; T. Tuomivaara, *On Idealizations in Ecology*; M. Kuokkanen and M. Häyry, *Early Utilitarianism and Its Idealizations from a Systematic Point of View*. **Idealization, Approximation and Measurement** – R. Westermann, *Measurement-Theoretical Idealizations and Empirical Research Practice*; U. Konerding, *Probability as an Idealization of Relative Frequency. A Case Study by Means of the BTL-Model*; R. Suck and J. Wienöbst, *The Empirical Claim of Probality Statements, Idealized Bernoulli Experiments and their Approximate Version*; P.J. Lahti, *Idealizations in Quantum Theory of Measurement*.

VOLUME 43 (1995)

Witold Marciszewski and Roman Murawski
MECHANIZATION OF REASONING IN A HISTORICAL PERSPECTIVE

Chapter 1: *From the Mechanization of Reasoning to a Study of Human Intelligence*; Chapter 2: *The Formalization of Arguments in the Middle Ages*; Chapter 3: *Leibniz's Idea of Mechanical Reasoning at the Historical Background*; Chapter 4: *Between Leibniz and Boole: Towards the Algebraization of Logic*; Chapter 5: *The English Algebra of Logic in the 19th Century*; Chapter 6: *The 20th Century Way to Formalization and Mechanization*; Chapter 7: *Mechanized Deduction Systems*.

VOLUME 44 (1995)

THEORIES AND MODELS IN SCIENTIFIC PROCESSES
(Edited by William Herfel, Władysław Krajewski,
Ilkka Niiniluoto and Ryszard Wójcicki)

Introduction; **Part 1. Models in Scientific Processes** – J. Agassi, *Why there is no Theory of Models?*; M. Czarnocka, *Models and Symbolic Nature of Knowledge*; A. Grobler, *The Representational and the Non-Representational in Models of Scientific Theories*; S. Hartmann, *Models as a Tool for the Theory Construction: Some Strategies of Preliminary Physics*; W. Herfel, *Nonlinear Dynamical Models as Concrete Construction*; E. Kałuszyńska, *Styles of Thinking*; S. Psillos, *The Cognitive Interplay Between Theories and Models: the Case of 19th Century Optics*. **Part 2. Tools of Science** – N.D. Cartwright, T. Shomar, M. Suarez, *The Tool-Box of Science*; J. Echeverria, *The Four Contexts of Scienctific Activity*; K. Havas, *Continuity and Change; Kinds of Negation in Scientific Progress*; M. Kaiser, *The Independence of Scientific Phenomena*; W. Krajewski, *Scientific Meta-Philosophy*; I. Niiniluoto, *The Emergence of Scientific Specialties: Six Models*; L. Nowak, *Antirealism, (Supra-) Realism and Idealization*; R.M. Nugayev, *Classic, Modern and Postmodern Scientific Unification*; V. Rantala, *Translation and Scientific Change*; G. Schurz, *Theories and Their Applications – a Case of Nonmonotonic Reasoning*; W. Strawiński, *The Unity of Science Today*; V. Torosian, *Are the Ethics and Logic of Science Compatible?* **Part 3. Unsharp Approaches in Science** – E.W. Adams, *Problems and Prospects in a Theory of Inexact First-Order Theories*; W. Balzer, G. Zoubek, *On the Comparision of Approximative Empirical Claims*; G. Cattaneo, M. Luisa Dalla Chiara, R. Giuntini, *The Unsharp Approaches to Quantum Theory*; T.A.F. Kuipers, *Falsification Versus Effcient Truth Approximation*; B. Lauth, *Limiting Decidability and Probability*; J. Pykacz, *Many-Valued Logics in Foundations of Quantum Mechanics*; R.R. Zapatrin, *Logico-Algebraic Approach to Spacetime Quantization*.

VOLUME 45 (1995)

COGNITIVE PATTERNS IN SCIENCE AND COMMON SENSE.
GRONINGEN STUDIES IN PHILOSOPHY OF SCIENCE,
LOGIC, AND EPISTEMOLOGY
(Edited by Theo A.F. Kuipers and Anne Ruth Mackor)

L. Nowak, *Foreword*; **General Introduction** – T.A.F. Kuipers and A.R. Mackor, *Cognitive Studies of Science and Common Sense*; **Part I: Conceptual Analysis in Service of Various Research Programmes** – H. Zandvoort, *Concepts of Interdisciplinarity and Environmental Science*; R. Vos, *The Logic and Epistemology of the Concept of Drug and Disease Profile*; R.C. Looijen, *On the Distinction Between Habitat and Niché, and Some Implications for Species' Differentiation*; G.J. Stavenga, *Cognition, Irreversibility and the Direction of Time*; R. Dalitz, *Knowledge, Gender and Social Bias*; **Part II: The Logic of the Evaluation of Arguments, Hypotheses, Rules, and Interesting Theorems** – E.G.W. Krabbe, *Can We Ever Pin One Down to a Formal Fallacy?*; T.A.F. Kuipers, *Explicating the Falsificationist and Instrumentalist Methodology by Decomposing the Hypothetico-Deductive Method*; A. Keupink, *Causal Modelling and Misspecification: Theory and Econometric Historical*

Practice; M.C.W. Janssen and Y.-H. Tan, *Default Reasoning and Some Applications in Economics*; B. Hamminga, *Interesting Theorems in Economics*; **Part III: Three Challenges to the Truth Approximation Programme** – S.D. Zwart, *A Hidden Variable in the Discussion About 'Language Dependency' of Truthlikeness*; H. Hettema and T.A.F. Kuipers, *Sommerfeld's Atombau: A Case Study in Potential Truth Approximation*; R. Festa, *Verisimilitude, Disorder, and Optimum Prior Probabilities*; **Part IV: Explicating Psychological Intuitions** – A.R. Mackor, *Intentional Psychology is a Biological Discipline*; J. Peijnenburg, *Hempel's Rationality. On the Empty Nature of Being a Rational Agent*; L. Guichard, *The Causal Efficacy of Propositional Attitudes*; M. ter Hark, *Connectionism, Behaviourism and the Language of Thought*.

VOLUME 46 (1996)

POLITICAL DIALOGUE: THEORIES AND PRACTICE
(Edited by Stephen L. Esquith)

Introduction – S.L. Esquith, *Political Dialogue and Political Virtue*. **Part I: The Modern Clasics** – A.J. Damico, *Reason's Reach: Liberal Tolerance and Political Discourse*; T.R. Machan, *Individualism and Political Dialogue*; R. Kukla, *The Coupling of Human Souls: Rousseau and the Problem of Gender Relations*; D.F. Koch, *Dialogue: An Essay in the Instrumentalist Tradition*. **Part II: Toward a Democratic Synthesis** – E. Simpson, *Forms of Political Thinking and the Persistence of Practical Philosophy*; J.B. Sauer, *Discoursee, Consensus, and Value: Conversations about the Intelligible Relation Between the Private and Public Spheres*; M. Kingwell, *Phronesis and Political Dialogue*, R.T. Peterson, *Democracy and Intellectual Mediation – After Liberalism and Socialism*. **Part III: Dialogue in Practice** – S. Rohr Scaff, L.A. Scaff, *Political Dialogue in the New Germany: The Burdens of Culture and an Asymmetrical Past*; J.H. Read, *Participation, Power, and Democracy*; S.E. Bennett, B. Fisher, D. Resnick, *Speaking of Politics in the United States: Who Talks to Whom, Why, and Why Not*; J. Forester, *Beyond Dialogue to Transformative Learning: How Deliberative Rituals Encourage Political Judgement in Community Planning Processes*; A. Fatić, *Retribution in Democracy*.

VOLUME 47 (1996)

EPISTEMOLOGY AND HISTORY. HUMANITIES AS A PHILOSOPHICAL PROBLEM AND JERZY KMITA'S APPROACH TO IT
(Edited by Anna Zeidler-Janiszewska)

A. Zeidler-Janiszewska, *Preface*. **Humanistic Knowledge** – K.O. Apel, *The Hermeneutic Dimension of Social Science and its Normative Foundation*; M. Czerwiński, *Jerzy Kmita's Epistemology*; L. Witkowski, *The Frankfurt School and Structuralism in Jerzy Kmita's Analysis*; A. Szahaj, *Between Modernism and Postmodernism: Jerzy Kmita's Epistemology*; A. Grzegorczyk, *Non-Cartesian Coordinates in the Contemporary Humanities*; A. Pałubicka, *Pragmatist Holism as an Expression of Another Disenchantment of the World*; J. Sójka, *Who is Afraid of Scientism?*; P. Ozdowski, *The Broken Bonds with the World*; J. Such, *Types of Determination vs. the Development of Science in Historical Epistemology*; P. Zeidler, *Some Issues of Historical Epistemology in the Light of the Structuralist Philosophy of Science*; M. Buchowski, *Via Media: On the Consequences of Historical Epistemology for the Problem of Rationality*; B. Kotowa, *Humanistic Valuation and Some Social Functions of the Humanities*. **On Explanation and Humanistic Interpretation** – T.A.F. Kuipers, *Explanation by Intentional, Functional, and Causal Specification*; E. Świderski, *The Interpretational Paradigm in the Philosophy of the Human Sciences*; L. Nowak, *On the*

Limits of the Rationalistic Paradigm; F. Coniglione, Humanistic Interpretation between Hempel and Popper; Z. Ziembiński, Historical Interpretation vs. the Adaptive Interpretation of a Legal Text; W. Mejbaum, Explaining Social Phenomena; M. Ziółkowski, The Functional Theory of Culture and Sociology; K. Zamiara, Jerzy Kmita's Social-Regulational Theory of Culture and the Category of Subject; J. Brzeziński, Theory and Social Practice. One or Two Psychologies?; Z. Kwieciński, Decahedron of Education (Components and aspects). The Need for a Comprehensive Approach; J. Paśniczek, The Relational vs. Directional Concept of Intentionality. **The Historical Dimension of Culture and its Studies** – J. Margolis, The Declension of Progressivism; J. Topolski, Historians Look at Historical Truth; T. Jerzak-Gierszewska, Three Types of the Theories of Religion and Magic; H. Paetzold, Mythos und Moderne in der Philosophie der symbolishen Formen Ernst Cassirers; M. Siemek, Sozialphilosophische Aspekte der Übersetzbarkeit. **Problems of Artistic Practice and Its Interpretation** – S. Morawski, Theses on the 20th Century Crisis of Art and Culture; A. Erjavec, The Perception of Science in Modernist and Postmodernist Artistic Practice, G. Dziamski, The Avant-garde and Contemporary Artistic Consciousness; H. Orłowski, Generationszugehörigkeit und Selbsterfahrung von (deutschen) Schriftstellern; T. Kostyrko, The "Transhistoricity" of the Structure of Work of Art and the Process of Value Transmission in Culture; G. Banaszak, Musical Culture as a Configuration of Subcultures; A. Zeidler-Janiszewska, The Problem of the Applicability of Humanistic Interpretation in the Light of Contemporary Artistic Practice; J. Kmita, Towards Cultural Relativism "with a Small 'r' "; The Bibliography of Jerzy Kmita.

VOLUME 48 (1996)

THE SOCIAL PHILOSOPHY OF ERNEST GELLNER
(Edited by John A. Hall and Ian Jarvie)

J.A. Hall, I. Jarvie, Preface; J.A. Hall, I. Jarvie, The Life and Times of Ernest Gellner. **Part 1: Intelectual Background** – J. Musil, The Prague Roots of Ernest Gellner's Thinking; Ch. Hahn, Gellner and Malinowski: Words and Things in Central Europe; T. Dragadze, Ernest Gellner in Soviet East. **Part 2: Nations and Nationalism** – B. O'Leary, On the Nature of Nationalism: An Appraisal of Ernest Gellner's Writings on Nationalism; K. Minogue, Ernest Gellner and the Dangers of Theorising Nationalism; A.D. Smith, History and Modernity: Reflection on the Theory of Nationalism; M. Mann, The Emergence of Modern European Nationalism; N. Stagardt, Gellner's Nationalism: The Spirit of Modernisation? **Part 3: Patterns of Development** – P. Burke, Reflections on the History of Encyclopaedias; A. MacFarlane, Ernest Gellner and the Escape to Modernity; R. Dore, Soverein Individuals; S. Eisenstadt, Japan Non-Axial Modernity; M. Ferro, L'Indépendance Telescopée: De la Décolonisation a L'Impérialisme Multinational. **Part 4: Islam** – A. Hammoudi, Segmentarity, Social stratification, Political Power and Sainthood: Reflections on Gellner's Theses; H. Munson, Jr., Rethinking Gellner's Segmentary Analysis of Morocco's Ait'Atta; J. Baechler, Sur le charisme; Ch. Lindholm, Despotism and Democracy: State and Society in PreModern Middle East; H. Munson, Jr. Muslism and Jew in Morocco: Reflections on the Distinction between Belief and Behaviour; T. Asad, The Idea of an Anthropology of Islam. **Part 5: Science and Disenchantment** – P. Anderson, Science, Politics, Enchantment; R. Schroeder, From the Big Divide to the Rubber Cage: Gellner's Conception of Science and Technology; J. Davis, Irrationality in Social Life. **Part 6: Relativism and Universals** – J. Skorupski, The Post-Modern Hume: Ernest Gellner's 'Enlightenment Fundamentalism'; J. Wettersten, Ernest Gellner: A Wittgensteinian Rationalist; I. Jarvie, Gellner's Positivism; R. Boudon, Relativising Relativism: When Sociology Refutes the Sociology of Science; R. Aya, The Empiricist Exorcist. **Part 7: Philosophy of History** – W. McNeill, A Swang Song for British Liberalism?; A. Park, Gellner and the Long Trends of History; E. Leone, Marx, Gellner, Power; R. Langlois, Coercion, Cognition and Production: Gellner's Challenge to

Historical Materialism and Post-Modernism; E. Gellner, *Reply to my Critics*; I. Jarvie, *Complete Bibliography of Gellner's Work*.

VOLUME 49 (1996)

THE SIGNIFICANCE OF POPPER'S THOUGHT
(Edited by Stefan Amsterdamski)

Karl Popper's Three Worlds – J. Watkins, *World 1, World 2 and the Theory of Evolution*; A. Grobler, *World 3 and the Cunning of Reason*. **The Scientific Method as Ethics** – J. Agassi, *Towards Honest Public Relations of Science*; S. Amsterdamski, *Between Relativism and Absolutism: the Popperian Ideal of Knowledge*. **The Open Society and its Prospects** – E. Gellner, *Karl Popper – The Thinker and the Man*; J. Woleński, *Popper on Prophecies and Predictions*.

VOLUME 50 (1996)

THE IDEA OF THE UNIVERSITY
(Edited by Jerzy Brzeziński and Leszek Nowak)

Introduction – K. Twardowski, *The Majesty of the University*. **I** – Z. Ziembiński, *What Can be Saved of the Idea of the University?*; L. Kołakowski, *What Are Universities for?*; L. Gumański, *The Ideal University and Reality*; Z. Bauman, *The Present Crisis of the Universities*. **II** – K. Ajdukiewicz, *On Freedom of Science*; H. Samsonowicz, *Universities and Democracy*; J. Topolski, *The Commonwealth of Scholars and New Conceptions of Truth*; K. Szaniawski, *Plus ratio quam vis*. **III** – L. Koj, *Science, Teaching and Values*; K. Szaniawski, *The Ethics of Scientific Criticism*; J. Brzeziński, *Ethical Problems of Research Work of Psychologists*. **IV** – J. Goćkowski, *Tradition in Science*; J. Kmita, *Is a "Creative Man of Knowledge" Needed in University Teaching?*; L. Nowak, *The Personality of Researchers and the Necessity of Schools in Science*. **Recapitulation** – J. Brzeziński, *Reflections on the University*.

VOLUME 51 (1997)

KNOWLEDGE AND INQUIRY: ESSAYS ON JAAKKO HINTIKKA'S EPISTEMOLOGY AND PHILOSOPHY OF SCIENCE
(Edited by Matti Sintonen)

M. Sintonen, *From the Science of Logic to the Logic of Science*. **I: Historical Perspectives** – Z. Bechler, *Hintikka on Plentitude in Aristotle*; M.-L. Kakkuri-Knuuttila, *What Can the Sciences of Man Learn from Aristotle?*; M. Kusch, *Theories of Questions in German-Speaking Philosophy Around the Turn of the Century*; N.-E. Sahlin, *'He is no Good for My Work': On the Philosophical Relations between Ramsey and Wittgenstein*. **II: Formal Tools: Induction, Observation and Identifiability** – T.A.F. Kuipers, *The Carnap-Hintikka Programme in Inductive Logic*; I. Levi, *Caution and Nonmonotic Inference*; I. Niiniluoto, *Inductive Logic, Atomism, and Observational Error*; A. Mutanen, *Theory of Identifiability*. **III: Questions in Inquiry: The Interrogative Model** – S. Bromberger, *Natural Kinds and Questions*; S.A. Kleiner, *The Structure of Inquiry in Developmental Biology*; A. Wiśniewski, *Some Foundational Concepts of Erotetic Semantics*; J. Woleński, *Science and Games*. **IV: Growth of Knowledge: Explanation and Discovery** – M. Sintonen, *Explanation: The Fifth Decade*; E. Weber, *Scientific Explanation and the Interrogative Model of Inquiry*; G. Gebhard, *Scientific Discovery, Induction, and the Multi-Level*

Character of Scientific Inquiry; M. Kiikeri, On the Logical Structure of Learning Models. V: Jaakko Hintikka: Replies.

VOLUME 52 (1997)

Helena Eilstein
LIFE CONTEMPLATIVE, LIFE PRACTICAL.
AN ESSAY ON FATALISM

Preface. **Chapter One: Oldcomb and Newcomb** – 1. *In the King Comb's Chamber of Game*; 2. *The Newcombian Predicaments*. **Chapter Two: Ananke** – 1. *Fatalism: What It Is Not?*; 2. *Fatalism: What Is It?*; 3. *Fatalism and* a priori *Arguments*; 4. *Fatalism and 'Internal' Experience*; 5. *Determinism, Indeterminism and Fatalism*; 6. *Transientism, Eternism and Fatalism*; 7. *Fatalism: What It Does Not Imply?*. **Chapter Three: Fated Freedom** – 1. *More on Libertarianism*; 2. *On the Deterministic Concept of Freedom*; 3. *Moral Self and Responsibility in the Light of Probabilism*; 4. *Fated Freedom*. **Chapter Four: The Virus of Fatalism** – 1. *Fatalism and Problems of Cognition*; 2. *The Virus of Fatalism: Why Mostly Harmless?*

VOLUME 53 (1997)

Dimitri Ginev
A PASSAGE TO THE HERMENEUTIC PHILOSOPHY OF SCIENCE

Preface; **Introduction**: *Topics in the Hermeneutic Philosophy of Science*; **Chapter 0**: *On the Limits of the Rational Reconstruction of Scientific Knowledge*; **Chapter 1**: *On the Hermeneutic Nature of Group Rationality*; **Chapter 2**: *Towards a Hermeneutic Theory of Progressive Change in Scientific Development*; **Chapter 3**: *Beyond Naturalism and Traditionalism*; **Chapter 4**: *A Critical Note on Normative Naturalism*; **Chapter 5**: *Micro and Macrohermeneutics of Science*; *Concluding Remarks*.

VOLUME 54 (1997)

IN ITINERE. EUROPEAN CITIES AND THE BIRTH OF MODERN
SCIENTIFIC PHILOSOPHY
(Edited by Roberto Poli)

Introduction – R. Poli, *In itinere. Pictures from Central-European Philosophy*. *Stages of the Tour* – K. Schuhmann, *Philosophy and Art in Munich around the Turn of the Century*; M. Libardi, *In itinere: Vienna 1870-1918*; W. Baumgartner, *Nineteenth-Century Würzburg: The Development of the Scientific Approach to Philosophy*; L. Dappiano, *Cambridge and the Austrian Connection*; J. Sebestik, *Prague Mosaic. Encounters with the Prague Philosophers*; J.J. Jadacki, *Warsaw: The Rise and Decline of Modern Scientific Philosophy in the Capital City of Poland*; J. Woleński, *Lvov*; L. Albertazzi, *Science and the Avant-Garde in Early Nineteenth-Century Florence*; F. Minazzi, *The Presence of Phenomenology in Milan between the Two World Wars. The Contribution of Antonio Banfi and Giulio Preti*.

VOLUME 55 (1997)

REALISM AND QUANTUM PHYSICS
(Edited by Evandro Agazzi)

Introduction – E. Agazzi. **Part One: Philosophical Considerations** – P. Horwich, *Realism and Truth*, E. Agazzi, *On the Criteria for Establishing the Ontological Status of Different Entities*; A. Baltas, *Constraints and Resistance: Stating a Case for Negative Realism*; M. Paty, *Predicate of Existence and Predicability for a Theoretical Object in Physics*. **Part Two: Observability and Hidden Entities** – F. Bonsak, *Atoms: Lessons of a History*; A. Cordero, *Arguing for Hidden Realities*; B. d'Espagnat, *On the Difficulties that Attributing Existence to "Hidden" Quantities May Raise*; M. Pauri, *The Quantum, Space-Time and Observation*. **Part Three: Applications to Quantum Physics** – D. Albert, *On the Phenomenology of Quantum-Mechanical Superpositions*; G.C. Ghiraldi, *Realism and Quantum Mechanics*; M. Crozon, *Experimental Evidence of Quark Structure Inside Hadrons*.

VOLUME 56 (1997)

IDEALIZATION VIII: MODELLING IN PSYCHOLOGY
(Edited by Jerzy Brzeziński, Bodo Krause and Tomasz Maruszewski)

Part I: Philosophical and Methodological Problems of Cognition Process – J. Wane, *Idealizing the Cartesian-Newtonian Paradigm as Reality: The Impact of New-Paradigm Physics on Psychological Theory*; E. Hornowska, *Operationalization of Psychological Magnitudes. Assumptions-Structure-Consequences*; T. Bachmann, *Creating Analogies – On Aspects of the Mapping Process between Knowledge Domains*; H. Schaub, *Modelling Action Regulation*. **Part II: The Structure of Ideal Learning Process** – S. Ohlson, J.J. Jewett, *Ideal Adaptive Agents and the Learning Curve*; B. Krause, *Towards a Theory of Cognitive Learning*; B. Krause, U. Gauger, *Learning and Use of Invariances: Experiments and Network Simulation*; M. Friedrich, *"Reaction Time" in the Neural Network Module ART 1*. **Part III: Control Processes in Memory** – J. Tzelgov, V. Yehene, M. Naveh-Benjamin, *From Memory to Automaticity and Vice Versa: On the Relation between Memory and Automaticity*; H. Hagendorf, S. Fisher, B. Sá, *The Function of Working Memory in Coordination of Mental Transformations*; L. Nowak, *On Common-Sense and (Para-)Idealization*; I. Nowakowa, *On the Problem of Induction. Toward an Idealizational Paraphrase*.

VOLUME 57 (1997)

EUPHONY AND LOGOS
ESSAYS IN HONOUR OF MARIA STEFFEN-BATÓG AND TADEUSZ BATÓG
(Edited by Roman Murawski, Jerzy Pogonowski)

Preface. **Scientific Works of Maria Steffen-Batóg and Tadeusz Batóg** – *List of Publications of Maria Steffen-Batóg*; *List of Publications of Tadeusz Batóg*; J. Pogonowski, *On the Scientific Works of Maria Steffen-Batóg*; Jerzy Pogonowski, *On the Scientific Works of Tadeusz Batóg*; W. Lapis, *How Should Sounds Be Phonemicized?*; P. Nowakowski, *On Applications of Algorithms for Phonetic Transcription in Linguistic Research*; J. Pogonowski, *Tadeusz Batóg's Phonological Systems*. **Mathematical Logic** – W. Buszkowski, *Incomplete Information Systems and Kleene 3-valued Logic*; M. Kandulski, *Categorial Grammars with Structural Rules*; M. Kołowska-Gawiejnowicz, *Labelled*

Deductive Systems for the Lambek Calculus; R. Murawski, *Satisfaction Classes – a Survey*; K. Świrydowicz, *A New Approach to Dyadic Deontic Logic and the Normative Consequence Relation*; W. Zielonka, *More about the Axiomatics of the Lambek Calculus*. **Theoretical Linguistics** – J.J. Jadacki, *Troubles with Categorial Interpretation of Natural Language*; M. Karpiński, *Conversational Devices in Human-Computer Communication Using WIMP UI*; W. Maciejewski, *Qualitative Orientation and Gramatical Categories*; Z. Vetulani, *A System of Computer Understanding of Text*; A. Wójcik, *The Formal Development of van Sandt's Presupposition Theory*; W. Zabrocki, *Psychologism in Noam Chomsky's Theory (Tentative Critical Remarks)*; R. Zuber, *Defining Presupposition without Negation*. **Philosophy of Language and Methodology of Sciences** – J. Kmita, *Philosophical Antifundamentalism*; A. Luchowska, *Peirce and Quine: Two Views on Meaning*; S. Wiertlewski, *Method According to Feyerabend*; J. Woleński, *Wittgenstein and Ordinary Language*; K. Zamiara, *Context of Discovery – Context of Justification and the Problem of Psychologism*.

VOLUME 58 (1997)

THE POSTMODERNIST CRITIQUE OF THE PROJECT OF ENLIGHTENMENT
(Edited by Sven-Eric Liedman)

S.-E. Liedman, *Introduction*; R. Wokler, *The Enlightenment Project and its Critics*; M. Benedikt, *Die Gegenwartsbedeutung von Kants aufklärender Akzeptanz und Zurückweisung des Modells der Naturwissenschaft für zwischenmenschliche Verhältnisse: Verfehlte Beziehungen der Geisterwelt Swedenborgs*; S.-E. Liedman, *The Crucial Role of Ethics in Different Types of Enlightenment (Condorcet and Kant)*; S. Dahlstedt, *Forms of the Ineffable: From Kant to Lyotard*; P. Magnus Johansson, *On the Enlightenment in Psycho-Analysis*; E. Lundgren-Gothlin, *Ethics, Feminism and Postmodernism: Seyla Benhabib and Simone de Beauvoir*; E. Kiss, *Gibt es ein Projekt der Aufklärung und wenn ja, wie viele (Aufklärung vor dem Horizont der Postmoderne)*; E. Kennedy, *Enlightenment Anticipations of Postmodernist Epistemology*; L. Nowak, *On Postmodernist Philosophy: An Attempt to Identify its Historical Sense*; M. Castillo, *The Dilemmas of Postmodern Individualism*.

VOLUME 59 (1997)

BEYOND ORIENTALISM. THE WORK OF WILHELM HALBFASS AND ITS IMPACT ON INDIAN AND CROSS-CULTURAL STUDIES
(Edited by Eli Franco and Karin Preisendanz)

E. Franco, K. Preisendanz, *Introduction and Editorial Essay on Wilhelm Halbfass*; Publications by Wilhelm Halbfass; W. Halbfass, *Research and Reflections: Responses to my Respondents. Beyond Orientalism? Reflections on a Current Theme.* **Part I: Cross-Cultural Encounter and Dialogue** – F. X. Clooney, SJ, *Wilhelm Halbfass and the Openness of the Comparative Project*; F. Dallmayr, *Exit from Orientalism: Comments on Wilhelm Halbfass*; S. D. Serebriany, *Some Marginal Notes on India and Europe*; R. Sen (née Mookerjee), *Some Reflections on India and Europe: An Essay in Understanding*; K. Karttunen, *Greeks and Indian Wisdom*; D. Killingley, *Mlecchas, Yavanas and Heathens: Interacting Xenologies in Early Nineteenth-Century Calcutta*; W. Halbfass, *Research and Reflections: Responses to my Respondents. Cross-Cultural Encounter and Dialogue.* **Part II: Issues of Comparative Philosophy** – J. Nath Mohanty, *Between Indology and Indian Philosophy*; J. S. O'Leary, *Heidegger and Indian Philosophy*; S. Rao, *"Subordinate" or "Supreme"? The Nature of Reason in India and the West*; R. Ivekoviæ, *The Politics of Comparative Philosophy*; B.-A. Scharfstein, *The Three Philosophical Traditions*; W. Halbfass, *Research and Reflections: Responses to my Respondents. Issues of Comparative Philosophy.* **Part III: Topics in Classical Indian Philosophy** – J. E. M. Houben, *Bhartṛhari's Perspectivism: The Vṛtti and*

Bhartṛhari's Perspectivism in the First kāṇḍa of the Vākyapadīya; J. Bronkhorst, Philosophy and the Vedic Exegesis in the Mīmāṃsā; J. Taber, The Significance of Kumārila's Philosophy; K. Harikai, Kumārila's Acceptance and Modification of Categories of the Vaiœeṣika School; V. Lysenko, The Vaiœeṣika Notions of ākāsa and diœ from the Perspective of Indian Ideas of Space; B. M. Perry, Early Nyāya and Hindu Orthodoxy: ānvīkṣikī and adhikāra; W. Halbfass, Research and Reflections: Responses to my Respondents: Topics in Classical Indian Philosophy. **Part IV: Developments and Attitudes in Neo-Hinduism** – A. O. Fort, Jīvanmukti and Social Service in Advaita and Neo-Vedānta; S. Elkman, Religious Plurality and Swami Vivekananda. **Part V: Indian Religion, Past and Present** – M. Hara, A Note on dharmasya sūkṣmā gatiḥ; A. Wezler, The Story of Aṇī-Māṇḍavya as told in the Mahābhārata: Its significance for Indian Legal and Religious History; Y. Grinshpon, Experience and Observation in Traditional and Modern Pātañjala Yoga; F. J. Korom, Language Belief and Experience in Bengali Folk Religion; W. Halbfass, Research and Reflection: Responses to my Respondents. Developments and Attitudes in Neo-Hinduism; Indian religion, Past and Present.

VOLUME 60 (1998)

MARX'S THEORIES TODAY
(Edited by Ryszard Panasiuk and Leszek Nowak)

R. Panasiuk, Introduction; **Part I: On Dialectics and Ontology** – S.-E. Liedman, Engels and the Laws of Dialectics; R. Panasiuk, On Dialectics in Marxism Again; R. Albritton, The Unique Ontology of Capital; R. Washner, It is not Singularity that Governs the Nature of Things. The Principle of Isolated Individual and Its Negation in Marx's Doctoral Thesis; **Part II: On Historical Materialism and Social Theories** – Z. Cackowski, The Continuing Validity of the Marxian Thought; P. Casal, From Unilineal to Universal Historical Materialism; I. Hunt, A Dialectical Interpretation and Resurrection of Historical Materialism; W. Krajewski, The Triumph of Historical Materialism; L. Nowak, The Adaptive Interpretation of Historical Materialism: A Survey. On a Contribution to Polish Analytical Marxism; M. Kozłowski, A New Look at Capitalism. Between the Decommunisation of Marx's and the Defeudalisation of Hegel's Visions of Capitalism; F. Moseley, An Empirical Appraisal of Marx's Economic Theory; Ch. Bertram and A. Carling, Stumbling into Revolution. Analytical Marxism, Rationality and Collective Action; K. Graham, Collectives, Classes and Revolutionary Potential in Marx; U. Himmelstrand, How to Become and Remain a Marxicising Sociologist. An Egocentric Report; **Part III: On Axiology and the Socialist Project** – P. Kamolnick, Visions of Social Justice in Marx: An Assessment of Recent Debates in Normative Philosophy; W. Schmied-Kowarzik, Karl Marx as a Philosopher of Human Emancipation; H. J. Sandkühler, Marx – Welche Rationalität? Epistemische Kontexte und Widersprüche der Transformation von Philosophie in Wissenschaft; J. Kmita, The Production of "Rational Reality" and the "Systemic Coercion"; J. Bidet, Metastructure and Socialism; T. Andreani, Vers une Issue Socialiste à la Crise du Capitalisme; W. Becker, The Bankruptsy of Marxism. About the Historical End of a World Philosophy; D. Aleksandrowicz, Myth, Eschatology and Social Reality in the Light of Marxist Philosophy.

VOLUME 61 (1997)

REPRESENTATIONS OF SCIENTIFIC REALITY
CONTEMPORARY FORMAL PHILOSOPY OF SCIENCE IN SPAIN
(Edited by Andoni Ibarra and Thomas Mormann)

Introduction – A. Ibarra, T. Mormann, *The Long and Winding Road to Philosophy of Science in Spain*. **Part 1: Representation and Measurement** – A. Ibarra, T. Mormann, *Theories as Representations*; J. Garrido Garrido, T*he Justification of Measurement*; O. Fernandez Prat, D. Quesada, *Spatial Representations and Their Physical Content*; J.A. Díez Calzada, *The Theory-Net of Interval Measurement Theory*. **Part 2: Truth, Rationality, and Method** – J.C. García-Bermejo Ochoa, *Realism and Truth Approximation in Economic Theory*; W.J.Gonzáles, *Rationality in Economics and Scientific Predictions*; J.P. Zamora Bonilla, *An Invitation to Methodonomics*. **Part 3: Logics, Semantics and Theoretical Structures** – J.L.Falguera, *A Basis for a Formal Semantics of Linguistic Formulations of Science*; A. Sobrino, E. Trillas, *Can Fuzzy Logic Help to Pose Some Problems in the Philosophy of Science?*; J. de Lorenzo, *Demonstrative Ways in Mathematical Doing*; M. Casanueva, *Genetics and Fertilization: A Good Marriage*; C.U. Moulines, *The Concept of Universe from a Metatheoretical Point of View*.

VOLUME 62 (1998)

IN THE WORLD OF SIGNS
(Edited by Jacek Juliusz Jadacki and Witold Strawiński)

Introduction. *How to Move in the World of Signs*. **Part I: Theoretical Semiotics** – A. Bogusławski, *Conditionals and Egocentric Mental Predicates*; W. Buszkowski, *On Families of Languages Generated by Categorial Grammar*; K.G. Havas, *Changing the World – Changing the Meaning. On the Meanings of the "Principle of Non-Contradiction"*; H. Hiż, *On Translation*; S. Marcus, *Imprecision, Between Variety and Uniformity: The Conjugate Pairs*; J. Peregrin, P. Sgall, *Meaning and "Propositional Attitudes"*; O.A. Wojtasiewicz, *Some Applications of Metric Space in Theoretical Linguistic*. **Part II: Methodology** – E. Agazzi, *Rationality and Certitude*; I. Bellert, *Human Reasoning and Artifical Intelligence. When Are Computers Dumb in Simulating Human Reasoning?*; T. Bigaj, *Analyticity and Existence in Mathematics*; G.B. Keene, *Taking up the Logical Slack in Natural Languages*; A. Kertész, *Interdisciplinarity and the Myth of Exactness*; J. Srzednicki, *Norm as the Basis of Form*; J.S. Stepanov, *"Cause" in the Light of Semiotics*; J.A. Wojciechowski, *The Development of Knowledge as a Moral Problem*. **Part III: History of Semiotics** – E. Albrecht, *Philosophy of Language, Logic and Semiotics*; G. Deledalle, *A Philosopher's Reply to Questions Concerning Peirce's Theory of Signs*; J. Deledalle-Rhodes, *The Transposition of Linguistic Sign in Peirce's Contributions to "The Nation"*; R. E. Innis, *From Feeling to Mind: A Note on Langer's Notion of Symbolic Projection*; R. Kevelson, *Peirce's Semiotics as Complex Inquiry: Conflicting Methods*; J. Kopania, *The Cartesian Alternative of Philosophical Thinking*; Xiankun Li, *Why Gonsung Long (Kungsun Lung) Said "White Horse Is Not Horse"*; L. Melazzo, *A Report on an Ancient Discussion*; Ding-fu Ni, *Semantic Thoughts of J. Stuart Mill and Chinese Characters*; I. Portis-Winner, *Lotman's Semiosphere: Some Comments;* J. Réthoré, *Another Close Look at the Interpretant*; E. Stankiewicz, *The Semiotic Turn of Breal's "Semantique"*; **Part IV: Linguistic** – K. Heger, *Passive and Other Voices Seen from an Onomasiological Point of View*; L.I. Komlószi, *The Semiotic System of Events, Intrinsic Temporal and Deictic Tense Relations in Natural Language. On the Conceptualization of Temporal Schemata*; W. M. Osadnik, E. Horodecka, *Polysystem Theory, Translation Theory and Semiotics*; A. Wierzbicka, *THINK – a Universal Human Concept and a Conceptual Primitive*. **Part V: Cultural Semiotics** – G. Bettetini,

Communication as a Videogame; W. Krysiński, Joyce, Models, and Semiotics of Passions; H. Książek-Konicka, "Visual Thinking" in the Poetry of Julian Przyboś and Miron Białoszewski; U. Niklas, The Space of Metaphor; M. C. Ruta, Captivity as Event and Metaphor in Some of Cervantes' Writings; E. Tarasti, From Aestetics to Ethics: Semiotics Observations on the Moral Aspects of Art, Especially Music; L. Tondl, Is It Justified to Consider the Semiotics of Technological Artefacts?; V. Voigt, Poland, Finland and Hungary (A Tuatara's View); T.G. Winner, Czech Poetism: A New View of Poetics Language; J. Wrede, Metaphorical Imagery – Ambiguity, Explicitness and Life. **Part VI: Psycho-Socio-Semiotics** – E.M. Barth, A Case Study in Empirical Logic and Semiotics. Fundamental Modes of Thought of Nazi Politician Vidkun Quisling, Based on Unpublished Drafts and Notebooks; P. Bouissac, Why Do Memmes Die? W. Kalaga, Threshold of Signification, A. Podgórecki, Do Social Sciences Evaporate?

VOLUME 63 (1998)

IDEALIZATION IX: IDEALIZATION IN CONTEMPORARY PHYSICS
(Edited by Niall Shanks)

N. Shanks, *Introduction*; M. Bishop, *An Epistemological Role for Thought Experiments*; I. Nowak & L. Nowak, *"Models" and "Experiments" as Homogeneous Families of Notions*; S. French & J. Ladyman, *A Semantic Perspective on Idealization in Quantum Mechanics*; Ch. Liu, *Decoherence and Idealization in Quantum Measurement*; S. Hartmann, *Idealization in Quantum Field Theory*; R. F. Hendry, *Models and Approximations in Quantum Chemistry*; D. Howard, *Astride the Divided Line: Platonism, Empiricism, and Einstein's Epistemological Opportunism*; G. Gale, *Idealization in Cosmology: A Case Study*; A. Maidens, *Idealization, Heuristics and the Principle of Equivalence*; A. Rueger & D. Sharp, *Idealization and Stability:A Perspective from Nonlinear Dynamics*; D. L. Holt & R. G. Holt, *Towards a Very Old Account of Rationality in Experiment: Occult Practices in Chaotic Sonoluminescence*.

VOLUME 64 (1998)

PRAGMATIC IDEALISM. CRITICAL ESSAYS ON NICHOLAS RESCHER'S SYSTEM
OF PRAGMATIC IDEALISM
(Edited by Axel Wüstehube and Michael Quante)

Introduction: A. Wüstehube, *Is Systematic Philosophy still Possible?*; T. Airaksinen, *Moral Facts and Objective Values*; L. Rodríguez Duplá, *Values and Reasons*; G. Gale, *Rescher on Evolution and the Intelligibility of Nature*; J Kekes, *The Nature of Philosophy*; P. Machamer, *Individual and Other-Person Morality: A Plea for an Emotional Response to Ethical Problems*; D. Marconi, *Opus Incertum*; M. Marsonet, *Scientific Realism and Pragmatic Idealism*; R. Martin, *Was Spinoza a Person?*; H. Pape, *Brute Facts, Real Minds and the Postulation of Reality: Resher on Idealism and the Ontological Neutrality of Experience*; J. C. Pitt, *Doing Philosophy: Rescher's Normative Methodology*; L. B. Puntel, *Is Truth "Ideal Coherence"?*; M. Quante, *Understanding Conceptual Schemes: Rescher's Quarrel with Davidson*; A. Siitonen, *The Ontology of Facts and Values*; M. Willaschek, *Skeptical Challenge and the Burden of Proof: On Rescher's Critique of Skepticism*; N. Rescher, *Responses*.

VOLUME 65 (1999)

THE TOTALITARIAN PARADIGM AFTER THE END OF COMMUNISM.
TOWARDS A THEORETICAL REASSESSMENT.
(Edited by Achim Siegel)

A. Siegel, **Introduction**: *The Changing Fortunes of the Totalitarian Paradigm in Communist Studies*. **On Recent Controversies Over The Concept Of Totalitarianism** – K. von Beyme, *The Concept of Totalitarianism – A Reassessment after the End of Communist Rule*; K. Mueller, *East European Studies, Neo-Totalitarianism and Social Science Theory*; L. Nowak, *A Conception that is Supposed to Correspond to the Totalitarian Approach to Realsocialism*; E. Nolte, *The Three Versions of the Theory of Totalitarianism and the Significance of the Historical-Genetic Version*; E. Jesse, *The Two Major Instances of Totalitarianism: Observations on the Interconnection between Soviet Communism and National Socialism*. **Classic Concept Of Totalitarianism: Reassessment And Reinterpretation** – J.P. Arnason, *Totalitarianism and Modernity: Franz Borkenau's "Totalitarian Enemy" as a Source of Sociological Theorizing on Totalitarianism*; A. Sölner, *Sigmund Neumann's "Permanent Revolution": A Forgotten Classic of Comparative Research into Modern Dictatorship*; F. Pohlmann, *The "Seeds of Destruction" in Totalitarian Systems. An Interpretation of the Unity in Hannah Arendt's Political Philosophy*; W.J. Patzelt, *Reality Construction under Totalitarianism: An Ethnomethodological Elaboration of Martin Draht's Concept of Totalitarianism*; A. Siegel, *Carl Joachim Friedrich's Concept of Totalitarianism: A Reinterpretation*; M.R. Thompson, *Neither Totalitarian nor Authoritarian: Post-Totalitarianism in Eastern Europe*.

VOLUME 66 (1999)

Leon Gumański

TO BE OR NOT TO BE? IS THAT THE QUESTION?
AND OTHER STUDIES IN ONTOLOGY, EPISTEMOLOGY AND LOGIC

Preface; *The Elements of a Judgment and Existence*; *Traditional Logic and Existential Presuppositions*; *To Be Or Not To Be? Is That The Question?*; *Some Remarks On Definitions*; *Logische und semantische Antinomien*; *A New Approach to Realistic Epistemology*; *Ausgewählte Probleme der deontischen Logik*; *An Attempt at the Definition of the Biological Concept of Homology*; *Similarity*.

VOLUME 67 (1999)

Kazimierz Twardowski

ON ACTIONS, PRODUCTS AND OTHER TOPICS IN PHILOSOPHY
(Edited by Johannes Brandl and Jan Woleński)

Introduction; *Translator's Note*; *Self-Portrait (1926/91)*; *Biographical Notes*. **I. On Mind, Psychology, and Language:** *Psychology vs. Physiology and Philosophy (1897)*; *On the Classification of Mental Phenomena (1898)*; *The Essence of Concepts (1903/24)*; *On Idio- and Allogenetic Theories of Judgment (1907)*; *Actions and Products (1912)*; *The Humanities and Psychology (1912/76)*; *On the Logic of Adjectives (1923/27)*. **II. On Truth and Knowledge:** *On So-Called Relative Truths (1900)*; *A priori, or Rational (Deductive) Sciences* and *a posteriori, or*

Empirical (Inductive) Sciences (1923); Theory of Knowledge. A Lecture Course (1925/75). **III. On Philosophy:** *Franz Brentano and the History of Philosophy (1895); The Historical Conception of Philosophy (1912); On Clear and Unclear Philosophical Style (1920); Symbolomania and Pragmatophobia (1921); Address at the 25th Anniversary Session of the Polish Philosophical Society (1929/31); On the Dignity of the University (1933).* **Bibliography.**

VOLUME 68 (2000)

Tadeusz Czeżowski

KNOWLEDGE, SCIENCE AND VALUES. A PROGRAM FOR SCIENTIFIC PHILOSOPHY
(Edited by Leon Gumański)

L. Gumański, *Introduction*. **Part 1: Logic, Methodology and Theory of Science** – *Some Ancient Problems in Modern Form; On the Humanities; On the Method of Analytical Description; On the Problem of Induction; On Discussion and Discussing; On Logical Culture; On Hypotheses; On the Classification of Sentences and Propositional Functions; Proof; On Traditional Distinctions between Definitions; Deictic Definitions; Induction and Reasoning by Analogy; The Classification of Reasonings and its Consequences in the Theory of Science; On the so-called Direct Justification and Self-evidence; On the Unity of Science; Scientific Description.* **Part 2: The World of Human Values and Norms** – *On Happiness; How to Understand "the Meaning of Life"?; How to Construct the Logic of Goods?; The Meaning and the Value of Life; Conflicts in Ethics; What are Values?; Ethics, Psychology and Logic.* **Part 3: Reality–Knowledge–World** – *Three Attitudes towards the World; On Two Views of the World; A Few Remarks on Rationalism and Empiricism; Identity and the Individual in Its Persistence; Sensory Cognition and Reality; Philosophy at the Crossroads; On Individuals and Existence.* J.J. Jadacki, *Trouble with Ontic Categories or Some Remarks on Tadeusz Czeżowski's Philosophical Views;* W. Mincer, *The Bibliography of Tadeusz Czeżowski.*

VOLUME 69 (2000)

Izabella Nowakowa, Leszek Nowak

THE RICHNESS OF IDEALIZATION

Preface; **Introduction** – *Science as a Caricature of Reality.* **Part I: THREE METHODOLOGICAL REVOLUTIONS** – *1. The First Idealizational Revolution. Galileo's-Newton's Model of Free Fall; 2. The Second Idealizational Revolution. Darwin's Theory of Natural Selection; 3. The Third Idealizational Revolution. Marx's Theory of Reproduction.* **Part II: THE METHOD OF IDEALIZATION** – *4. The Idealizational Approach to Science: A New Survey; 5. On the Concept of Dialectical Correspondence; 6. On Inner Concretization. A Certain Generalization of the Notions of Concretization and Dialectical Correspondence; 7. Concretization in Qualitative Contexts; 8. Law and Theory: Some Expansions; 9. On Multiplicity of Idealization.* **Part III: EXPLANATIONS AND APPLICATIONS** – *10. The Ontology of the Idealizational Theory; 11. Creativity in Theory-building; 12. Discovery and Correspondence; 13. The Problem of Induction. Toward an Idealizational Paraphrase; 14. "Model(s) and "Experiment(s). An Analysis of Two Homogeneous Families of Notions; 15. On Theories, Half-Theories, One-fourth-Theories, etc.; 16. On Explanation and Its Fallacies; 17. Testability and Fuzziness; 18. Constructing the Notion; 19. On Economic Modeling; 20. Ajdukiewicz, Chomsky and the Status of the Theory of Natural Language; 21. Historical Narration; 22. The Rational Legislator.* **Part IV: TRUTH AND IDEALIZATION** – *23. A Notion of Truth for Idealization; 24. "Truth is a System": An Explication; 25. On the Concept of Adequacy of Laws; 26. Approximation and the Two Ideas of Truth; 27. On the Historicity of Knowledge.* **Part V: A GENERALIZATION OF IDEALIZATION** – *28. Abstracts Are Not Our*

Constructs. The Mental Constructs Are Abstracts; 29. Metaphors and Deformation; 30. Realism, Supra-Realism and Idealization. **REFERENCES** – *I. Writings on Idealization*; *II. Other Writings*.

VOLUME 70 (2000)

QUINE. NATURALIZED EPISTEMOLOGY, PERCEPTUAL KNOWLEDGE AND ONTOLOGY
(Edited by Lieven Decock and Leon Horsten)

Introduction. **Naturalized Epistemology** – T. Derksen, *Naturalistic Epistemology, Murder and Suicide? But what about the Promises!*; Ch. Hookway, *Naturalism and Rationality*; M. Gosselin, *Quine's Hypothetical Theory of Language Learning. A Comparison of Different Conceptual Schemes and Their Logic*. **The Nature of Perceptual Knowledge** – J. van Brakel, *Quine and Innate Similarity Spaces*; D. Koppelberg, *Quine and Davidson on the Structure of Empirical Knowledge*; E. Picardi, *Empathy and Charity*. **Ontology** – S. Laugier, *Quine: Indeterminacy, 'Robust Realism', and Truth*; R. Vergauwen, *Quine and Putnam on Conceptual Relativity and Reference: Theft or Honest Toil?*; I. Douven, *Empiricist Semantics and Indeterminism of Reference*; L. Decock, *Domestic Ontology and Ideology*; P. Gochet, *Canonical Notation, Predication and Ontology*.

VOLUME 71 (2000)

LOGIC, PROBABILITY AND SCIENCE
(Edited by Niall Shanks)

N. Shanks & R.R. Gardner, *Introduction*; C. Morgan, *Canonical Models and Probabilistic Semantics (Commentary by François Lepage; Reply by Morgan)*; F. Lepage, *A Many-Valued Probabilistic Logic (Commentary by Charles Morgan; Reply by Lepage)*; P. Rawling, *The Exchange Paradox, Finite Additivity, and the Principle of Dominance (Commentary by Robert R. Gardner; Reply by Rawling)*; S. Vineberg, *The Logical Status of Conditional and its Role in Confirmation (Commentary by Piers Rawling; Reply by Vineberg)*; D. Mayo, *Science, Error Statistics, and Arguing from Error (Commentary by Susan Vineberg; Reply by Mayo)*; M.N. Lance, *The Best is the Enemy of the Good: Bayesian Epistemology as a Case Study in Unhelpful Idealization (Commentary by Leszek Nowak; Reply by Lance)*; R.B. Gardner & M.C. Wooten, *An Application of Bayes' Theorem to Population Genetics (Commentary by Lynne Seymour; Reply by Gardner and Wooten)*; P.D. Johnson, Jr., *Another Look at Group Selection (Commentary by Niall Shanks; Reply by Johnson)*; C.F. Juhl, *Teleosemantics, Kripkenstein and Paradox (Commentary by Daniel Bonevac; Reply by Juhl)*; D. Bonevac, *Constitutive and Epistemic Principles (Commentary by Mark Lance; Reply by Bonevac)*; O. Bueno, *Empiricism, Mathematical Truth and Mathematical Knowledge (Commentary by Chuang Liu; Reply by Bueno)*; Ch. Liu, *Coins and Electrons: A Unified Understanding of Probabilistic Objects (Commentary by Steven French; Reply by Liu)*; A. Maidens, *Are Electrons Vague Objects? (Commentary by David Over; Reply by Maidens)*.

VOLUME 72 (2000)

ON COMPARING AND EVALUATING SCIENTIFIC THEORIES
(Edited by Adam Jonkisz and Leon Koj)

L. Koj, *Preface*; L. Koj, *Methodology and Values*; L. Koj, *Science as System*; A. Grobler, *Explanation and Epistemic Virtue*; P. Giza, *"Intelligent" Computer System and Theory Comparison*; H. Ogryzko-Wiewiórowski, *Methods of Social Choice of Scientific Theories*; K. Jodkowski, *Is the*

Causal Theory of Reference a Remedy for Ontological Incommensurability?; W. Balzer, On Approximative Reduction; C. Ulises Moulines, Is There Genuinely Scientific Progress?; A. Jonkisz, On Relative Progress in Science.

VOLUME 73 (2000)

THE RATIONALITY OF THEISM
(Edited by Adolfo García de la Sienra)

Preface; A. García de la Sienra, *Introduction*; W. Redmond, *A Logic of Religious Faith and Development*; J.M. Bocheński, O.P., *The Five Ways*; M. Beuchot, *Saint Thomas' Third Way: Possibility and Necessity, Essence and Existence*; R. Swinburne, *Cosmological and Teleological Arguments*; A. García de la Sienra, *The Ontological Argument*; A. García de la Sienra, *Pascal's Wager*; A. García de la Sienra & A. Araujo, *The Experience of God in Moral Obligation*; A. Plantinga, *The onus probandi of Theism*; R. A. Clouser, *Is God Eternal?*; A. Tomasini, *The Presence and Absence of God*; L. Nowak, *On the Common Structure of Science and Religion*.

VOLUME 74 (2000)

POLISH PHILOSOPHERS OF SCIENCE AND NATURE IN THE 20th CENTURY
(Edited by Władysław Krajewski)

W. Krajewski, *Introduction*; **I. Philosophers** J. Woleński, *Tadeusz Kotarbiński – Reism and Science*; A. Jedynak, *Kazimierz Ajdukiewicz – From Radical Conventionalism to Radical Empiricism*; L. Gumański, *Tadeusz Czeżowski – Our Knowledge though Uncertain is Probable*; M. Tałasiewicz, *Jan Łukasiewicz – The Quest for the Form of Science*; I. Szumilewicz-Lachman, *Zygmunt Zawirski – The Notion of Time*; A. Jedynak, *Janina Hosiasson-Lindenbaumowa – The Logic of Induction*; T. Bigaj, *Joachim Metallmann – Causality, Determinism and Science*; J. Woleński, *Izydora Dąmbska – Between Conventionalism and Realism*; A. Koterski, *Henryk Mehlberg – The Reach of Science*; I. Nowakowa, *Adam Wiegner's Nonstandard Empiricism*; W. Krajewski, *Janina Kotarbińska – Logical Methodology and Semantic*; M. Tałasiewicz, *Maria Kokoszyńska-Lutmanowa – Methodology, Semantics, Truth*; T. Batóg, *Seweryna Łuszczewska-Romahnowa – Logic and Philosophy of Science*; M. Omyła, *Roman Suszko – From Diachronic Logic to Non-Fregean Logic*; J. Woleński, *Klemens Szaniawski – Rationality and Statistical Methods*; A. Jedynak, *Halina Mortimer – The Logic of Induction*; K. Zamiara, *Jerzy Giedymin – From the Logic of Science to the Theoretical History of Science*; J. M. Dołęga, *B. J. Gawecki – A Philosopher of the Natural Sciences*; A. Bronk, *Stanisław Kamiński – A Philosopher and Historian of Science*; Z. Hajduk, *Stanisław Mazierski – A Theorist of Natural Lawfulness*. **II. Scientists** W. Krajewski, *Marian Smoluchowski – A Forerunner of the Chaos Theory*; A. Motycka, *Czesław Białobrzeski's Conception of Science*; M Tempczyk, *Leopold Infeld – The Problem of Matter and Field*; M. Czarnocka, *Grzegorz Białkowski – Science and Its Subject*; J. Płazowski, *Jerzy Rayski – Physicist and Philosopher of Physics*; J. Misiek, *Zygmunt Chyliński – Physics, Philosophy, Music*; W. Sady, *Ludwik Fleck – Thought Collectives and Thought Styles*. **II. General Surveys** K. Ajdukiewicz, *Logicist Anti-Irrationalism in Poland*; K. Szaniawski, *Philosophy of Science in Poland*; I. Nowakowa, *Main Orientations in the Contemporary Polish Philosophy of Science*.

VOLUME 75 (2000)

STRUCTURALIST KNOWLEDGE REPRESENTATION
PARADIGMATIC EXAMPLES
(Edited by Wolfgang Balzer, Joseph D. Sneed and C. Ulises Moulines)

W. Balzer, U. Moulines, *Introduction*; J. A Diez Calzada, *Structuralist Analysis of Theories of Fundamental Measurement*; A. García de la Sienra, P. Reyes, *The Theory of Finite Games in Extensive Form*; H. J. Burscheid, H. Struve, *The Theory of Stochastic Fairness – its Historical Development, Formulation and Justification*; W. Balzer, R. Mattessich, *Formalizing the Basis of Accounting*; W. Diederich, *A Reconstruction of Marxian Economics*; B. Hamminga, W. Balzer, *The Basic Structure of Neoclassical General Equilibrium Theory*; K. Manhart, *Balance Theories: Two Reconstructions and the Problem of Intended Applications*; R. Westermann, *Festinger's Theory of Cognitive Dissonance: A Structuralist Theory-Net*; R. Reisenzein, *Wundt's Three-Dimensional Theory of Emotion*; P. Lorenzano, *Classical Genetics and the Theory-Net of Genetics*; H. Hettema, T.A.F. Kuipers, *The Formalisation of the Periodic Table*; C. Ulises Moulines, *The Basic Core of Simple Equilibrium Thermodynamics*; T. Bartelborth, *An Axiomatization of Classical Electrodynamics*; *Author's Index*; *Subject Index*.

VOLUME 76 (2000)

EVENTS, FACTS AND THINGS
(Edited by J. Faye, U. Scheffler and Max Urchs)

J. Faye, U. Scheffler and M. Urchs, *Philosophical Entities: An Introduction*; J. Faye, *Facts as Truth Makers*; J. Persson, *Examining the Facts*; U. Scheffler and Y. Shramko, *The Logical Ontology of Negative Facts: On What is Not*; W. Stelzner, *The Impact of Negative Fact for the Imaginary Logic of N.A. Vasil'ev*; B. Rode Meinertsen, *Events, Facts and Causation*; U. Meixner, *Essential Conception of Events*; P. Stekeler-Weithofer, *Questions and Theses Concerning (Mental) Events and Causation*; E. Tegtmeier, *Events as Facts*; M. Urchs, *Events of Episystems*; J. Seibt, *The Dynamic Constitution of Things*; K. Trettin, *Tropes and Things*; D. von Wachter, *A World of Fields*; A. Bartels, *Quantum Field Theory: A Case for Event Ontologies?*; M. Dorato, *Facts, Events, Things and the Ontology of Physics*; M. Kuhlmann, *Processes as Objects of Quantum Field Theory: Consequences for the Interpretation of QFT*; J. Paśniczek, *Objects vs. Situations*; A. Siitonen, *Effects or Consequences of Action*; P. Needham, *Hot Stuff*; L. Bo Gundersen, *Goodman's Gruesome Modal Fallacy*; Th. Mormann, *Topological Representations of Mereological Systems*; U. Scheffer & M. Winkler, *Tools*.

VOLUME 77 (2003)

KNOWLEDGE AND FAITH
(Edited by J. J. Jadacki and Kordula Świętorzecka)

Editorial Note; J.J. Jadacki and K. Świętorzecka, *On Jan Salamucha's Life and Work*. **Part I. Logic and Theology** - *On the «Mechanization» of Thinking*; *On the Possibilities of a Strict formalization of the Domain of Analogical Notion*; *The Proof ex motu for the Existence of God. Logical Analysis of St. Thomas Aquinas' Arguments*. **Part II. History of Logic** - *The Propositional Logic in William Ockham*; *The Appearance of Antinomial Problems within Medieval Logic*; *From the History of Medieval Nominalism*. **Part III. Metaphysics and Ethics** - *From the History of One Word*

("Essence"); *The Structure of the Material World*; *Faith*; *The Relativity and Absoluteness of Catholic Ethics*; *The Problem of Force in Social Life*; *A Vision of Love.* **Comments and Discussions** – J. M. Bocheński, *J. Salamucha The Notion of Deduction in Aristotle and St. Thomas Aquinas*; J. M. Bocheński, *J. Salamucha, "The Proof ex motu for the Existence of God. Logical Analysis of St. Thomas Aquinas' Arguments"*; J.F. Drewnowski, *J. Salamucha, "The Proof ex motu for the Existence of God. Logical Analysis of St. Thomas Aquinas' Arguments"*; H. Scholz, *The Mathematical Logic and the Metaphysics*; H. Scholz, *J. Salamucha "The Appearance of Antinomial Problems within Medieval Logic*; J. Bendiek, *On the Logical Structure of Proofs for the Existence of God*; K. Policki, *On the formalization of the Proof ex motu for Existence of God*; J. Herbut, *Jan Salamucha's Efforts Towards the Methodological Modernization of Theistic Metaphysics*; F. Vandamme, *Logic, Pragmatics and Religion*; E. Nieznański, *Logical Analysis of Thomism. The Polish Programme that Originated in 1930s.* **Bibliography.**

VOLUME 78 (2003)

Jacek Juliusz Jadacki
FROM THE VIEWPOINT OF THE LVOV-WARSAW SCHOOL

Preface; *Introduction: Philosophy and Precision.* **Part I. Being and Essence** - *On What Seems Not to Be*; *On the Controversy about Universals*; *On Forms of Objects*; *On Good, Necessity, and Sufficiency; On Essence.* **Part II. Truth and Nonsense** - *On the Definition and Criteria of Truth*; *On Linguistic Categories*; *On Questions*; *On Semiotic Function of Conditionals*; *On Nonsense.* **Part III. Understanding and Silence** - *On Misunderstandings about Understanding*; *On Definition, Explication, and Paraphrase*; *On Reasoning*; *On Simplicity*; *On Silence*; *Conclusion: Science and Creation*; *References*; *Index of Names*; *Index of Subjects*.

VOLUME 79 (2003)

Jan Such
MULTIFORMITY OF SCIENCE

Preface; **Part One: Contributions to the Idealizational Theory of Science** - *Idealization and Concretization in the Natural Sciences*; *Plato's Philosophy and the Essence of the Scientific Method*; *The Idealizational Theory of Science and Physics of the Microworld*; *The Idealizational Conception of Science and the Structure of the Law of Universal Gravitation.* **Part Two: The Nature of Scientific Cognition** - *On Kinds of Knowledge*; *Scientific and Everyday Knowledge*; *Universality of Scientific Laws*; *The Role of Theory in Physical Sciences*; *The Leibniz-Einstein Principle of the Minimization of Premises*; *On Kinds of Interpretation Procedures in Science*; *The Problem of the Rationality of Science*; *Principles and Kinds of Scientific Rationality*; *The Rationality of Science and Limitations of Scientific Methods*; *What has Changed in the Philosophical View of Science?* **Part Three: The Development of Science** - *Types of Determination vs. the Development of Science in Historical Epistemology*; *Relation of Correspondence and Logical Consequence*; *Experiment and Science*; *Hegel's Historicism and Contemporary Conceptions of the Development of Science.* **Part Four: Problems of Verification of Knowledge** - *Are there Definitively Falsifying Procedures in Science?*; *On the so-called Complementary Experiments. The Example of Fizeau's and Michelson's Experiments*; *Testability of Knowledge at Various Levels of its Development*; *Atomistic Empiricism or Holistic Empiricism?*; *The Notion of an ad hoc Hypothesis.* **Part Five: Philosophy of Physics and Cosmology** - *On the Peculiarity of Physics and its Divisions*; *Models of*

Rationality in Physics; *Transcendental Philosophy and the Physics of the Microworld*; *The Universality of Scientific Laws and the Evolution of the Universe*; *Aspects of the Problem of the Spatiotemporal Infinity of the World*; *The Peculiar Status of Cosmology as a Science*; *The Origin of the Universe and Contemporary Cosmology and Philosophy*; *Newton's Fields of Study and Methodological Principles*; *Hegel and Contemporary Natural Sciences*. **Part Six: Some Problems of the Theory of Reality** - *Unity or Variety of Nature?*; *The Place of Processes in the Structure of Reality*; *Science and Technology and the Current Trends in the Development of Culture*; *Hegel's Category of Totality and His Concept of State*; *The Being of Beings in Heidegger's* Sein und Zeit.

VOLUME 80 (2003)

ANALYTIC PHILOSOPHY IN FINLAND
(Edited by L. Haaparanta and I. Niiniluoto)

Preface; **Part I: The Background** – I. Niiniluoto, *Philosophy in Finland – the Cultural Setting*; E. Westermarck, *Normative and Psychological Ethics*; E. Kaila, *On Scientific and Metaphysical Explanation of Reality*; E. Kaila, *On the Method of Philosophy. Extracts from a Statement to the Section of History and Philology at the University of Helsinki*; G. H. von Wright, *What Philosophy is for Me*; J. Hintikka, *Contemporary Philosophy and the Problem of Truth*; J. Woleński, *Formal Metaphilosophy in Finland*. **Part II: Logic and Philosophy of Language** – A. Korhonen, *Logical Semantics – Truth and Analyticity*; V. Rantala, *Possible Worlds*; T. Aho, *Propositional Attitudes*; V. Svoboda, *Forms of Norms and Validity*. **Part III: Philosophy of Science** – R. Festa, *Induction, Probability, and Bayesian Epistemology*; M. Sintonen, *Realism and Growth of Knowledge – Philosophy of Science since Eino Kaila*; M. Kusch, *Explanation and Understanding: The Debate over von Wright's Philosophy of Action Revisited*. **Part IV: History of Philosophy** – M. Yrjönsuuri, *Finnish Studies in the History of Ancient and Mediaeval Philosophy*; O. Koistinen, *Finnish Studies in Seventeenth-Century Rationalism*; J. Schulte, *The Reception of Wittgenstein's Philosophy in Finland*. **Part V: Ethics and Social Philosophy** – M. Salmela, *Analytic Moral Philosophy in Finland*; M. Häyry, *Applied Ethics in Finland*; E. Lagerspetz, *Analytical Philosophy of Institutions*. **Part VI: Interfaces of Analytical Philosophy** – L. Haaparanta, *Finnish Studies in Phenomenology and Phenomenological Studies in Finland: Interfaces of Analytic Philosophy and Phenomenology*; S. Pihlström, *Pragmatistic Influences in Twentieth Century Finnish Philosophy: From Pre-analytic to Post-analytic Thought*; T. Wallgren, *Critical Theory*.

VOLUME 81 (2004)

Evandro Agazzi
RIGHT, WRONG, AND SCIENCE.
THE ETHICAL DIMENSIONS OF THE TECHNO-SCIENTIFIC ENTERPRISE
(Edited by C. Dilworth)

Editor's Introduction; **Evandro Agazzi: RIGHT, WRONG AND SCIENCE. THE ETHICAL DIMENSIONS OF THE TECHNO-SCIENTIFIC ENTERPRISE.** *Preface*; *Introduction*. **Part I: The World of Science and Technology** – 1. *What is Science?*; 2. *Science and Society*; 3. *Is Science Neutral?*; 4. *Science, Technique and Technology*; 5. *The Techno-Scientific Ideology*; 6. *The Techno-Scientific System*. **Part II: Encounter with the Ethical Dimension** – 7. *Norms and Values in Human Action*; 8. *The Role of Values in the Human Sciences*; 9. *Theoretical Rationality and Practical Rationality*; 10. *The Moral Judgment of Science and Technology*; 11. *The Problem of Risk*; 12. *The Responsibility of*

Science in a Systems-Theoretic Approach; 13. The Ethical Dimension; 14. An Ethics for Science and Technology. **COMMENTARIES.** J. González, The Challenge of the Freedom and Responsibility of Science; F. Miró Quesada, The Full Dimensions of Rationality; V. Lektorsky, Science, Society and Ethics; M. Bunge, The Centrality of Truth; D.P. Chattopadhyaya, Some Reflections on Agazzi's Philosophy of Science; E. Berti, Practical Rationality and Technical Rationality; B. Yudin, Knowledge, Activity and Ethical Judgement; G. Hottois, Techno-Sciences and Ethics; P.T. Durbin, The Alleged Error of Social Epistemology; J.Boros, Evandro Agazzi's Ethical Pragmatism of Science; H. Lenk, A Scheme-Interpretationist Sophistication of Agazzi's Systems Approach to Science and Ethics; J. Ladrière, A Note on the Construction of Norms; L. Fleischhacker, The Non-Linearity of the Development of Technology and the Techno-Scientific System; J. Echeverría, Some Questions from the Point of View of an Axiology of Science; E. Agazzi, Replies to the Commentaries.

VOLUME 82 (2004)

HISTORICAL STUDIES ON ABSTRACTION AND IDEALIZATION
(Edited by F. Coniglione, R. Poli and R. Rollinger)

Preface; **General Perspectives** – I. Angelelli, Adventures of Abstraction; A. Bäck, What is Being qua Being?; F. Coniglione, Between Abstraction and Idealization: Scientific Practice and Philosophical Awareness. **Case Studies** – D.P. Henry, Anselm on Abstracts; L. Spruit, Agent Intellect and Phantasms. On the Preliminaries of Peripatetic Abstraction; R. D. Rollinger, Hermann Lotze on Abstraction and Platonic Ideas; R. Poli, W.E. Johnson's Determinable-Determinate Opposition and his Theory of Abstraction; M. van der Schaar, The Red of a Rose. On the Significance of Stout's Category of Abstract Particulars; C. Ortiz Hill, Abstraction and Idealization in Edmund Husserl and Georg Cantor prior to 1895; G. E. Rosado Haddock, Idealization in Mathematics: Husserl and Beyond; A. Klawiter, Why Did Husserl not Become the Galileo of the Science of Consciousness?; G. Camardi, Ideal Types and Scientific Theories.

VOLUME 83 (2004)

CONFIRMATION, EMPIRICAL PROGRESS AND TRUTH APPROXIMATION
ESSAYS IN DEBATE WITH THEO KUIPERS, VOL. 1
(Edited by Roberto Festa, Atocha Aliseda and Jeanne Peijnenburg)

R. Festa, A. Aliseda, J. Peijnenburg, Introduction; T.A.F. Kuipers, The Threefold Evaluation of Theories: A Synopsis of From Instrumentalism to Constructive Realism. On Some Relations between Confirmation, Empirical Progress, and Truth Approximation (2000).. **Confirmation and the HD Method** — P. Maher, Qualitative Confirmation and the Ravens Paradox; J.R. Welch, Gruesome Predicates; A. Aliseda, Lacunae, Empirical Progress and Semantic Tableaux. **Empirical Progress by Abduction and Induction** — J. Meheus, Empirical Progress and Ampliative Adaptive Logics; D. Batens, On a Logic of Induction; G. Schurz, Bayesian H-D Confirmation and Structuralistic Truthlikeness: Discussion and Comparison with the Relevant-Element and the Content-Part Approach. **Truth Approximation by Abduction** — I. Niiniluoto, Abduction and Truthlikeness; I. Douven, Empirical Equivalence, Explanatory Force, and the Inference to the Best Theory. **Truth Approximation by Empirical and Nonempirical Means** — B. Hamminga, Constructive Realism and Scientific Progress; D. Miller, Beauty, a Road to the Truth?; J.P. Zamora Bonilla, Truthlikeness with a Human Face: On Some Connections between the

Theory of Verisimilitude and the Sociology of Scientific Knowledge. **Truthlikeness and Updating** — S.D. Zwart, *Updating Theories*; J. Van Benthem, *A Note on Modeling Theories.* **Refined Truth Approximation** — T. Mormann, *Geometry of Logic and Truth Approximation*; I.C. Burger, J. Heidema, *For Better, for Worse: Comparative Orderings on States and Theories.* **Realism and Metaphors** — J.J.A. Mooij, *Metaphor and Metaphysical Realism*; R. Festa, *On the Relations between (Neo-Classical) Philosophy of Science and Logic*; *Bibliography of Theo A.F. Kuipers*; *Index of Names.*

VOLUME 84 (2004)

COGNITIVE STRUCTURES IN SCIENTIFIC INQUIRY
ESSAYS IN DEBATE WITH THEO KUIPERS, VOL. 2
(Edited by Roberto Festa, Atocha Aliseda and Jeanne Peijnenburg)

R. Festa, A. Aliseda, J. Peijnenburg, *Introduction*; T.A.F. Kuipers, *Structures in Scientific Cognition: A Synopsis of Structures in Science. Heuristic Patterns Based on Cognitive Structures. An Advanced Textbook in Neo-Classical Philosophy of Science (2001).* **Types of Research and Research Programs** — D. Atkinson, *A New Metaphysics: Finding a Niche for String Theory*; T. Nickles, *Problem Reduction: Some Thoughts*; M. Franssen, *Design Research Programs.* **Types of Explanation** — E. Weber, H. De Preester, *Micro-Explanations of Laws*; E.R. Scerri, *On the Formalization of the Periodic Table*; J. Peijnenburg, *Classical, Nonclassical and Neoclassical Intentions*; A.R. Mackor, *Erklären, Verstehen and Simulation: Reconsidering the Role of Empathy in the Social Sciences*; A. Wouters, *Functional Explanation in Biology*; A. Grobler, A. Wiśniewski, *Explanation and Theory Evaluation.* **Computational Approaches** — J. Kamps, *The Ubiquity of Background Knowledge*; A.P.M. Van Den Bosch, *Structures in Neuropharmacology*; P. Thagard, *Why Is Beauty a Road to the Truth?*; G.A.W. Vreeswijk, *Direct Connectionistic Methods for Scientific Theory Formation.* **Theories and Structures** — E. Ruttkamp, *Overdetermination of Theories by Empirical Models: A Realist Interpretation of Empirical Choices*; R.L. Causey, *What Is Structure?*. **Science and Ethics** — H. Zandvoort, *Knowledge, Risk, and Liability. Analysis of a Discussion Continuing within Science and Technology*; *Bibliography of Theo A.F. Kuipers*; *Index of Names.*

VOLUME 85 (2004)

John Wettersten

WHEWELL'S CRITICS
HAVE THEY PREVENTED HIM FROM DOING GOOD?
(Edited by L. Haaparanta and I. Niiniluoto)

J.A. Bell, *Foreword*; *Preface and Acknowledgments*; *Analytical Table of Contents*; *Introduction: Whewell's Image and Impact; Two Conflicting Tales.* **PART ONE: THE BUILDING OF WHEWELL'S IMAGE** — *1. Immediate Rejection*; *2. Embarrassed Silence.* **PART TWO: ENCOUNTER WITH THE ETHICAL DIMENSION** — *3. Disturbing Recollections Fail to Pass Away*; *4. The 20th Century Sneaks a Worried Look at Old Judgments.* **PART THREE: THE IMAGE REINSTATED. THE REALITY COVERED OVER** — *5. The Return to Old Misconceptions*; *6. Quixotic Attempts to Revive*

Mill's Program; 7. *The Reappraisal of Whewell's Place in the History of the Philosophy of Science Begins*. **PART FOUR: WHEWELL REAPPRAISED TODAY** — 8. *An Overview: Whewell's Philosophy in Retrospect*; 9. *The Good that Whewell Can Still Do*. **COMMENTARIES** — M. Segre, *Whewell's Legacy and the Art of Argumentation*; J. Agassi, *The Case-Study and Its Import: Wettersten on Whewell*; R. Curtis, *The Theological Deduction*; M.A. Finocchiaro, *Was Whewell an Inductivist?*; G. Guillaumin J., *William Whewell's Idea of Historical Causation*; W. Margolis, *A Small Appreciation of William Whewell*. **REPLIES TO THE COMMENTARIES** — J. Wettersten, *Replies to the Commentaries*; *Name Index*.

VOLUME 86 (2005)

CORRECTING THE MODEL
IDEALIZATION AND ABSTRACTION IN THE SCIENCES
(Edited by Martin R. Jones and Nancy Cartwright)

Preface; *Analytical Table of Contents*; K.D. Hoover, *Quantitative Evaluation of Idealized Models in the New Classical Macroeconomics*; J. Pemberton, *Why Idealized Models in Economics Have Limited Use*; A. Funkenstein, *The Revival of Aristotle's Nature*; J.R. Griesemer, *The Informational Gene and the Substantial Body: On the Generalization of Evolutionary Theory by Abstraction*; N.J. Nersessian, *Abstraction via Generic Modeling in Concept Formation in Science*; M. Morrison, *Approximating the Real: The Role of Idealizations in Physical Theory*; M.R. Jones, *Idealization and Abstraction: A Framework*; D.S. Nivison, *Standard Time*; J. Bogen, J. Woodward, *Evading the IRS*; M.N. Wise, *Realism Is Dead*; R.N. Giere, *Is Realism Dead?*

VOLUME 87 (2005)

Adam Wiegner

OBSERVATION, HYPOTHESIS, INTROSPECTION
(Edited by Izabella Nowakowa)

I. Nowakowa, *Introduction: Adam Wiegner's Nonstandard Empiricism*. **Adam Wiegner, OBSERVATION, HYPOTHESIS, INTROSPECTION** — *Translator's Note*; *List of Translational Decisions*. **HOLISTIC EMPIRICISM** — *A Note on Holistic Empiricism (1964)*; *The Problem of Knowledge in light of L. Nelson's Critical Philosophy (1925)*; *The "Proton Pseudos" in Wundt's Criticism of R. Avenarius' Philosophy (1963)*; *Philosophical Significance of Gestalt Theory (1948)*; *The Idea of a Logic of Knowledge (1934)*. **OTHER EPISTEMOLOGICAL AND METHODOLOGICAL CONTRIBUTIONS** — *Remarks on Indeterminism in Physics (1932)*; *A Note on the Concept of Relative Truth (1964)*; *On the so-called "Relative Truth" (1963)*; *On Abstraction and Concretization (1960)*. **PHILOSOPHY OF MIND AND PHILOSOPHY OF PSYCHOLOGY** — *On the Nature of Mental Phenomena (1933)*; *On the Debate about Imaginative Ideas (1932)*; *On the Subjective and Objective Clarity in Thought and Word (1959)*; *References*; *Original Sources*; Appendix: J. Kmita, *Wiegner's Conception of Holistic Empiricism*.

International Studies in the Philosophy of Science

EDITOR:
James W. McAllister, *University of Leiden, The Netherlands*

International Studies in the Philosophy of Science is a scholarly journal dedicated to publishing original research in philosophy of science and in philosophically informed history and sociology of science. Its scope includes the foundations and methodology of the natural, social, and human sciences, philosophical implications of particular scientific theories, and broader philosophical reflection on science. The editors invite contributions not only from philosophers, historians, and sociologists of science, but also from researchers in the sciences. The journal publishes articles from a wide variety of countries and philosophical traditions. The editors encourage participation in the annual Philosophy of Science conference at the Inter-University Centre, Dubrovnik, a forum for high-quality research and international debate in philosophy of science.

This journal is also available online.
For further information please visit www.tandf.co.uk/journals

To request an online sample copy please visit:
www.tandf.co.uk/journals/onlinesamples.asp

SUBSCRIPTION RATES
2005 – Volume 19 (3 issues)
Print ISSN 0269-8595
Online ISSN 1469-9281
Institutional rate: US$665; £403
(includes free online access)
Personal rate: US$209; £126 (print only)

ORDER FORM cisp

PLEASE COMPLETE IN BLOCK CAPITALS AND RETURN TO THE ADDRESS BELOW
Please invoice me at the ❏ institutional rate ❏ personal rate

Name _____

Address _____

_____

_____

Email _____

Please contact Customer Services at either:
Taylor & Francis Ltd, Rankine Road, Basingstoke, Hants RG24 8PR, UK
Tel: +44 (0)1256 813002 **Fax:** +44 (0)1256 330245 **Email:** enquiry@tandf.co.uk **Website:** www.tandf.co.uk

Taylor & Francis Inc, 325 Chestnut Street, 8th Floor, Philadelphia, PA 19106, USA
Tel: +1 215 6258900 **Fax:** +1 215 6258914 **Email:** info@taylorandfrancis.com **Website:** www.taylorandfrancis.com

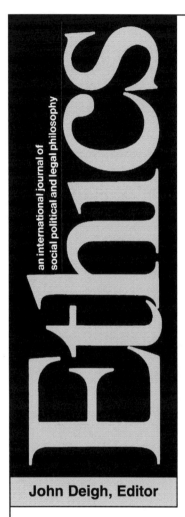

Founded in 1890, **Ethics** is an international journal of moral, political, and legal philosophy presenting scholarly work from a variety of intellectual perspectives, including social and political theory, law, and economics. **Ethics** also publishes book reviews and review essays.

Ethics Online
www.journals.uchicago.edu/ET
- Links to author references, tables, and figures
- Easy, printable PDF format
- Full-text articles searchable by keyword

Quarterly. ISSN: 0014-1704

 -TOC
Sign up for e-TOC, the FREE Tables of Contents Alerting Service at
www.journals.uchicago.edu/ET

John Deigh, Editor

To Subscribe:
Online: *www.journals.uchicago.edu/ET*
E-mail: *subscriptions@press.uchicago.edu*
Phone: toll-free (877) 705-1878 or (773) 753-3347
Fax: toll-free (877) 705-1879 or (773) 753-0811

2/05

 The University of Chicago Press
Journals Division • Box 37005 • Chicago, IL 60637

THE JOURNAL OF THE BRITISH SOCIETY FOR PHENOMENOLOGY

An International Review of Philosophy and the Human Sciences

EDITOR: DR ULLRICH HAASE

Volume 36, No.2, May 2005
Husserl and Derrida

Articles

Presence and Origin: On the Possibility of the Static-Genetic Distinction, by Michael K. Shim

Husserl, Derrida and Genetic Phenomenology, by Gary Banham

Derrida's Intentional Skepticism: a Husserlian Response, by Pol Vandevelde

Klein and Derrida on the Historicity of Meaning and the Meaning of Historicity in Husserl's *Crisis*-Texts, by Burt C. Hopkins

Husserl, Freud, *A Suivre*: Derrida on Time, by Joanna Hodge

Derrida's 'New Thinking' A Response to Leonard Lawlor's *Derrida and Husserl*, by James R. Mensch

'*Verstellung*' (Misplacement): Completions of Immanence, by Leonard Lawlor

---

The *JBSP* publishes papers on phenomenology and existential philosophy as well as contributions from other fields of philosophy. Papers from workers in the Humanities and human sciences interested in the philosophy of their subject will be welcome. All papers and books for review to be sent to the Editor: Dr Ullrich Haase, Department of Politics and Philosophy, The Manchester Metropolitan University, Manchester M15 6LL, England. Subscription and advertisement enquiries to be sent to the publishers: Jackson Publishing and Distribution, 3 Gibsons Road, Heaton Moor, Stockport, Cheshire, SK4 4JX, England.

Mobilizing Place, Placing Mobility.
The Politics of Representation in a Globalized World.

Edited by Ginette Verstraete and Tim Cresswell.

Amsterdam/New York, NY 2002. 195 pp.
(Thamyris/Intersecting 9)
ISBN: 90-420-1144-0   € 40,-/US $ 48.-

What role does 'place' have in a world marked by increased mobility on a global scale? What strategies are there for representing 'place' in the age of globalization? What is the relationship between 'place' and the varied mobilities of migrancy, tourism, travel and nomadism?

These are some of the questions that run through the ten essays in this collection. The combined effect of these essays is to participate in the contemporary project of subjecting the links between place, mobility, identity, representation and practice to critical interdisciplinary scrutiny. Such notions are not the property of particular disciplines. In the era of globalization, transnationalism and readily acknowledged cultural hybridity these links are more important than ever. They are important because of the taken-for-grantedness of: the universal impact of globalization; the receding importance of place and the centrality of mobile identities. This taken-for-grantedness masks the ways place continues to be important and ways in which mobility is differentiated by race, gender, ethnicity, nationality and many other social markers. This book is a concerted attempt to stop taking for granted these themes of the age. Material discussed in the essays include the creation of cultural routes in Europe, the video's of Fiona Tan, artistic and literary representations of the North African desert, the production of indigenous videos in Mexico, mobile forms of ethnography, the film *Existenz*, Jamaica Kincaid's writing on gardens, the video representation of sex tourism and ways of imagining the global.

USA/Canada: One Rockefeller Plaza, Ste. 1420, New York, NY 10020,
Tel. (212) 265-6360, Call toll-free (U.S. only) 1-800-225-3998,
Fax (212) 265-6402
All other countries: Tijnmuiden 7, 1046 AK Amsterdam, The Netherlands.
Tel. ++ 31 (0)20 611 48 21, Fax ++ 31 (0)20 447 29 79
Orders-queries@rodopi.nl   www.rodopi.nl
Please note that the exchange rate is subject to fluctuations

Africa and Its Significant Others.
Forty Years of Intercultural Entanglement.

Edited by Isabel Hoving, Frans-Willem Korsten and Ernst van Alphen.

Amsterdam/New York, NY 2003. 208 pp.
(Thamyris Intersecting Place, Sex and Race 11)
ISBN: 90-420-1029-0 € 40,/US$ 50.-

When did the intimate dialogue between Africa, Europe, and the Americas begin? Looking back, it seems as if these three continents have always been each other's significant others. Europe created its own modern identity by using Africa as a mirror, but Africans traveled to Europe and America long before the European age of discovery, and African cultures can be said to lie at the root of European culture. This intertwining has become ever more visible: Nowadays Africa emerges as a highly visible presence in the Americas, and African American styles capture Europe's youth, many of whom are of (North-) African descent. This entanglement, however, remains both productive and destructive. The continental economies are intertwined in ways disastrous for Africa, and African knowledge is all too often exported and translated for US and European scholarly aims, which increases the intercontinental knowledge gap.

This volume proposes a fresh look at the vigorous and painful, but inescapable, relationships between these significant others. It does so as a gesture of gratitude and respect to one of the pioneering figures in this field. Dutch Africanist and literary scholar Mineke Schipper, who is taking her leave from her chair in Intercultural Literary Studies at the University of Leiden. Where have the past four decades of African studies brought us? What is the present-day state of this intercontinental dialogue?

USA/Canada: 906 Madison Avenue, UNION, NJ 07083, USA
Call toll-free (USA only)1-800-225-3998, Tel. 908 206 1166, Fax 908-206-0820
All other countries: Tijnmuiden 7, 1046 AK Amsterdam, The Netherlands.
Tel. ++ 31 (0)20 611 48 21, Fax ++ 31 (0)20 447 29 79
<u>Orders-queries@rodopi.nl</u>   <u>www.rodopi.nl</u>
Please note that the exchange rate is subject to fluctuations

Africa's Quest for a Philosophy of Decolonization

Messay Kebede

Amsterdam/New York, NY 2004.
XIII, 256 pp.
(Value Inquiry Book Series 153)

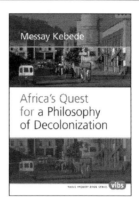

ISBN: 90-420-0810-5 €52,-/ US$ 70.-
ISBN: 90-420-0840-7 €22,-/US$ 29.70 *
*Textbook; minimum order 10 copies

"Kebede (Dayton) positions this important contribution on the status of ethnophilosophy within the context of how best to emancipate African philosophy from Western domination. His well-stated argument regarding the strategic importance of negritude's appropriation-of-otherness mythmaking as counter as counter to Western whiteness propaganda sets the stage for his own view of the role of cultural traditions and mysticism in the modernization of Africa. ... Jam packed with issues and citations, each chapter is a literature survey that could be expanded into a book. ... Recommended."
　　　　　　　　　　　　　　CHOICE January 2005 – Vol. 42 No. 5

"If you have time to read only one book to learn about the intricacies of African philosophy, then read *Africa's Quest for a Philosophy of Decolonization.* The beauty of this volume is Kebede's clear presentation and thoughtful evaluation of each of the main schools in African Philosophy."
　　　　　　　　　　　　　　Joseph C. Kunkel

"*Africa's Quest for a Philosophy of Decolonization* is an exceptionally clear introduction to African philosophy."　　Filosofie magazine

---

USA/Canada: One Rockefeller Plaza, Ste. 1420, New York, NY 10020,
Tel. (212) 265-6360, Call toll-free (U.S. only) 1-800-225-3998,
Fax (212) 265-6402

All other countries: Tijnmuiden 7, 1046 AK Amsterdam, The Netherlands.
Tel. ++ 31 (0)20 611 48 21, Fax ++ 31 (0)20 447 29 79

Orders@rodopi.nl　　　　　　　　　　**www.rodopi.nl**

Please note that the exchange rate is subject to fluctuations